# Practical Mathematics

## APPRAISAL of the

# LEARNING DISABLED

# Contributors

Colleen S. Blankenship
Mary E. Cronin
Henry A. Goodstein
Anne M. Fitzmaurice Hayes
Mahesh C. Sharma
Robert A. Shaw
Raymond E. Webster

# Practical Mathematics

# APPRAISAL of the

# LEARNING DISABLED

Editor
**John F. Cawley, Ph.D.**
University of New Orleans
Lakefront

AN ASPEN PUBLICATION®
Aspen Systems Corporation
Rockville, Maryland
Royal Tunbridge Wells
1985

Library of Congress Cataloging in Publication Data

Main entry under title:

Practical mathematics appraisal of the learning disabled.

"An Aspen publication."
Includes bibliographies and index.
1. Mathematics—Study and teaching. 2. Learning disabilities.
I. Cawley, John F.
QA11.P634   1985      371.9′044      84-20499
ISBN: 0-89443-559-0

Publisher: John R. Marozsan
Associate Publisher: Jack W. Knowles, Jr.
Editorial Director: Margaret Quinlin
Executive Managing Editor: Margot G. Raphael
Managing Editor: M. Eileen Higgins
Editorial Services: Jane Coyle
Printing and Manufacturing: Debbie Collins

Library of Congress Catalog Card Number: 84-20499
ISBN: 0-89443-559-0

*Printed in the United States of America*

1   2   3   4   5

# Table of Contents

# Preface

The process of appraisal is perceived as a comprehensive technique that leads toward the development of an appropriate education for the learning disabled.

Much has been written about appraisal as it relates to the broad issues of development, reading, language, and overall academic achievement. Little attention has been directed toward mathematics.

This book has been developed with an emphasis on the practical aspects of appraisal. Substantive theoretical issues were not considered as primary topics. Rather, the direction is toward the development of a basic understanding of mathematics appraisal and the learning disabled.

Chapter 1 introduces the topic of appraisal in mathematics for the learning disabled. Distinctions are made among measurement, assessment, and diagnosis and the roles each play in the process of appraisal.

Chapter 2 discusses background issues in measurement. Considerable emphasis is directed toward domain-referenced testing and its implications for mathematics.

Chapter 3 brings together the topics of assessment, curriculum, and instruction. The approach highlights curriculum-based assessment and its interrelationships with curriculum and instruction.

The next three chapters, 4, 5, and 6, explore appraisal across the developmental span that encompasses preschool through entrance into the real world. The illustrations and examples accentuate the reality that mathematics content needs to be an integral consideration in any appraisal program.

Appraisal in areas other than mathematics is an essential component of efforts with the learning disabled. Chapter 7 discusses the implications of this facet of appraisal. Building upon the general descriptions of appraisal in chapter 7, chapter 8 contains an analysis and descriptions of multidisciplinary appraisal in the clinical setting. Case studies serve as the primary medium of presentation.

No program of appraisal would be complete without reference to behavior and to those facets of behavior that have implications for the classroom setting. Chapter 9 emphasizes a teacher-oriented approach to behavioral appraisal.

Chapter 10 discusses approaches with individuals considered to be among the more severely handicapped in mathematics. The interview technique is highlighted.

The final chapter considers the topics of student evaluation and program evaluation. Student progress is an essential element of any program of evaluation. Chapter 11 is directed toward clarifying some of the issues of student evaluation as related to appraisal and to program evaluation.

Each component of *Practical Mathematics Appraisal of the Learning Disabled* was developed to provide a basic background and to serve as an aid in selecting or organizing mathematics appraisals for the learning disabled. The authors recognize the diversity that characterizes the field of learning disability. Amidst this mass of diversity are the problems and issues to be addressed in fulfilling our responsibilities to those we serve. It is hoped that this text will serve as a stimulant to those interested in the field of learning disability with the anticipated outcome being the production of more effective approaches to mathematics appraisals.

*John F. Cawley*
*Editor*

# Chapter 1

# Learning Disability and Mathematics Appraisal

*John F. Cawley*

The concepts of learning disability and mathematics appraisal are both invaluable and controversial. Perhaps the only truism that can be stated is that each of these concepts is characterized by its diversity. This diversity, while a stimulant to the research worker and theoretician, is a nuisance to the practitioner. Although they motivate inquiry and argument among some, multiple connotations and implications make it almost impossible for others to describe these concepts and to affix specifics to either of them.

Whenever appraisal is discussed the question of intelligence arises. Intelligence has been described as anything from a hypothetical construct to that which intelligence tests measure. The specific attributes associated with intelligence vary with the many divergent orientations and practices of the theoretician and practitioner. In some instances, intelligence is measured as a univariate trait. Such a case exists with the *Peabody Picture Vocabulary Test*. In other instances, intelligence is measured as a multivariate concept. The *Wechsler Intelligence Scale for Children-R* and the *Stanford-Binet, L-M* are examples of multitrait appraisal. Sternberg (1984) proposes a triarchic theory of intelligence for intelligence testing, a major purpose of which is to improve levels of prediction. Sternberg proposes to interrelate the appraisal of intelligence including the internal world of mechanisms that lead to intelligent behavior, those points along the continuum of experience or tasks that critically involve the use of intelligence, and the external world involving environmental adaptation, selection, and shaping.

What seems to be true regarding intelligence also seems true of the concept of learning disability and mathematics. The concept of learning disability encompasses a number of specific attributes, all of which may be measured through univariate or multivariate approaches. These specific attributes seem to exist independently more in regulations and in theory

1

than they do in practice. In fact, the attributes and abilities generally assigned to the concept of learning disability are so extensive and intertwined that the concept is more appropriately presented in the form of a Venn diagram, Figure 1-1, than in the form of individually listed abilities (Cawley, 1984). The concept of ability and achievement in mathematics must also be viewed in the form of a Venn diagram, Figure 1-2.

## WHAT IS INVOLVED IN APPRAISAL?

Among the learning disabled, mathematics appraisal and programming should include a minimum of six topics in the early years and a minimum of four topics in the later years. Skills and concepts should be appropriately represented and problem solving and applications should be included at all stages. Different orientations may be used to conduct these appraisals. For example, one might elect to include conservation of number within the strand of numbers or seriation within the strand of measurement. Some topics have values other than those specifically related to mathematics. Sets, for example, can be included for reasons other than those related to "set theory." Sets allow for appraisal of classification and conceptualization with diverse sets of materials and arrangements.

**Figure 1-1** Venn Diagram of Learning Disabilities

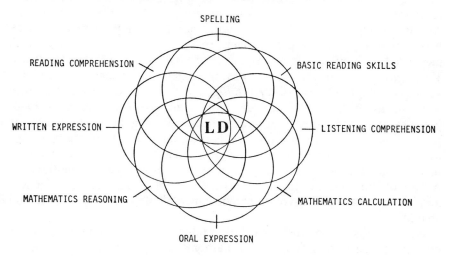

*Source:* Cawley, J.F. (1984). Learning Disabilities: Issues and Alternatives. Chapter 1 in *Developmental Teaching of Mathematics for the Learning Disabled* (J. Cawley, ed.) Rockville, Md: Aspen Systems.

**Figure 1-2** Venn Diagram of Mathematics

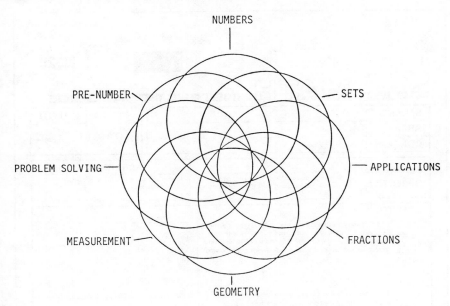

NUMBERS

PRE-NUMBER

SETS

PROBLEM SOLVING

APPLICATIONS

MEASUREMENT

FRACTIONS

GEOMETRY

*Source:* From *Developmental Teaching of Mathematics for the Learning Disabled*, J.F. Cawley, Ed., with permission of Aspen Systems Corp.,© 1984.

Adaptations can be made for appraisal in standardized tests or in curriculum or progress type evaluations. Exhibit 1-1 contains an illustration of the latter. In this illustration, the topic is grouping by tens. The evaluative item is designed to assess proficiency with the indicated topic in the same manner in which the instruction took place. If, as in the present case, instruction was conducted with pictures and by pointing, then appraisal would take place via the same interactions. Given the aforementioned, how do we reconcile the matter of diversity? There seem to be two choices. One of these is to recognize a rule-based approach. The other is to recognize an attribute-based approach.

**The Rule-Based Approach**

In the rule-based approach, standards are agreed upon, discrepancies are specified, and guidelines are established. With respect to intelligence, we can follow the rule that an IQ of 100 is average, an IQ of 70 represents

**Exhibit 1-1** Evaluation within Instruction

LEVEL 1                                          **N325**

PROJECT **MATH** INSTRUCTIONAL GUIDE

| STRAND | Numbers | INPUT | OUTPUT |
|---|---|---|---|
| AREA | Place Value | | |
| CONCEPT | Grouping by Tens | | |

| BEHAVIORAL OBJECTIVE | Presents pictures of a set which has been divided into groups of tens and remainders (10-99). | LEARNER Identifies picture of a set which has been similarly divided. |
|---|---|---|

**ACTIVITIES**

1. **Comparing Set Choices to a Model.** Begin the activity by saying to the learners, "We are going to work with sets that can be grouped into more than one set of 10 and also have some ones left over." Show the learners the following:

Then show the learners the following two pictures. Point out that one red chip is equal to a set of 10 blue chips.

Now ask a learner to point to the one picture that represents the same set as the model he was first shown. After he has chosen the correct picture (B), emphasize that he is correct because: Picture B has two red chips and each red chip equals one set of 10. The model picture has two sets of 10 and the correct answer also has three ones left over. Both pictures show us 23; that is, two sets of 10 and 3 ones. Repeat the activity for other numbers between 20 and 99. At times, use large blue chips to represent one set of 10, and change pictures accordingly.

**MATERIALS**

Pictures of sets divided into groups of tens and remainders (left overs).

**SUPPLEMENTAL ACTIVITIES** N325: a, b, c.

**EVALUATION**

Show the learner the following pictures and ask him to point to the sets which represent the same number.

*Source:* J.F. Cawley, A.M. Fitzmaurice, H.A. Goodstein, A. Lepore, R. Sedlak, and V. Athaus. *Project MATH.* Tulsa, Okla.: Educational Progress, Inc. 1976.

mild retardation, and an IQ of 130 represents brightness or possibly gift-edness.

We can establish a rule which states that an individual can be defined as learning disabled only when there is a discrepancy of at least two standard deviations between level of expectancy and present level of functioning when expectancy is measured by a test of ability and level of functioning is measured by a test of achievement. The rule can be limited to include only those with a minimum of average or near average ability. Or, the rule might stipulate that the discrepancy must exist between two areas of achievement. One of these areas has to reflect near average performance. The other has to be at least two standard deviations below. All individuals meeting these criteria would be eligible to receive special education services through any one of a variety of service delivery options.

In effect, the rules have established a basis for inclusion or placement. These rules have not provided a basis for individualized programming. That will have to be developed through an attribute approach. Tucker (1979) indicated that mathematics assessment should be used for the purposes of placement and instruction. The rule-based approach provides for the former. The attribute-based approach provides for the latter.

## The Attribute-Based Approach

Basically, the attribute-based appraisal is a combination of two factors. One is the manner of interaction between the individual and the examiner during the process of appraisal. The other is the actual content included in the appraisal.

Consider five different school districts, using five different approaches to mathematics appraisal, and that all five approaches differ in both content and the interaction between the examiner and the individual. The attribute approach would produce five different sets of attributes or characteristics and, theoretically, five different approaches to instruction. If special education is truly *specially designed instruction,* as defined in the regulations to P.L. 94-142, to include a direct and identifiable link between present levels of functioning and objectives (McDaniel, 1979), then the attributes that characterize learners in the different school districts should result in the development of divergent approaches to *specially designed instruction.* This is uncommon because the rule-based approach dominates. That is, one ordinarily determines a discrepancy and programs the individual on that basis. For example, an individual in the seventh grade with a present level of functioning at the 3.5 grade equivalent is likely to be given instruction at the third-grade level by the special education teacher. The level of mathematics instruction in the regular classroom will vary according to the criteria and procedures of the school district and the resources available to the regular class teacher.

## DEFINING *LEARNING DISABILITY*

All of the aforementioned bring us to the point at which we need to define the term *learning disability* in general and as a specific disability in mathematics. The following limitations apply:

1. A learning disability in mathematics will exist when there is a discrepancy between level of expectancy as measured by an ability test and level of functioning as measured by an achievement test. Educational performance in the regular classroom must be adversely affected.
2. Some individuals will demonstrate a significant discrepancy in mathematics, but not in reading, language, and other areas. Some may demonstrate discrepancies in all areas.
3. A learning disability in mathematics will not exist simply because the material is too hard. Failure alone does not justify a learning disability designation.
4. A learning disability should not exist because the individual has not been exposed to specific concepts or skills. A content gap alone is not sufficient to assign the term *learning disability*.
5. A learning disability will not necessarily exist when the child distorts a nonconventional algorithm. It is necessary to determine if the nonconventional algorithm has been taught to the child or whether the child has developed an aberration unknowingly.
6. A learning disability in mathematics may be accompanied by indicators of perceptual, language, or cognitive disturbance which interfere with performance in mathematics. (Reisman & Kauffman, 1980)

A learning disability will be said to exist when there is a significant discrepancy between expectancy and level of functioning to a degree stipulated by state or local standards. This discrepancy may be between overall expectancy such as that derived by contrasting intelligence and chronological age (i.e., mental age) with the present level of functioning as determined during the appraisal. Or, the learning disability may be said to exist when one or more areas of achievement are at expectancy (e.g., a child of 10 is reading at fourth-grade level) and one or more areas of achievement is discrepant (e.g., mathematics performance is at 1.6 grade level).

## THE APPRAISAL PROCESS

The appraisal process must provide for both the rule-based and the attribute-based approaches. The term *appraisal* as applied to mathematics and the learning disabled refers to a three-stage procedure that includes measurement, assessment, and diagnosis.

### Measurement

Measurement is that stage in appraisal in which the primary concern is to compare the performance of one or more individuals with that of others. Measurement is primarily a norm-referenced procedure that reports the status of the individual in terms such as grade equivalents, standard scores, percentiles, or normal curve equivalent scores. Measurement approaches do not give extended consideration to content representation or to the organization and sequencing of content. Items are developed on the basis of technical adequacy (e.g., their role in contributing to the reliability of a test) and inserted into the final version of the test in accordance with the statistical qualities of the item. Thus, items that are too easy or too difficult would be excluded.

The technical adequacy of tests tends to be a prime concern among reviewers and analysts. While there can be no doubt about the importance of norms, reliability, and validity, these are not the only considerations in mathematics assessment. While the statement may be speculative, it seems that relatively few users and practitioners understand technical adequacy; nor do they truly care about it. The issue is even more confusing when one looks to professional reviews for assistance. For example, Thurlow and Ysseldyke (1979) indicated that the *KeyMATH Diagnostic Test* is technically inadequate in terms of norms, reliability, and validity. In the same issue of the *Learning Disability Quarterly*, McCollough and Zaremba (1979) stated the *"KeyMATH"* and the *Woodcock* can be used with confidence for learning disabilities screening, diagnosis and research." How can a test that is technically inadequate be used with confidence? How do different sets of authors make such dissimilar remarks?

The format of tests and methods of administration are generally selected because of their efficiency or packaging. Some examples of measurement approaches are:

- *Wide Range Achievement Test* (arithmetic)
- *Peabody Individual Achievement Test*
- *K-ABC Arithmetic Test*

- *Woodcock-Johnson Math Cluster* (computations, applications)
- *Test of Early Mathematics Ability*

**Assessment**

Assessment is that stage of appraisal which intentionally evaluates the individual across a number of mathematical strands or content areas. Assessment requires that the developer plot sequences of content across mathematics areas for the level at which the assessment will take place. These might be plotted from the *Mathematics Concept Inventory* as shown in Table 1-1. Note that some degree of equivalence is given to all areas. The numerals show the number of items at each level for each topic.

Assessment consists of a search for patterns of strengths and weaknesses. A correct response is as valuable as an incorrect response. In assessment, the examiner does not seek a ceiling, per se. Rather, the search is directed toward curriculum placement, proficiency in many areas of mathematics, and the identification of a pattern of what the learner knows as well as a pattern of what the learner does not know. Examples of assessment instruments are:

- *Test of Mathematics Abilities*
- *KeyMATH Diagnostic Test*
- *Mathematics Concept Inventory*

*KeyMATH* was a sincere attempt to meet the needs of the field of special education as those needs might have been seen a decade ago. The question

**Table 1-1** Content Plot of *Mathematics Concept Inventory*

|  | Level 1 | Level 2 | Level 3 | Level 4 |
|---|---|---|---|---|
|  | Grade Equivalent K–1.5 | Grade Equivalent 1.5–3.0 | Grade Equivalent 3.0–4.5 | Grade Equivalent 4.5–6.0 |
| Sets | 6 | 5 |  |  |
| Patterns | 5 | 3 |  |  |
| Numbers | 20 | 21 | 19 | 17 |
| Fractions | 5 | 8 | 10 | 15 |
| Geometry | 10 | 13 | 14 | 11 |
| Measurements | 12 | 13 | 17 | 17 |
|  | 58 | 63 | 60 | 60 |

for us today relates to the standards of acceptance that have been set for instrumentation and approaches that are coming of age at this time. Things do not seem to have improved. If one looks at the instruments that are emerging today, the field seems to be in pretty much the same situation as in the past. This observation refers to the process of diagnosis and assessment, not measurement.

The measurement instruments we have today are generally well standardized and comprehensive in their validation. But, because they are limited to comparisons of the learner relative to other learners, these instruments do not assist us with the process of intervention or in the development of remedial activities. They do not cover the content of mathematics adequately enough or serve as the basis for individualizing instruction. They do serve to guide us through placement decisions or categorization.

The lack of *assessment* instruments seems unconscionable in this day and age. Is it the fact that arithmetic computation is so dominant a part of the thinking of special education that we fail to notice the value of geometry, measurement, and other topics? Would it not be of considerable value to know the type of progress the child is making in geometry and to determine if this is similar or different from that in arithmetic? If we consider seriously the notion of *learning styles* we must recognize that some youngsters might have styles such that geometry and measurement are preferred mathematics for them at given points in time.

## Diagnosis

Diagnosis is that stage of appraisal where the focus is upon intraindividual performance in a single or limited number of mathematics topics. The process of diagnosis will be undertaken with a restricted set of items. Diagnosis is a clinical process. As such, there is an ambience of informality.

Diagnosis may be described as a process that is applicable across any content area or it may be defined as the search for specific patterns of performance within a limited area. This chapter will accentuate the latter. There is a commitment to both testing and instruction as part of the diagnostic procedure. There is the further requirement that the diagnosis be interview-based and that there be considerable interaction between clinicians and learners.

Examples of instruments having a diagnostic approach are

- *Diagnostic Test of Arithmetic Skills (DTAS)*
- *Diagnostic Inventory of Basic Skills*

- *Diagnostic Chart for Fundamental Processes in Arithmetic*
- *Diagnostic Protocol for Mathematics (DPM)*

The difference among DTAS, the *Inventory,* the *Diagnostic Chart,* and the *Protocol* is that the first three concentrate on the identification of algorithmic variations in learner performance in what are primarily paper-pencil formats. The DPM is considerably more comprehensive, as will be shown momentarily.

## ACHIEVEMENT AND ABILITY

Wick (1973) distinguished aptitude or ability measures from achievement, not on the basis of content, but on the basis of use. If a test is used to determine present levels of functioning, it is an achievement test. If the results are used to make some sort of prediction or decision about a student's future, it is an ability test. The distinction may be somewhat circular in the sense that a test used to describe status is also used to predict status, which may then be confirmed by the original measure when it is given as a post-test.

The difficulty we face in using measures of achievement or aptitude to describe or to predict learner status is that the predictions are traditionally based upon there being a range of students in each sample. A mathematics test is developed. The test is administered to a sample of youngsters who range from very good in mathematics to quite poor in mathematics. When this test is administered to children, one could have confidence in the prediction that high scorers are likely to do better in mathematics than low scorers. Now, however, how will one use the results with individuals whose scores are so low that they are defined as being learning disabled in mathematics? Given the case of two learning-disabled individuals of comparable development in all areas and similar scores on the math test, how will the instructional and curriculum programs of each be differentiated? What kinds of predictions can be made relative to short-term growth (e.g., six months) and long-term growth (e.g., three years)? Do the results mean that if one teaches the individual at his or her grade level, the individual will perform satisfactorily in all areas of math that are first taught at that grade level? Does this mean that the individual will learn the math of the grade level at a rate of progress comparable to other individuals of similar ability who are working at the same grade level? Do these scores stipulate areas of strengths and weaknesses for each individual?

With the lack of emphasis on content and because administrative procedures in appraisal fail to provide the information needed for individualizing instruction, there is a need for alternatives. Percentile ranks, grade equivalent descriptors, and standard scores have little value in the development of curriculum or instructional options. Nor do these forms of reporting help one to make predictions with regard to different individuals within the subset referred to as learning disabled. The reason for this is that we use rule-based approaches to make attribute-based decisions.

It is proposed, therefore, that consideration be given to the development of sets of performance descriptors that report the p-value of each item across the ages for which the item is appropriate. Next it is suggested that the examiner arrange the items into patterns of strengths and weaknesses. Table 1-2 illustrates the arrangement of data for average, nonlearning-disabled children and Table 1-3 displays the data for the learning disabled. Given the data in each table, the examiner could analyze the performance of each child by each item. A 9-year-old learning-disabled child who missed item 1 would seem to be inordinately disabled. A 9-year old who missed item 9 is somewhat representative of the group and the same degree of concern might not be needed as in the case of the individual who missed item 1. If, however, the individual missed the item at 13 years of age, a serious discrepancy would be indicated.

For the appraisal of progress, each child could be plotted for each item, as shown in Table 1-4. This chart shows that the individual is making relatively good progress when compared to the learning disabled in Table 1-3. Item 5 seems to lack stability and should be tracked. As can be seen with item 6, the performance of the learning disabled reaches a level of mastery comparable to about 75 percent of the nonlearning disabled at age

**Table 1-2** Percent Correct by Age—Nonlearning Disabled

| Age | 6 | 7 | 8 | 9 | 10 | 11 | 12 | 13 |
|---|---|---|---|---|---|---|---|---|
| Item 1 | 96 | 99 | | | | | | |
| 2 | 92 | 96 | 99 | | | | | |
| 3 | 89 | 93 | 98 | | | | | |
| 4 | 86 | 92 | 97 | | | | | |
| 5 | 84 | 87 | 91 | 99 | | | | |
| 6 | 83 | 87 | 91 | 98 | | | | |
| 7 | 83 | 88 | 93 | 99 | | | | |
| 8 | 80 | 84 | 87 | 93 | 99 | | | |
| 9 | 80 | 83 | 86 | 91 | 97 | | | |
| 10 | 79 | 83 | 86 | 89 | 93 | 99 | | |
| 11 | 77 | 81 | 85 | 88 | 92 | 98 | | |

**Table 1-3** Item Percent Correct by Age—Learning Disabled

| Age | 6 | 7 | 8 | 9 | 10 | 11 | 12 | 13 |
|---|---|---|---|---|---|---|---|---|
| Item 1 | 83 | 91 | 97 | 97 | | | | |
| 2 | 81 | 90 | 94 | 99 | | | | |
| 3 | 80 | 90 | 93 | 96 | | | | |
| 4 | 91 | 77 | 86 | 91 | 97 | | | |
| 5 | 67 | 76 | 81 | 87 | 94 | 99 | | |
| 6 | 59 | 67 | 74 | 77 | 89 | 97 | | |
| 7 | 58 | 65 | 73 | 75 | 81 | 89 | 98 | |
| 8 | 56 | 65 | 71 | 73 | 79 | 87 | 94 | |
| 9 | 43 | 51 | 59 | 64 | 78 | 83 | 87 | 96 |
| 10 | | | | | | | | |
| 11 | | | | | | | | |

**Table 1-4** Item Plot of Individual

| | Year of testing | 1 | 2 | 3 | 4 |
|---|---|---|---|---|---|
| | Age at testing | 9 | 10 | 11 | 12 |
| Item 1 | | + | + | + | + |
| 2 | | + | + | + | + |
| 3 | | + | + | + | + |
| 4 | | − | + | + | + |
| 5 | | − | + | − | + |
| 6 | | + | − | + | + |
| 7 | | − | − | − | + |
| 8 | | − | − | + | + |
| 9 | | − | − | − | + |
| 10 | | − | − | − | − |

9 and to 97 percent of the nonlearning disabled at age 11. Items can be clustered by strand and growth across different content areas traced. Such an approach focuses attention on assessment rather than measurement in the appraisal process.

## APPRAISAL FORMATS

Most tests and test item formats are structured for ease of administration and packaging. Paper-pencil items of a multiple-choice format dominate measurement instruments. Spoken exchanges and the use of pictorial representations are common in assessment instruments.

Format selection is an essential aspect of test development. The *WISC-R Arithmetic Test* uses a combination of aural or written inputs and all answers are given orally. Levy (1981) studied the effectiveness of this test in differentiating children with learning disabilities in math. There were significant differences between the groups using the standard administrative format. Levy modified the format to provide combinations of written inputs and written responses and combinations of aural inputs and oral responses. Performance for both groups was higher for all written combinations. No computational errors were noted for any written combinations.

**The *K-ABC***

The *K-ABC* is a recently published test (Kauffman & Kauffman, 1983) that includes sets of subtests designed to measure mental processes and educational achievement. The Arithmetic Subtest consists of 38 items, two of which have two parts. The *K-ABC* clearly fits into the measurement component of the appraisal process. That is, its primary value is that it is designed to yield a score that can be contrasted with a set of norms.

The content of the Arithmetic Subtest does not seem to have been chosen from any curriculum-related scheme. It is an arithmetic test, not a mathematics test, a factor that clearly limits its use in attribute-based appraisal. Simply put, there is not sufficient representation of content to enable one to learn enough about a child to describe his or her characteristics in relation to the mathematics experiences of school. Though the *K-ABC,* probably more than any other battery other than the *Illinois Test of Psycholinguistic Abilities* (Kirk, McCarthy, & Kirk, 1968), suggests instructional or remedial implications, the lack of content representation indicates a serious shortcoming.

The administrative format of the *K-ABC* presents the learner with an informative display in the form of a picture and accompanies this with a set of oral directions. Thirteen of the thirty-eight items have picture cards that are not needed and in fact are irrelevant to the item itself. Illustrative of this is item 28. This item shows a picture of 5 elephants and is accompanied by aural directions which indicate that one elephant weighs 650 pounds and another elephant weighs 550 pounds. The question is then asked, "How much more does the big elephant weigh than the small one?" There is no use for the picture card. The information exchange is entirely verbal. Of the 40 items on the test, 35 require an oral response. Given the fact that little literature in the field of learning disabilities stresses the high quality of verbal development among the learning disabled, this verbal dependency would seem to limit our overall ability to obtain attribute-based data.

Format is important in the acquisition of attribute information. The inclusion of manipulatives in appraising the learning disabled, for example, is essential for two reasons. First, the youngster is generally unable to make the same mistakes with manipulatives that are made with paper-pencil formats. Second, by representing the algorithm manipulatively, the processes of instruction and learning are integrated into the appraisal. The use of manipulatives and other formats must take place in an orderly and systematic manner. One procedure to accomplish this utilizes the inter-active unit (IU).

### The Interactive Unit

The interactive unit is an effective organizer in that it provides a means:

to balance the format of the items contained in the appraisal. The number of items for each combination could be plotted.

to organize instruction so that multiple sets of tasks can be pre-pared for the same set of content. As many as 10 different formats for worksheets can be developed from the IU. (Cawley, 1984)

These factors enable the appraisal specialist to determine strengths and weaknesses and to relate these to content selection or to the selection of instructional alternatives.

Interactive programming is a process that defines interactions between teachers and children and among teachers, children, and materials. When used to meet the needs of learning-disabled children in mathematics, inter-active programming provides an orderly arrangement for variation in instructional practices and material modification. The interactive unit does no more than emulate good teaching. Its advantage is that it systematizes the management and selection of the alternatives in good teaching. The process is content free and can be implemented in any subject area (e.g., science, social studies) to develop concepts and skills within that subject area.

Exhibit 1-2 presents an example of an interactive unit. The grid is the controlling element in interactive programming. The terms used in an IU are:

MANIPULATE ......... Manipulation of objects (piling, arranging, and moving)

DISPLAY ............... (Instructor Interaction) Presentation of displays (pictures, arrangements of materials)

SAY ..................... Oral discussion

IDENTIFY .............. (Learner Interaction) Selection from multiple choices of nonwritten materials (pictures, objects)

WRITE ................. Written materials (letters, numerals, words, signs of operation) and marking of these types of materials

The grid describes 16 possible combinations of interaction between teacher and children. These 16 combinations serve to organize the manner in which instruction takes place and the manner in which instructional materials are developed or modified to represent selected principles and skills of mathematics.

The IU provides for systematic variation in teacher behavior and for constancy of learner behavior or for constancy of teacher behavior and variation in learner behavior. Examine Exhibit 1-2 by glancing back and forth across the rows. Note that the manner in which the teacher elects to represent a principle or skill changes with the move from one cell to another. Note also that the behavior of the learner is constant. In effect, the move across the rows makes it possible for the teacher to modify the means of input while holding the output behavior constant.

Look up and down the columns. Here we see that teacher behavior is held constant and it is the learner behavior that is changing. The move up or down any column seeks variation in learner behavior.

In the manipulate/manipulate task, Exhibit 1-2, the teacher would say something such as "Watch me," produce the flip, and then say, "Do what I did." In the write/write task the teacher would say, "I am going to show you a word. I want you to copy the word I show you." The teacher would show the word "flip" and the learner would copy the word. Numerous permutations are possible within each cell. Again, in the write/write cell, assume the teacher wanted to include short-term memory. The teacher would say, "I am going to show you a word and then I will take the word away. After I take it away, I want you to write the word." If the teacher wanted to stress comprehension, he or she might say, "I am going to show you a word. I want you to write a sentence in which the meaning of the word is properly used," or the teacher might elect a multiple-choice activity and say, "I am going to show you a word. There are three definitions

**Exhibit 1-2** Interactive Unit: FLIP

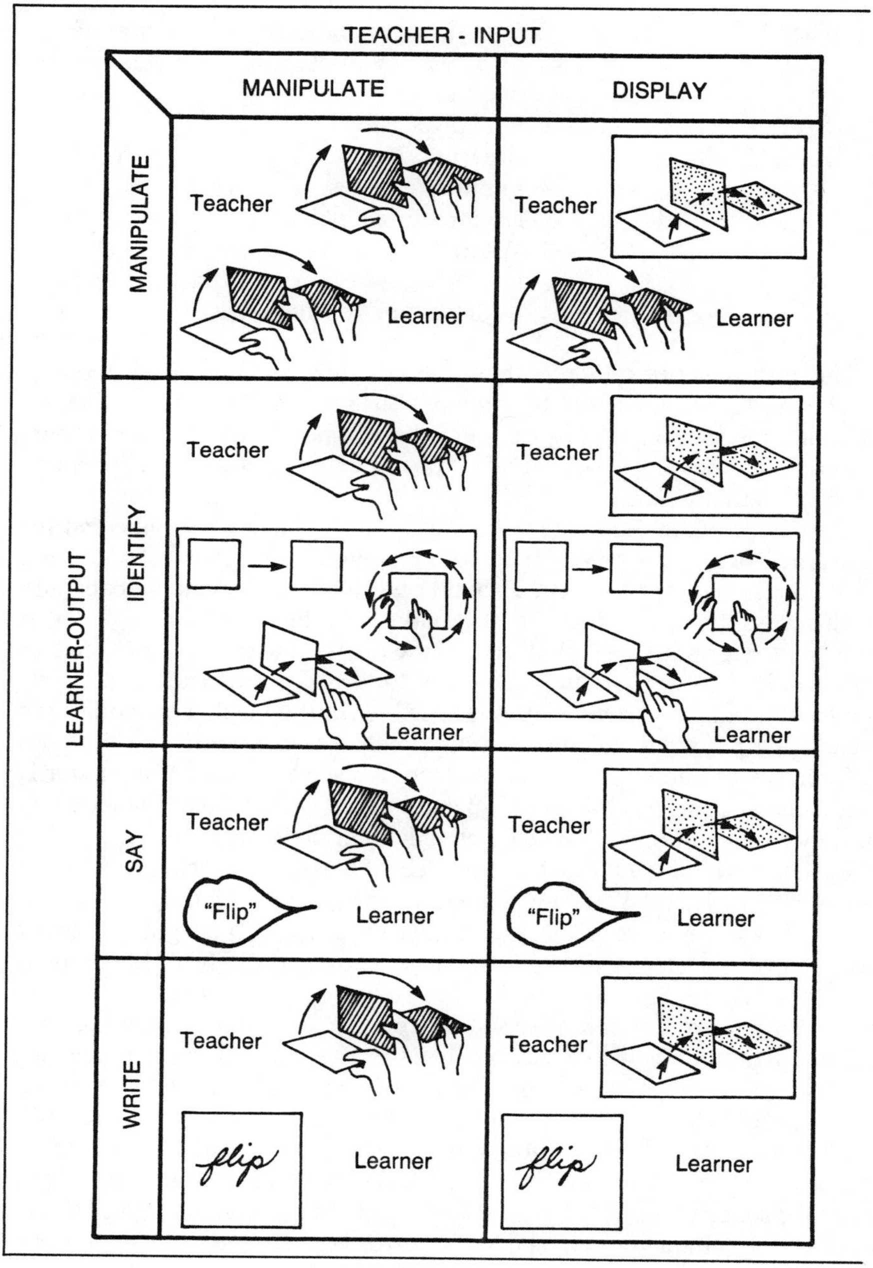

**Exhibit 1-2** continued

with the word. I want you to mark the choice that is the best definition for the word.''

If a teacher or diagnostician wanted to determine the character of response behavior, he or she need only select a given column and proceed up or down as desired. If, on the other hand, the teacher wanted to determine something about the nature of the child's receptive capabilities, he or she would go across the rows. There exists, therefore, a capability to determine something about the relative strengths and weaknesses of the learner in both expressive and receptive terms. This is important in programming for the learning-disabled child because the child might have a problem that is receptive (e.g., reading), one that is expressive (e.g., writing), one involving transferring from one combination (e.g., manipulate/identify) to another (e.g., write/say), or one in which there is an impairment in a combination of some receptive and expressive interactions (e.g., reading and writing), but no problem in other areas (e.g., say/identify).

If a teacher has a child with severe visual symbolic difficulties (i.e., material composed of letters, numerals, and codes or signs), he or she might eliminate interaction via the *write* column and utilize other combinations. If a teacher has a child whose success rate in group situations is low, he or she might eliminate the *say* and *manipulate* response options because these tend to expose the child to the group. The *identify* and *write* responses are somewhat more private and do not expose the child in front of others.

The IU can also be used as a guide in the development of instructional alternatives. This becomes important in meeting the needs of the learning disabled.

> If the learner is to be taught a set of knowledge that is new to the learner, it is essential that this be done using skills or procedures with which the learner is proficient. If, for example, the learner is not proficient in the use of manipulatives, then teaching a new content area such as division through manipulatives may be unwise.
>
> If the learner is to be taught a new procedure, this should be done within a known set of content. If, for example, the learner is knowledgeable in subtraction, the use of manipulatives should be introduced in subtraction before proceeding to use them in division.

## Combining Referenced-Based and Curriculum-Based Appraisal

Pupil appraisal can be conducted within a model that differentiates the stages of appraisal and that allows for the use of different techniques in any topic of mathematics. Table 1-5 shows one arrangement utilizing this approach.

A primary difference between curriculum-based and referenced-based appraisal is content. The content for curriculum-based assessment is taken directly from the material being taught in the class or school. The content for referenced-based appraisal is selected to be representative of that which any youngster in any school might encounter. The content for curriculum-based appraisal has more meaning in terms of the knowledge component of attribute-based approaches. That is, the teachers can tell if the material might have been taught and if the individual was in school during the time it was taught. Knowledge deficits might be curriculum related, rather than learner related.

In either case, attention should be given to the following item factors:

1. *Item clarity* — Does the examiner understand the item? Is it clear and efficient? Does the child understand the item?

2. *Item identification* — Does the learner locate the correct item amidst a set of items? How many items can be included on a page? In a set?

---

**Table 1-5** Curriculum-Based and Referenced-Based Appraisal

|  | *Curriculum-Based* | *Referenced-Based* |
|---|---|---|
| Measurement | Teacher-made quizzes or exams that are used to assign marks or to compare learners | Norm-referenced ability or achievement tests that are used to compare learners against a standard |
| Assessment | Teacher-made tests that sample many areas of math. Tests that accompany specific series | Norm-referenced tests of achievement that sample many areas of math |
| Diagnostics | Teacher-made devices where items are constructed to provide data on intraindividual performance. Teacher use of clinically validated techniques for classroom content | Standardized procedures or clinically validated techniques |

3. *Item specificity* — Does the learner attend to the relevant aspects of the item? Are there factors (spacing on the page, reading level, or something else) that mask performance? If the item is concept rooted, is the concept specifically clear so as to be certain that the concept was actually measured?

4. *Item accuracy* — Is the item mathematically accurate? Can it be reliably matched to a behavioral objective descriptor? Are the distractors logically consistent with the intent of the item?

5. *Item ease* — Is the item easy to administer? Does the examiner have difficulty locating materials, sequencing them, and keeping records?

6. *Item attractiveness* — Is the item attractive and appealing to the examiner? To the child?

Another major problem is nomenclature. Clinicians often utilize a set of descriptors that are not well understood by the professional who delivers instruction. This problem is discussed in Chapter 7.

Exhibit 1-3 displays a set of information concerning one individual. The items are plotted by strengths (i.e., those at the top) and weaknesses (i.e., those in the lower section) and by each content area. Given the fact that the content is specific, the user need only glance at the profile and read across the top to identify strengths and across the bottom to identify weaknesses. The instrument used to conduct this assessment was the *Mathematics Concept Inventory,* Level 3. The learner profile in Exhibit 1-3 lists each item by strand, area, and concept. Each item in the MCI is similar to that shown in Exhibit 1-4. Note that the item is coded by strand area and concept. The user knows precisely what the item assessed and can translate that into instructional activities.

## Level of Functioning and Level of Expectancy

Two types of comparisons of the learning disabled are necessary in the appraisal process. These comparisons occur at the present level of functioning and at the level of expectancy. Comparisons at the level of expectancy provide for rule-based decisions and the selection of a service delivery option. Comparisons at the present level of functioning provide for

**Exhibit 1-3** Learner Profile, Based on *Mathematics Concept Inventory,*
Level 3

|  | Numbers | Fractions | Measurements | Word Problems |
|---|---|---|---|---|
| Expectancy 4-0 |  |  |  |  |
| Level of Functioning 2-1 | Addition of 2 + 2 digit numbers<br>Grouping by 10s | Part-Size Relations | Linear Measures | Subtraction with Indefinite Quantifiers |
|  | Subtraction of 1-digit numbers<br>Addition: Sign of Operations<br>Addition of 1-digit numbers | Interchangeable Parts<br><br>Blended Parts | Liquid Measures<br><br>Height: High/Low<br><br>Speed: Rate | Addition with Indefinite Quantifiers |
|  | Cardinal Property to 19 | Discrete Parts |  | Counting: No Classification |

content selections. To illustrate, the appraisal data might indicate that Child A is learning disabled and that an appropriate service delivery model would be a combination of four hours per day of regular class and one hour per day of specially designed instruction in a resource center. Let us say that the individual in our example is 12 years of age and has average intellectual ability. The expectancy level approximates seventh grade. The youngster has an overall level of functioning approximating the third grade level. An analysis of the item plot such as that shown in Exhibit 1-3 indicates that no single area of performance in mathematics shows proficiency beyond the fourth grade level. About 40 percent of the correct responses were generated on items typically associated with first or second grade content.

What do the data suggest? Would Child A be appropriately served in a class with his or her age group? What difficulties would this present to the teachers? To the child? Should Child A remain in regular class during math instruction or would that be the time to send him or her to the resource room? What will happen if the child misses all the math of the

**Exhibit 1-4** Sample Test Items

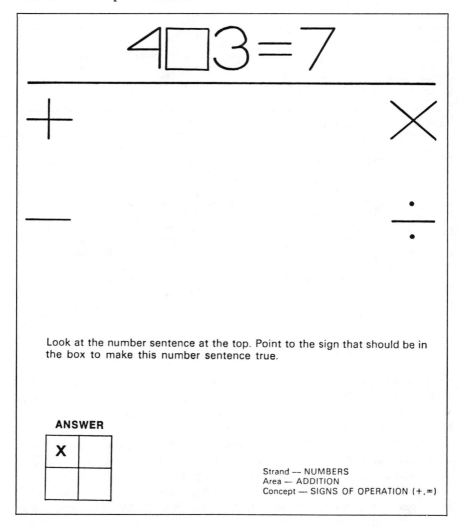

Look at the number sentence at the top. Point to the sign that should be in the box to make this number sentence true.

**ANSWER**

Strand — NUMBERS
Area — ADDITION
Concept — SIGNS OF OPERATION (+,=)

seventh grade during the time of actual enrollment? What topics will be covered in the resource room? Is it possible Child A could respond more effectively to the upper-level math if specially designed instruction was truly provided? What about goal setting and the selection of a course of study in the secondary school? Where will competency tests and graduation requirements fit in? Will the school exercise the option to absent the child from the competency requirements? What will happen if the specially designed instruction does impact Child A and he or she no longer meets the rule-based requirements for learning disability but is still educationally discrepant? If the specially designed instruction is working, how will the school arrange to continue it? If those who are providing the specially designed instruction were to leave, will it continue at the same level of quality? Can the new personnel interpret the appraisal information to arrive at the same conclusion as to an effective program for the learner?

## DIAGNOSTICS

Within the field of special education, the process of diagnosis in mathematics or arithmetic has suffered more neglect than any other facet of the appraisal-intervention process. This might be due to a number of factors, among which are the following:

1. the dominance of measurement and the feeling that if we know the grade-equivalent status of the child, we have sufficient information upon which to construct an intervention
2. the lack of research and interest in research in mathematics, a factor that has limited our knowledge of the magnitude and complexity of the existing problem
3. a lack of training in teacher education and inservice programs
4. the difficulty in developing the necessary knowledge and skills that would enable appraisal specialists to accomplish the process of diagnosis

## KeyMATH

Special education mistakenly took the terminology in one of the major tests as an indication that the test had the capability to serve the function of diagnosis. As a result, many special educators thought they were accomplishing the process of diagnosis because the name of the test included the word *diagnosis* in it. Specifically, the *KeyMATH Diagnostic Test* captured the hearts of special educators and many felt the process of diagnosis was operative within that test. As we know today, the content of *KeyMATH* is so lacking, the gaps between and among items so great, and the comparability of one subtest with another so limited it is unlikely that *Key-MATH* ever truly served any useful function.

### Inventory of Basic Arithmetic Skills

Recently, other measures claiming a diagnostic capability have emerged. The *Inventory of Basic Arithmetic Skills* (Enright, 1983) is a test of 144 computational skills across the four operations of addition, subtraction, multiplication, and division of numbers, fractions, and decimals. The inventory consists of a Wide Range Placement Test, a Skill Placement Test, and a set of Basic Facts Tests. The manual indicates that the inventory evolved through three levels of field testing and two levels of statistical analysis, although none are fully described. For example, given the fact that the inventory is predicated upon an analysis of algorithmic deficiencies and patterns, it is reasonable to expect that some report on the frequency of each algorithm would be included based on age and level of functioning. This would enable the user to know if a different algorithm was typical or atypical of a given age, a factor that has significant importance for diagnosis.

The inventory describes 233 discrete error types and has these grouped into the following error clusters:

- recognizing
- process
- substitution
- omission
- directional
- placement
- attention to sign
- guessing

The items in the inventory are presented in paper-pencil format, a factor that limits its diagnostic and interpretative capability.

Each section (e.g., division of whole numbers) of the *Inventory of Basic Arithmetic Skills* contains a set of worksheets including items that relate to specific characteristics (e.g., 1-digit number by a 1-digit number). These are sequenced by skill and grade level taught, although there is some uncertainty as to the basis of the sequencing. The data in the manual do not show whether the worksheets have been sequenced on the basis of the field test data or for some other reason. If grade level taught was the basis for the sequencing, the items do not follow this rule. To illustrate, the division items are sequenced as follows:

| Test Sequence | Grade Level Taught |
|---|---|
| D-1 | 3.0 |
| D-2 | 3.4 |
| D-3 | 3.7 |
| D-4 | 3.3 |
| D-5 | 3.5 |
| D-6 | 3.4 |
| D-7 | 3.8 |
| D-8 | 3.7 |
| D-9 | 4.1 |
| D-10 | 3.7 |

As can be seen, had the worksheets been sequenced by grade level taught, the sequence would be different.

The user needs to examine the performance of the learner within a total context. There might be more than one type of error within a problem or a combination of errors within a set of problems. The occurrence of a consistent error pattern with a set of items would signal one approach to remediation. The occurrence of an inconsistent error pattern within a set of items would signal an alternative and possibly easier approach to remediation.

**Diagnostic Test of Arithmetic Strategies**

The *Diagnostic Test of Arithmetic Strategies* (Ginsburg and Mathews, 1984) is designed to measure procedures children use to perform arithmetic operations. DTAS is an informal instrument. As an informal device, it allows one to make use of flexibility in testing procedures. DTAS focuses analysis on both successful and unsuccessful methods of individual computation across the four basic operations of addition, subtraction, multiplication, and division. Each operation is presented in three sections. There are sections on:

- Setting Up The Problem
    Addition:  Tell the child to write down eighty-five plus three.
    Subtraction:  Tell the child to write down fifty-six minus four.
    Multiplication:  Tell the child to write down sixty-three times two.
    Division:  Tell the child to write down forty-eight divided by two.
- Written Calculation
    Addition:  Give worksheet and have child do items.
    Subtraction:  Give worksheet and have child do items.

Multiplication: Give worksheet and have child do items.
Division: Give worksheet and have child do items.

- Informal Skills
I want you to do some problems in your head. Tell me how you are doing the problem in your head.
Addition: How much is fourteen and thirteen?
Subtraction: How much is seventeen minus four?
Multiplication: How much is thirteen times four?
Division: How much is forty-eight divided by two?

The scoring procedures emphasize informal analysis. These focus upon number-fact errors, bugs, slips, and skipping numbers. The user manual contains a chapter on interpretation and remediation, although the remedial recommendations are vague and seemingly unrelated to the diagnostic procedure. For example, there is a recommendation to use physical properties such as bundles of sticks, but there are no diagnostic components that specifically include diagnostics with "sticks." Nor are there any illustrations as to how the remediation would be carried out with sticks (e.g., how would you do 276 divided by 12 with sticks?).

**Diagnostic Chart for Fundamental Processes in Arithmetic**

The *Diagnostic Chart for Fundamental Processes in Arithmetic* (Buswell and John, 1925) seems to be the most comprehensive of the present-day diagnostic tests or inventories for arithmetic difficulties. The *Buswell-John* consists of 88 pairs of items that measure fundamental skills in addition, subtraction, multiplication, and division. The student is instructed to complete items on a worksheet. Because this is an individual appraisal, the teacher sits with the child during the procedure. The teacher instructs the child to think aloud in order to determine how the child is thinking during the completion of the task. Exhibit 1-5 shows the teacher diagnostic record for addition. The teacher maintains a record of the child's explanations and makes note of any response patterns from the child.

The frequency of the type of error uncovered during field testing is listed at the top of the diagnostic record. Thus, "errors in combinations" were the most frequently occurring errors and "added the same number twice" was the least frequently occurring error. All error patterns occurred at least five times in the field of testing. The manual provides explanations as to the general source of the difficulty for each pair of items. In effect, these explanations serve as the basis for remediation.

**Exhibit 1-5** Teacher's Diagnostic Chart

| | |
|---|---|
| Teacher's Diagnosis<br>for pupil _____ | **TEACHER'S DIAGNOSTIC CHART**<br>**FOR**<br>**INDIVIDUAL DIFFICULTIES**<br>**FUNDAMENTAL PROCESSES**     Printed in U.S.A.<br>**IN ARITHMETIC**<br>**Prepared by G.T. Buswell and Lenore John** |

Name _____ School _____

Grade _____ Age _____ IQ _____ Date of Diagnosis: _____

Add. _____; Subt. _____; Mult. _____; Div. _____

Teacher's preliminary diagnosis _____

---

**ADDITION: (Place a check before each habit observed in the pupil's work)**

| | |
|---|---|
| ___ a1  Errors in combinations | ___ a15  Disregarded column position |
| ___ a2  Counting | ___ a16  Omitted one or more digits |
| ___ a3  Added carried number last | ___ a17  Errors in reading numbers |
| ___ a4  Forgot to add carried number | ___ a18  Dropped back one or more tens |
| ___ a5  Repeated work after partly done | ___ a19  Derived unknown combination from familiar one |
| ___ a6  Added carried number irregularly | ___ a20  Disregarded one column |
| ___ a7  Wrote number to be carried | ___ a21  Error in writing answer |
| ___ a8  Irregular procedure in column | ___ a22  Skipped one or more decades |
| ___ a9  Carried wrong number | ___ a23  Carrying when there was nothing to carry |
| ___ a10  Grouped two or more numbers | ___ a24  Used scratch paper |
| ___ a11  Splits numbers into parts | ___ a25  Added in pairs, giving last sum as answer |
| ___ a12  Used wrong fundamental operation | ___ a26  Added same digit in two columns |
| ___ a13  Lost place in column | ___ a27  Wrote carried number in answer |
| ___ a14  Depended on visualization | ___ a28  Added same number twice |

Habits not listed above _____

---

**(Write observation notes on pupil's work in space opposite examples)**

| (1)                     | | (5)                 | |
|---|---|---|---|
| 5    6<br>2    3 | | 6 + 2 =<br>3 + 4 = | |

**Exhibit 1-5** continued

| (2) | | | (6) | | |
|---|---|---|---|---|---|
| 2 | 8 | | 52 | 40 | |
| 9 | 4 | | 13 | 39 | |
| (3) | | | (7) | | |
| 12 | 13 | | 78 | 46 | |
| 9 | 5 | | 71 | 92 | |
| (4) | | | (8) | | |
| 19 | 17 | | 3 | 8 | |
| 2 | 9 | | 3 | 8 | |
| | | | 5 | 7 | |
| | | | 8 | 9 | |
| | | | 2 | 7 | |

*Source:* Reprinted with the permission of Guy T. Buswell.

### Diagnostic Protocol for Arithmetic

The *Diagnostic Protocol for Arithmetic* (Cawley, in progress) is an informal process designed to appraise intraindividual characteristics in arithmetic. Figure 1-3 displays the format of the DPA. As can be seen, there are two points of entry. If the diagnostician feels the learner is capable of responding to arithmetic computation items, the learner is introduced to the process with computational items. If it is felt that the status of the learner is more characteristic of precomputational proficiency, the learner is introduced to the diagnostic process at the concept level. At the concept level, items 1–5 have a "cardinality" about them. Should the youngster experience difficulty with items 1–5, the examiner would go directly to the learning section. Here the youngster would be taught number/numeral names, sequencing of items by cardinal property, and rote counting. The appraisal would focus upon learning and the type of data collected would identify the number of repetitions needed to learn a given amount of material. Items are also derived from measurement, fractions, and geometry. The level of difficulty is equivalent to preschool.

The information obtained from the concepts and the learning sections provides direction for intervention based on choices of mathematics topics (e.g., measurement activities) or learning. One could focus on procedures that would increase the efficiency of learner performance by providing experiences based on strengths. The emphasis would be on rate, speed, and related components of performance.

Since the DPA is an informal instrument, one could substitute or add different content areas, weight, for example, as well as height. The computational component of the DPA can be directed toward the use of

**Figure 1-3** Format of *Diagnostic Protocol for Arithmetic*

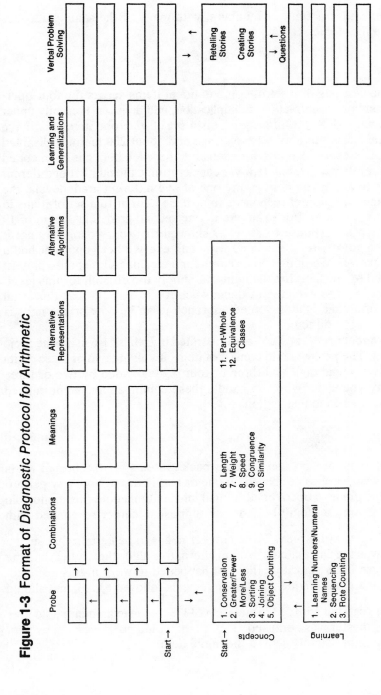

operations with fraction, or numbers, with many of the same guidelines used for either topic.

## Probe

A probe consists of a set of computational items across the four operations of addition, subtraction, multiplication, and division. Presently under study (Cawley & Kahn, in progress) is a set of 92 probe items that have been administered to about 200 average and about 200 learning-disabled children. The exact response for each child for each item has been coded and is presently being tabulated. We can determine the number of different responses to any given item at any one of five different grade levels, the number and variation of responses to a single item or to a set of items in any given classroom. For example, in one second grade classroom of 19 the variation in response to $85 + 39$ showed that four youngsters got it right, three got it wrong the same way, and every other youngster had a different answer. Obviously, the search for a meaningful response pattern was limited by the fact that the item was simply too difficult for this level. This is an important factor in diagnostics for it may be that the usual response of a child is an invented approach to an item he or she finds is unfamiliar or too difficult.

The components of the DPA are illustrated in Exhibit 1-6 using the topic of division. The probe would consist of items involving two or three digits divided by a single digit and three or four digits divided by two or three digits. Any youngster who can handle these combinations is not in need of specially designed instruction.

## Combinations

The combinations are designed as backup items for the probe. As is often the case, probes are based on one or two items without any permutation of the items to uncover additional information about the learner. To illustrate, given the item $8\overline{)488}$, let us suppose a learner responded with $8\overline{)488}$ with quotient $1$ and then with $8\overline{)488}$ with quotient $61$. The examiner needs to be certain that such a response was the calculated use of an alternative algorithm rather than the incorrect use of an algorithm that just happened to work in this instance. The combinations provide additional items as follows: $6\overline{)376}$, and should the learner respond with $6\overline{)376}$ with quotient $1$ and then $6\overline{)376}$ with quotient $61$ R , the examiner would note that the youngster was confused. This factor would not have been evident had the examiner simply scored the initial item.

**Exhibit 1-6** Sample Items, *Diagnostic Protocol for Arithmetic*

|              PROBE              |       COMBINATIONS       |        MEANINGS         |

PROBE

$119 \overline{\smash{)}406}$

$15 \overline{\smash{)}243}$

$12 \overline{\smash{)}276}$

$9 \overline{\smash{)}192}$

COMBINATIONS

$12 \overline{\smash{)}214}$

$21 \overline{\smash{)}294}$

$13 \overline{\smash{)}256}$

$16 \overline{\smash{)}208}$

MEANINGS

1. Estimation
   See this:
   $$21 \overline{\smash{)}294}$$
   About how many times
   will twenty-one go into
   the number?

2. Place Value
   See the number with the
   line under it. How much
   is that number?
   $$12 \overline{\smash{)}2\underline{56}}$$

ALTERNATIVE
REPRESENTATIONS

ALTERNATIVE
ALGORITHMS

LEARNING AND
GENERALIZATIONS

Learn these:

(IIIII)  0000  111111

(IIIII)  000

(IIIII)

(IIIII)

Bundles of toothpicks

$$
\begin{array}{r}
12 \overline{\smash{)}276} \quad 10 \\
\underline{120} \\
156 \quad 10 \\
\underline{120} \\
36 \quad 3
\end{array}
$$

$$
\begin{array}{ccc}
 & C & H & L \\
M \overline{\smash{)}J} & A \overline{\smash{)}P} & B \overline{\smash{)}T}
\end{array}
$$

Do these:

$$
\begin{array}{ccc}
M \overline{\smash{)}J} & H \overline{\smash{)}P} & C \overline{\smash{)}J} \\
M \overline{\smash{)}P} & L \overline{\smash{)}T} & A \overline{\smash{)}T}
\end{array}
$$

$$C \times M = H \times A =$$
$$B \times L = A \times H =$$

VERBAL PROBLEM
SOLVING

A boy has 12 sets of apples and 23 sets of
pears. He has 276 apples in all. How many
apples in each set?

A boy divided his apples among his 12
friends so that each friend got 23 apples.
How many apples did the boy start with?

QUESTIONS

A boy has 276 apples.
The boy has 12 friends.

*Meanings*

The section devoted to meanings focuses on three factors in addition and subtraction and three factors in multiplication and division. These are *estimation* and *place value* in each instance and in the case of addition and subtraction, the *interrelationships among* the addends (2 + 3 = 5; 5 − 3 = 2), which connotes reversibility, and in the case of multiplication and division, the factor × factor product relationship (e.g., 2 × 3 = 6; 6 ÷ 3 = 2; 6 ÷ 2 = 3).

*Alternative Representations*

In conducting the diagnostic appraisal across alternative representations, the interactive unit (IU) is utilized. To the extent necessary, all 16 combinations of the interactive unit might be utilized with a given learner. The purposes of this are twofold: first, to identify the effectiveness of performance across alternative representations (i.e., can the child do the item with blocks; does the child have any idea as to how to do the item with toothpicks; specifically, can the youngster represent the item in any format other than paper-pencil); second, to develop a basis on which the examiner can select alternative representations for the purpose of initiating the intervention. Whereas some approaches recommend the use of physical properties (Ginsburg & Mathews, 1984), they fail to conduct any appraisal that would indicate the performance characteristics in using these properties. Also, many teachers change the algorithm when they change formats of representation. Both the algorithm and the representation need to be systematically manipulated for true diagnosis. The illustration of 276 divided by 12 maintains the integrity of the algorithm (Cawley, 1984) and allows for the completion of the item across each of the interactive combinations.

**Alternative Algorithms**

The question of the conventional algorithm must ultimately be addressed. Is this algorithm best for a given youngster at a given point in time? We know, for example, that one does not need to borrow to subtract, and that operations done left-to-right can be done as effectively as those done right-to-left. Why then do we insist on the use of only one algorithm for each youngster? It may be that successful intervention can be initiated with the use of alternative algorithms rather than a rehashing of the one that has produced the failure. The introduction of an alternative algorithm brings the factor of novelty into the diagnostic process. Here the student is likely to deal with an approach that has never been used before. The number of repetitions or the procedures used when learning new algorithms can be carefully recorded. A key element in the use of alternative algorithms is the combined strategies of teaching and appraisal. In effect, the clinician needs to be teaching during the process of diagnosis. Over time, each clinician will develop a sense as to which algorithms are more or less appropriate for children with certain attributes. For this reason it is important to incorporate a number of algorithms for each of the operations into the diagnostic repertoire.

**Learning and Generalization**

Learning and generalization are integral components of any diagnostic procedure. Learning appraisal provides a basis for determining the efficiency with which the learner responds to new or to novel demands. It is most useful to identify the number of items or amount of time or repetitions it will take to learn new items. Without acquisition at the original learning stage, retention and generalization will be less than optimal. This means that the learner must meet criteria (e.g., two perfect repetitions in a row without assistance and again in three to five minutes). Once criteria have been obtained and the examiner is satisfied that the material has been acquired and retained, the learner can be asked to perform selected generalization tasks. The illustration in Exhibit 1-6 shows three simple paired-associate learning combinations. These would be practiced until the criterion is met. The learner would then be given a series of items to work similar to the ones shown.

There are many types of learning and different forms of stimuli and criteria that can be established. In an informal procedure, the examiner has the latitude to specify these. The information fed back to the teacher would indicate the number of times something has to be repeated for the child, the number of items that can be included in a set of materials to be learned, and the extent to which the child might be able to work with these items after they have been learned.

**Verbal Problem Solving**

The word problems shown in Exhibit 1-6 show two illustrations from division. In reality, any diagnostic approach to word problems needs to emanate from some form of matrix or plan by which the problems are developed. In the main, it is important to make the reading easy. Performance in verbal problems should not be interfered with by complex vocabulary and terms with which the individual is not familiar. The learner should be presented with material that can be analyzed and processed.

If problem solving is the desired activity, the problems should be presented in a manner that permits the learner to solve them. Devard (1973) did a study that illustrates this point. She constructed sets of two types of problems, one containing extraneous information and the other without extraneous information. Addition and subtraction were the designated operations. Problems were written at three different vocabulary levels and with three different syntactical arrangements. Each problem was read aloud and the number of errors recorded. The next week the learner was given the problems to solve. What Devard found was that the number of reading errors increased as the vocabulary level increased. However, the type of problem error was independent of this. Problems with extraneous information were generally incorrect whether the child could read them or not. In another study, Ballew and Cunningham (1982) found varying patterns of reading, computation, and problem solving to affect percent correct.

The inclusion of word problems in the diagnostic process requires that the characteristics of each problem be delineated so that response patterns can be determined. Problems can be constructed using a matrix approach (Cawley et al., 1979). The process begins by specifying the characteristics of a matrix and then developing sets of problems for the cells within the matrix. Many matrices need to be developed. Exhibit 1-7 contains a matrix with the following characteristics:

Sentence Structure:
    Simple sentence
    Simple sentence with prepositional phrase
Computational Complexity:
    Single digit × single digit
    Two digit × single digit, no regrouping
    Two digit × two digit, no regrouping
Information Processing:
    No classification
    Classification
    Direct addition
    Indirect addition
Reading Vocabulary Level:
    Second–Fourth

Each problem or set of problems in the matrix is numbered. By examining the position of the number in the matrix, the teacher can determine the characteristics of each problem. Consider the following:

**Exhibit 1-7** Problem-Solving Matrix

| | Second | | Third | | Fourth | | |
|---|---|---|---|---|---|---|---|
| | Direct | Indirect | Direct | Indirect | Direct | Indirect | |
| Simple Sentence | 1 | 2 | 3 | 4 | 5 | 6 | Single Digit |
| Simple Sentence with Prepositional Phrase | 7 | 8 | 9 | 10 | 11 | 12 | |
| Simple Sentence | 13 | 14 | 15 | 16 | 17 | 18 | Two digit × one digit, no regrouping |
| Simple Sentence with Prepositional Phrase | 19 | 20 | 21 | 22 | 23 | 24 | |
| Simple Sentence | 25 | 26 | 27 | 28 | 29 | 30 | Two digit × two digit, no regrouping |
| Simple Sentence with Prepositional Phrase | 31 | 32 | 33 | 34 | 35 | 36 | |
| Simple Sentence | 37 | 38 | 39 | 40 | 41 | 42 | Three digit × two digit, no regrouping |
| Simple Sentence with Prepositional Phrase | 43 | 44 | 45 | 46 | 47 | 48 | |

*Source:* From "Math Word Problems: Suggestions for Learning Disabled Students," *Learning Disability Quarterly,* Vol. 2, pp. 25–41, 1979. Reprinted with the permission of the Council for Learning Disability.

3. John bought 3 coyotes.
   He then bought 2 more coyotes.
   How many coyotes did John buy?
4. John bought 3 coyotes.
   John now has 5 coyotes.
   How many coyotes did John start with?
32. John placed 13 new frogs on the rock.
    There are now 15 frogs on the rock.
    How many frogs did he start with?
34. John purchased 13 coyotes from the hunter.
    He now has 15 coyotes on his ranch.
    How many coyotes did he start with?
36. John pursued 13 alligators after the disease came.
    John has now pursued 15 alligators into the swamp.
    How many alligators did he pursue before the disease came?

The difference between problems 3 and 4 lies in information processing. Each is a simple sentence, at the third reader vocabulary level, using single-digit combinations. The distinction is in the use of the direct versus indirect problems.

Contrast 4 and 34. There are two key differences. One difference is the use of two-digit combinations, which makes the arithmetic more appropriate. Another difference consists of the inclusion of the prepositional phrase, which extends the amount of information that has to be processed.

Contrast 32, 34, and 36. The only difference is in reading vocabulary level.

If Child A was an able reader but a limited "arithmetiker," the sequence of assignments would likely go from 1 and 2 to 5 and 6. If Child B was a limited reader but an able "arithmetiker," the sequence of assignments would go downward from 1 and 2 to 31 and 32.

Once the needed matrices are established, the development of individual assignments is a relatively efficient procedure. To illustrate, what might be the next logical assignment for Child A and for Child B? Why might 11 and 12 be appropriate for Child A and 43 and 44 (notice the skipping of 37 and 38) be appropriate for Child B? As can be seen, error patterns can be determined and direct intervention initiated.

**Retelling Stories**

How children use quantifiers within context is something that should be determined in the diagnostic process. The child's relationship to quantity and to mathematical stimuli can be distorted and disorganized. Children may not be able to mentally manipulate contradictions in situations and to interpret these in contextual settings. The retelling of stories presents us with an interesting opportunity to observe how children manage information and respond to quantitative stimuli. For example, ask a child to tell the story of the Three Little Pigs, but limit the child to the fact that there are only two pigs present for the story. Or have the child tell the story of the Three Bears, but indicate that there are four bears instead of three at this time.

## Questions

Observations of the performance of some learning-disabled children suggest that interpreting questions may be more of a problem than giving answers. Often, these children do not understand the question, the idea of a question, or the manner in which the question relates to the set of information. As a result their answers are incorrect. However, the problem may not lie in their inability to provide the correct answer to a given set of information. The problem might lie in the question. For this reason, the systematic variation of question types is important in diagnosis. One of the most egregious errors the special educator can make is to link specific types of questions with specific types of responses. Questions such as "How many does the boy have left?" where the child is cued to certain key words as a signal for an operation can be devastating in comprehensive problem-solving programs. A task that requires the child to create the questions to certain types of stimuli has considerable diagnostic value. The question cues the examiner as to the manner in which the child is using the set of information.

## MICROCOMPUTER APPRAISAL

Thompson (1983) indicates that statistical capability, software flexibility, and microcomputer accessibility are combinations of factors that suggest an exciting future for systems of microcomputer appraisal.

A unique and significant component of appraisal will involve both "test-tailoring" and microcomputer test administration. "Tailoring" refers to the practice of individualizing which item subjects complete so as to maximize both the appropriateness and the reliability of the measurement. Reliability is essentially a function of score variance. If students are given items that are much too hard for them, they select answers by random guessing and chance scores are produced. If the items are consistently too easy for students, scores have little or no variance and the measurement provides little insight except that the students are above the "ceiling" of the measure.

Traditionally, efforts were made to minimize these difficulties by "centering" tests, giving groups of students tests "centered" at the ability level of the *average* student in the group. This raises the reliability of the ability estimates for the students of a group. However, unless the students are quite homogeneous, the procedure produces less accurate estimates for students at the two ability extremes in the group.

"Latent trait" measurement offers some important advances over traditional measurement practice by allowing students to take individualized sets of items centered at their individual ability levels. This results in optimal measurement of each individual. Latent trait mathematics then allows conversion of the scores into comparable measures even though the individuals may have taken different items with varying levels of difficulty. As Wright and Stone (1979, p. 141) note, "A calibrated item bank provides a resource from which subtests of items can be selected to form specifically designed tests with optimal characteristics. Scores on these tests, although stemming from different combinations or 'correct' responses to different selections of items, can nevertheless be converted through the bank calibrations into comparable measures." Typically, students are given a wide range of items and remaining items are "centered" at the ability level identified from this initial estimate. Furthermore, the initial ability estimate can be iteratively revised during the administration process.

This statistically feasible process becomes practical if the test is administered by a microcomputer processor. Such units are becoming increasingly available in schools (Weiss, 1983). The benefits of application of microcomputers in research and testing are also increasingly being recognized. As catalogued by Johnson (1982), they include the following:

1. Sequences in which one or a few factors at a time are altered are simple to conduct with microcomputers.
2. Observation and recording of responses can be done accurately and unobtrusively.
3. Examiner presence and thus demand characteristics can be reduced or eliminated.
4. Random assignment of subjects to conditions can be left to the computer itself.
5. Random presentation of material can be handled by the computer.
6. Administration time and paperwork can be reduced greatly since all data are stored on diskettes, and multiple copies of materials can be made quickly from the original.

One additional advantage to this application, not mentioned by Johnson, is that children are usually motivated to participate in computer-related activities.

## SUMMARY

This chapter described the process of appraisal as having three stages: measurement, assessment, and diagnosis. Of the three, only measurement has received more than scant attention in the field. Little attention has been devoted to assessment and still less to diagnosis.

Extensive work in assessment is needed to ensure that the attributes ascribed to the learning disabled are based on a reasonable representation of mathematics topics. Work in diagnosis is needed so a full range of individual characteristics can be more fully understood.

---

### REFERENCES

Ballew, H., & Cunningham, J. (1982). Diagnosing strengths and weaknesses of sixth-grade students in solving word problems. *Journal for Research in Mathematics Education, 13,* 202–210.

Buswell, G.T., & John, L. (1925). *Diagnostic Chart for Fundamental Processes in Arithmetic*. Indianapolis: Bobbs-Merrill.

Cawley, J.F. (in progress). *The diagnostic protocol for arithmetic*. New Orleans: University of New Orleans.

Cawley, J.F. (1984). Selection, adaptation and development of curriculum and instructional materials, Chapter 10. In *Developmental Teaching of Mathematics to the Learning Disabled*. Rockville, MD: Aspen Systems.

Cawley, J.F., & Kahn, H. (in progress). *A study of computational characteristics of learning-disabled and nonlearning-disabled children*. New Orleans: University of New Orleans.

Cawley, J.F., Fitzmaurice, A.M., Goodstein, H.A., Lepore, A., Sedlak, R., & Athaus, V. (1976). *Project MATH*. Tulsa, OK: Educational Progress Corp.

Cawley, J.F., Fitzmaurice, A.M., Shaw, R.A., Kahn, H., & Bates, H. (1979). Math word problems and suggestions for LD students. *Learning Disability Quarterly, 2,* 25–41.

Devard, A.J. (1973). *Oral reading of arithmetical problems by educable mentally retarded children*. Unpublished doctoral dissertation, University of Connecticut, Storrs, CT.

Enright, B. (1983). *Inventory of Basic Arithmetic Skills*. North Billerica, MA: Curriculum Associates.

Ginsburg, H.P., & Mathews, S. (1984). *Diagnostic Test of Arithmetic Strategies*. Austin, TX: ProEd.

Johnson, C.W. (1982). Microcomputer-administered research: What it means for educational researchers. *Educational Researcher, 11,* 12–16.

Kauffman, A., & Kauffman, N. (1983). *K-ABC Kauffman Assessment Battery For Children*. Circle Pine, MI: American Guidance Service.

Kirk, S., McCarthy, J., & Kirk, W. (1968). *Illinois test of psycholinguistic abilities* (Rev. ed.). Urbana, Ill: University of Illinois Press.

Levy, W. (1981). *WISC-R Arithmetic Subtest performance of mathematically handicapped and nonhandicapped learning disabled students as a function of presentations/response behaviors and vocabulary intervention.* Unpublished doctoral dissertation, University of Connecticut, Storrs, CT.

McCollough, B.C., & Zaremba, B.A. (1979). Standardized achievement tests used with learning disabled and non-learning disabled adolescent boys. *Learning Disability Quarterly, 2,* 65–70.

McDaniel, G. (1979). *DAS Information Bulletin No. 50.* Washington, DC: Department of Education.

Reisman, F.K., & Kauffman, S.H. (1980). *Teaching mathematics to children with special needs.* Columbus, OH: Charles E. Merrill.

Sternberg, R.J. (1984). What should intelligence tests test? Implications of a triarchic theory of intelligence for testing. *Educational Researcher, 13,* 5–15.

Thompson, B. (1983). Microcomputer Appraisal. (Personal Communication)

Thurlow, M., & Ysseldyke, J.E. (1979). Current assessment and decision making practices in mild learning disabled programs. *Learning Disability Quarterly, 2,* 15–24.

Tucker, J. (1979). The assessment of mathematics, spelling, and written expression. In D. Sabatino & T.L. Miller, (Eds.), *Describing Learner Characteristics of Handicapped Children and Youth.* Boston: Allyn & Bacon.

Weiss, R.P. (1983). Micro-Workshop—And what it's doing to our kids. *Electronic Learning, 2,* 24–28.

Wick, J. (1973). *Educational measurement: Where are we going and how will we know when we get there?* Columbus, OH: Charles E. Merrill.

Wright, B.D., & Stone, M.H. (1979). *Best test design.* Chicago: MESA Press.

# Chapter 2

# Measurement

*Henry A. Goodstein*

Assessment has been described as a systematic process for determining the current status of learner knowledge and skill and identifying any additional information required for effective instructional planning (Goodstein, 1984). The assessment process includes both quantitative and qualitative descriptions of the learner, weighted and synthesized through a process that considers value judgments (Gronlund, 1981). Measurement is the process of obtaining those quantitative descriptions.

Typically, the measurement of educational aptitude and achievement derives from the administration of a test. A test is an instrument designed to sample behavior in such a way that reliable (consistent) and valid (appropriate) inferences can be made from the test scores about the characteristics of the person taking the test. Test theory has been described as the mathematical formulation of principles through which observed behavior can be described and related to a substantive theory of behavior in such a way that the quality of description can be evaluated and refined (Allen & Yen, 1979).

This chapter will provide an overview of topics in test theory and measurement technology that should enhance the interpretation and application of test data for the instructionally relevant assessment of specific mathematics disabilities. Emphasis will be placed on the treatment of test theory from a criterion-referenced (domain-referenced) perspective, as it is this measurement technology that provides the greatest opportunity to improve the quality of teacher-constructed or teacher-adapted testing practices. More complete treatments of test theory (specifically, norm-referenced test score interpretation) and its application to the assessment of exceptional children can be found in the many excellent textbooks devoted to these topics.

## CATEGORIES OF EDUCATIONAL TESTS

Most authorities distinguish two broad categories of educational tests, aptitude and achievement tests. *Aptitude* tests are designed to predict future performance in some activity. *Achievement* tests are intended to measure knowledge and skill attained as a result of instruction. The two broad categories are not mutually exclusive as achievements predict future performance and all aptitude tests to a degree tap knowledge and skill attained as a result of instruction.

The focus on this chapter will be on achievement testing. Significant measurement issues are concerned with the interpretation of aptitude test scores (e.g., intelligence tests or psychoeducational process tests) or aptitude-achievement discrepancies in the identification and diagnosis of specific learning disabilities (see especially Berk, 1981; Salvia & Ysseldyke, 1981). However, for the classroom teacher faced with the challenge of designing a compensatory, developmental, or remedial program of mathematics instruction (and evaluating its effectiveness) for learners with a mathematics disability, many of these issues lack relevance.

## ALTERNATIVE MEASUREMENT TECHNOLOGIES

Two alternative measurement technologies are available for measuring achievement. The two technologies differ in the meaning one wishes to attach to test scores. Norm-referenced measurement is the older, more traditional technology. Performance on a norm-referenced test is evaluated as a *relative* measurement. The test score obtained by the student is evaluated in reference to the test scores obtained by others (the current population of a classroom or a school or some more broadly defined reference group at local, state, or national levels).

In the past twenty years increasing attention has been given to an alternative measurement technology that many instructional and measurement specialists believe is more appropriate for the planning and evaluation of student achievement (Goodstein, 1982). This technology has been referred to variously as *objectives-referenced, criterion-referenced,* or *domain-referenced.* The term *domain-referenced* will be used in this chapter as it most clearly describes the appropriate interpretation of such tests. Performance on a domain-referenced test is considered an *absolute* measurement. The test score obtained by the student is evaluated in reference to a *well-defined performance domain* (Hambleton, 1980a). Reference to the performance of others is not required to provide meaning to the obtained scores.

## NORM-REFERENCED MEASUREMENT

Typically, norm-referenced achievement tests assess a wider range of objectives with a limited number of items to measure each objective (in contrast to domain-referenced achievement tests). Efforts are made in the construction of a norm-referenced test to provide for maximum variation in individual scores. A wide range of obtained scores is useful in that it facilitates the ranking of students, an essential component of relevant measurement systems. While raw scores may be used for norm-referenced interpretations of performance at the local (classroom or school) level, typically raw scores are converted to derived scores (e.g., grade- or age-equivalents, percentiles, or some form of standard score such as T-scores or stanines) to allow for the comparison of a student's performance with that of some clearly defined reference group.

Historically, grade-equivalent scores have been the most popular form of derived scores for norm-referenced achievement tests. However, in recent years grade-equivalent scores have been the target of many criticisms and have been eliminated or deemphasized by test publishers. Cole (1982) provides an excellent review of these criticisms. The following overview derives from her analysis:

1. *Not an equal interval scale.* One grade-equivalent (GE) unit does not have the same meaning in different portions of the scale. The expected normal growth is not the same for students at different score levels. GE curves smooth uneven growth rates within the school year and fail to consider summer losses.
2. *Not comparable across school subjects.* A GE score in one school subject should not be compared with a GE score from another subject to infer relative strength in the two areas.
3. *Does not indicate grade level at which student can perform.* GE scales are constructed to give the grade level at which other students score the same as this student on the content tested, but do not provide information as to the level of content that a student should be taught. The notion of performing at grade level has questionable meaning beyond the elementary years.

Berk (1981) adds to this list of criticisms the observations that GE scores are derived primarily from interpolation and extrapolation rather than from real data and that GE scores tend to exaggerate the significance of small differences in performance. Berk concludes that there is no technically sound reason to justify the use of GE scores in the identification, diagnosis, or remediation of learning disabilities.

Given the possibilities for misinterpretation of grade-equivalent (or age-equivalent) scores, many test publishers are reporting norm-referenced test scores as percentile ranks, standard scores, or both. Percentile ranks identify a student's position or relative standing in the norm group. They indicate the percentage of students that scored at or below a given raw score. Their interpretation is direct and easily understood and they are therefore recommended for individual test score interpretation by many measurement authorities (Berk, 1981; Gronlund, 1981).

Standard scores are linear transformations of raw scores to one of a variety of scales based on a normal distribution of test scores. Each of these scales would have a set mean and standard deviation. By comparing a student's standard score with the mean and standard deviation of the scale, the student's percentile rank can be identified. An advantage of standard scores is their equal-interval scale, which allows for a variety of statistical or arithmetical operations to be performed on test data (e.g., calculating average performance) that cannot be performed on GE scores (not an equal-interval scale) or percentiles (an ordinal scale). Stanines, T-scores, Z-scores, and deviation IQs are just some of the examples of standard scores.

Any appropriate norm-referenced interpretation of student achievement ultimately rests with the comparability of the student(s) being assessed and the samples of students comprising normative population. The measurements of performance are most reliable and valid for students who score closest to the mean of a norm-referenced achievement test (Berk, 1981). Several authorities have pointed out the difficulty in differentiating performance of exceptional students (at either end of the achievement continuum) when either all items are answered correctly or almost no items are answered correctly on a particular level of an achievement test (Horst, Tallmadge, & Wood, 1974; Jones, 1973). There is the natural inclination to assess a student with a specific learning disability using an achievement test whose content may be more appropriate (i.e., easier level of difficulty), even if the test or level of the test was intended to be administered to younger students. This is often referred to as out-of-level testing (Berk, 1981; Salvia & Ysseldyke, 1981).

Out-of-level testing involves administration of a test or a level of a test whose normative population differs fundamentally from the student being assessed (age, number of years of school, etc.). Derived scores based on norm tables provided by the test publisher will be invalid for the student. A domain-referenced interpretation of the test scores may be possible if sufficient items are provided to assess each objective (Goodstein, 1984).

Recently, several test publishers have attempted to address this problem of out-of-level testing with strategies for the vertical equating of scaled scores between levels of the same achievement test. While this process is subject to some systematic errors, these new strategies provide for more appropriate norm-referenced interpretations of performance on out-of-level achievement tests (Berk, 1981). The classroom teacher should seek advice from a psychometrician, testing specialists, or consultants for the test publisher on the proper interpretation of test scores when out-of-level testing is accomplished with a vertically equated series of achievement tests.

## DOMAIN-REFERENCED MEASUREMENT

A key recommendation of the NIE Conference on Research on Testing (Tyler & White, 1979) was a call for more effective integration of testing with teaching. The report suggested that instructional guidance was not well served by existing tests and recommended a sustained effort to improve the use of testing in instructional guidance. Standardized (norm-referenced) tests tend to be limited when it comes to day-to-day application to classroom instruction. The tests generally underrepresent the curricular content and instructional objectives of classroom teachers and are tied to the multiple-choice format.

For integrating classroom testing and instruction, teacher-developed tests are often strongest where standardized testing is weakest. Teacher-developed tests are readily adapted to curricular decisions, varying instructional objectives, and scheduling requirements. They can include a range of testing modes such as short-answer questions, structured writing assignments, and laboratory assignments in addition to multiple-choice items. Because of these properties, teacher-developed tests are potentially highly valid for instructional decision making.

The construction of a technically sound norm-referenced test is a significant challenge to a classroom teacher. Yet, historically it was this measurement technology that was emphasized in teacher preparation programs (if any measurement background was provided). The lack of knowledge and skill in test construction was cited by Tyler and White (1979) as a major limitation for the valid use of classroom tests for instructional planning and decision making. However, recent advances in measurement technology and test development practices, *specifically in domain-referenced measurement,* offer significant promise for improving the quality of teacher-developed tests and more closely linking those tests to commercially available tests and, more important, to effective classroom instructional planning.

**Constructing a Domain-Referenced Test**

Efforts are made in the construction of a domain-referenced test to adequately sample a performance domain. Items selected for a test are viewed as merely a sample of items selected from a larger universe of potential items (not necessarily actually written). This universe of potential items is conceptualized as a *domain*. For domain-referenced testing, the score one wishes to estimate for the student is the score that student would have obtained on all actual or potential items in the domain (Linn, 1980). Note that no intentional effort must be made in the construction of a domain-referenced test to cause variation in individual test scores (as is the case with norm-referenced test development). Reference to (comparison with) the performance of others is not required to provide meaning to the obtained scores.

It is clearly both impossible and/or undesirable in most testing situations to administer to a student all test items from a domain. Thus, one must *estimate* the student's domain score (true score in a classical sense) from the student's observed (actual) score on the *sample* of items that comprise the specific test.

The measurement precision optimally desired would result in a perfect correspondence between a student's test score obtained from a single administration of the test (typically stated as a proportion correct) and the student's true domain score. For example, if a student scored 80 percent on a particular domain-referenced test, one would want to predict with perfect confidence that the student would pass 80 percent of all the items in the measurement domain. Alternatively, if the student were to be retested with a different (random) sample of items from the domain, one would want to be totally confident that the student would again score 80 percent.

Obviously, the ideal aspired to can never be achieved because of a variety of factors that influence the performance of a student on a test. Collectively, these factors are referred to as *errors of measurement*. However, the magnitude of these errors of measurement will be affected by how well the test functions as a representative sample of the performance domain. For example, to the extent that the test is biased towards including more easy or difficult items or towards one of several topics within the domain, the domain score that one would estimate from actual performance on that test would be similarly biased (Linn, 1981).

To the extent that one can clearly describe the performance domain, representative sampling can be ensured and errors of measurement reduced. This allows one to speak with more confidence about the level of performance indicated by the student's test score. A well-defined measurement domain improves the quality of our interpretation of what the test score really means (Cronbach, 1980).

## Defining the Domain

Typically, the boundaries of domains are provided by instructional objectives. Broad instructional objectives provide for broad domains. Narrow or precise instructional objectives provide for more narrow instructional domains. Considerable effort in recent years has been directed towards improving the quality of descriptions of performance domains.

Most processes that have been explored to date for providing clarity and definition of measurement domains have resulted in narrowing the domains, often significantly (Linn, 1980). Prevailing opinion favors more intensive measurement of selected skills or content (more test items for fewer objectives) over a thinner sampling of a wider range of skills or content (fewer test items for more objectives) (Popham, 1981). This position assumes that considerable deliberative care is taken in the selection of the most representative or important skills or content.

There are typically two primary dimensions of domain specifications for most domain-referenced tests. The first describes rules (a plan) for sampling the content to be assessed. The second involves the determination of test item format(s) or measurement tactic(s) for assessing the content. In the explication of the item domain it is often assumed that minor variations in item format or content would be trivial and have an inconsequential impact on performance. However, seemingly minor variations in item format have been shown to substantially influence performance on domain-referenced tests containing division computational problems (Alderman, Swinton, & Braswell, 1979). The inference that a student could not perform certain types of division problems (a content inference) might have to be modified to refer to only those items presented in a particular format. Linn (1980) has observed that item format may be a critical component in the definition of a universe of test items in any domain-referenced test design.

Goodstein, Howell, and Williamson (1982) administered a battery of domain-referenced tests to 48 special education and 48 regular education students. The tests were designed to systematically measure four subsets of skills in subtraction with items using four formats (short-answer, multiple-choice, true-false, and a mixed format). For both samples of students, short-answer tests were significantly more difficult (and more reliable for decision making). Relatively minor differences in content definition resulted in significant differences in level of performance.

These results suggest that caution be exercised in the interpretation of performance on domain-referenced tests with rather broad content domains. Consolidated content domains (inclusive of several subskills) may not always provide sufficient items of varying content characteristics to allow for valid estimates of performance and contribute to valid instructional decisions.

While many teachers do not construct multiple-choice (or true-false) tests (especially in mathematics), the multiple-choice format remains popular with commercial test publishers. As more domain-referenced tests with multiple-choice formats are developed by commercial test publishers, differences in performance with respect to format become an important issue in the interpretation of test results. The results of the study by Goodstein, Howell, and Williamson suggested that multiple-choice tests may inflate performance estimates (in comparison with equivalent short-answer tests) by as much as one-third. Obviously, results from multiple-choice tests in mathematics should be viewed cautiously with respect to instructional planning and evaluation decisions.

**Detailed Test Specifications**

While instructional objectives fix or establish the domain, they are not sufficiently detailed to allow for precise description (Popham, 1978). Instructional objectives serve a variety of purposes, the direction of test construction processes being only one (and not always the most prominent). There is often a contradiction between level of detail included in an instructional objective for its role in communication as opposed to its role in evaluation (Kapfer, 1978).

One popular process used in the construction of domain-referenced achievement tests for minimal-competency testing programs is the use of detailed test specifications (Popham, 1978), a form of expanded instructional objectives. Starting with a broad general description of the domain to be assessed (which may or may not be stated as an instructional objective), the stimulus properties of potential test items are carefully described. In addition, rules for judging the adequacy of responses that will be supplied by students are enumerated. If multiple-choice items are to be created, attributes of the correct response and incorrect alternatives (foils) are clearly stated. Exercises or test items are then written to conform to these detailed test specifications.

Experience in the use of such specifications for designing minimal-competency tests is only beginning to accumulate. The process seems to require considerable sophistication and experience when it is applied to broader measurement domains. This results from the increasing number of factors that must be considered as important to success on the various tasks within the performance domain (Quelmallz, 1981). Often an outcome of the analysis process is the determination that the domain as conceptualized is simply too broad. Sometimes, only a decision to subdivide the domain will lead to a clear measurement strategy.

If classroom teachers were to use a process similar to the test specifications approach described above in the design of their teacher-developed tests, they would improve the clarity of the performance domain they seek to assess. Clarity of definition of the performance domain is also a prerequisite for effective instructional planning. Students in the preservice teacher education programs of Peabody College of Vanderbilt University were trained to use detailed test specifications in the development of domain-referenced inventories for instructional planning and evaluation.

While these students could have used a commercially available inventory for assessment, they would have been denied the opportunity to engage in the process of test design. It is this process that is as important as the quality of the achievements tests actually developed and that results in the improvement of instructional planning and decision making. It is the process of test design that confronts teachers with the task of examining the performance domain they are expecting to teach. Logical analysis of the performance domain, sequencing or hierarchically arranging subtasks within the domain, and selecting the most important or critical skills in the domain are as essential to effective instructional planning as to test development.

**Types of Domain-Referenced Interpretations**

Two types of domain-referenced interpretations can be distinguished. The first interpretation involves the use of the actual observed test score as an estimate of potential performance. The other more typical interpretation involves comparing the observed score with some standard that has been established. Most frequently, this interpretation is associated with making mastery/nonmastery decisions. In the first instance the measurement of performance is the sole objective of giving the test. In the latter instance that goal is supplanted in importance by the need to make a valid decision as a result of obtaining a particular score.

One of the reasons that prominent measurement professionals do not prefer the more commonly used term *criterion-referenced measurement* revolves around confusion that has existed over the meaning of the term *criterion* (Nitko, 1980). In most achievement testing situations, the only criterion that can be validated is that provided through the clear definition of the measurement domain. Unfortunately, many persons have confused the intended use of the term *criterion* with a standard for making a classification or placement (advancement) decision. This has tended to place a disproportionate emphasis on the selection of a standard over careful definition of the measurement domain in the test construction process (Millman, 1980). One can construct a domain-referenced (criterion-referenced) test with an explicit standard. One cannot construct a domain-referenced test without a well-defined measurement domain (even if one has set a standard of performance).

### Item Analysis for Domain-Referenced Tests

Regardless of how well-defined the measurement domain may be, the quality of the resulting measurements (and decisions to be made as a result of those measurements) will ultimately rest with the quality of the test items. Item analysis serves a different purpose for domain-referenced test construction than for the construction of norm-referenced tests (Berk, 1980). For norm-referenced tests, items are sought that contribute to the differentiation and ranking of students. Such items discriminate between students who score well on the test as a whole and those who score poorly. Perfectly valid items that prove to be too easy or too difficult and thus may not discriminate between students may be discarded in favor of items with higher discrimination indices.

Since the purpose of domain-referenced testing is not to compare individual performances, items that fail to discriminate between students would be retained if they were found not to be technically flawed. To eliminate such items would negatively affect the test as a representative sample of the performance domain. However, items that have negative discrimination indices (where poor performers on the test as a whole performed better on that item than good performers on the test as a whole) most probably are technically flawed and should be revised or eliminated.

The issue of judging the appropriate difficulty of items for domain-referenced tests is quite complex. For norm-referenced tests, items of average difficulty levels are sought in an effort to provide for maximum discrimination among examinees (Gronlund, 1981). For domain-referenced tests, the difficulty level of items should reflect the difficulty of the outcomes being measured. Some have argued that as long as the item can be shown to have been congruent with the test specifications for its construction, variation in item difficulty among parallel items on a test is acceptable (Popham, 1978, 1980). Such items would be judged as *derivatively homogeneous*.

Others have suggested that for most domain-referenced tests, items should have similar difficulty levels if it is intended that they function as parallel measurements of the same class of outcomes (Brennan, 1980). Such items would be judged as *functionally homogeneous*. Functional homogeneity as a goal must be balanced against many other considerations and should not be blindly pursued. One suggestion is that if a test item is at a level of difficulty *significantly* at variance with other items purportedly measuring similar outcomes, it is best to revise or eliminate it. Minor variations in item difficulty can be tolerated in most instances.

**Reliability**

Reliability is an essential characteristic of any measurement device. Consistency of measurement is a necessary (but not sufficient) condition for valid inferences regarding achievement. However, as with other features of measurement theory, one cannot directly study reliability. Rather, it must be *estimated* statistically. Classical test theory recognized three different approaches to estimating reliability, each approach employing a different methodology and suitable for responding to different concerns.

*Test-retest reliability* addresses the stability of measurements over time. *Parallel forms* (or equivalent forms) *reliability* addresses the equivalence of measurements over alternative forms of the same test. *Internal consistency reliability* (KR-20, KR-21, Coefficient Alpha, etc.) addresses the homogeneity of items within a test and provides an estimate of the magnitude of the other reliability coefficients from the administration of a single test.

Estimation of the reliability coefficient is only a means of estimating how much error is inherent in the actual observed score (errors of measurement). The higher the estimate of reliability, the lower would be the estimated errors of measurement and the more confident one would be that the student's true score was quite close to the score the student obtained on the test.

Similarly, the reliability of domain-referenced tests is a critical concern. The more confidence one has that the student's observed score is quite close to the student's domain score, the higher the probability of making dependable instructional decisions. Two divergent views regarding reliability have gained prominence with respect to domain-referenced tests— reliability of the measurements and reliability of the decisions based upon those measurements (mastery/nonmastery; advance/retain) (Traub & Rowley, 1980). Goodstein (1982) presents a comparison of these two approaches.

In general, a test with high measurement reliability will result in more reliable decisions than a test with lower measurement reliability. Two factors are prominent in their impact on measurement reliability—item homogeneity and test length. To the extent that items are similar in levels of difficulty, estimates of reliability are enhanced. To the extent that tests are longer, estimates of reliability are enhanced. As test item difficulties begin to vary, tests of increasing length must be constructed to achieve the same level of reliability.

Reflecting upon the test item sampling model that has been introduced above, this empirical finding makes sense. For those measurement domains that are broader, variance in item difficulties would be expected. To adequately sample those domains, a larger number of test items should be included on the test to ensure a representative sample of the divergent tasks being assessed (Wilcox, 1980). If the number of items to be sampled on the test was overly restricted, the risk of having a biased sample is increased. This would imply that the student's score on the set of items selected for one test might not predict how well the student might perform on an alternate set of items—hence, lower reliability. By increasing test length we increase the probability of accurately reflecting domain performance (across all items). Of course, if our domain is so broad and undefined as to limit the ability to make judgments about what might be a representative sample of items, the proper course is not to increase test length but to restructure the measurement domain.

## Validity

Validity refers to the intent or purposes for which the test is designed and scores are used (Berk, 1981). Just as a test cannot be judged as to reliability independently of a specification of methodology and population, neither can validity be judged absolutely. The appropriate way to frame a validity question is to ask, "Is the test (scores) valid for a particular purpose with a specific population of students?" Traditional classifications of validity consider content validity (fidelity of the test to the curriculum content it purports to measure), criterion-related validity (concurrent and predictive—the statistical relationship between scores on the test and a current or future criterion measure), and construct validity (the relationship of the test to the psychological construct it purports to measure). Berk (1981) extends this traditional listing to include curricular validity (the relationship of the test to the curriculum used by a particular school or school district) and discriminant validity (how well does this test differentiate groups of children, i.e., learning-disability children from nonlearning-disability children).

Historically, the most prominent validity consideration for domain-referenced tests was content validity (Popham & Husek, 1969). In fact, for some it was the only validity data sought. Focus was restricted to ensuring that the items were representative of the measurement domain. More recent efforts have been directed to the broader issue of construct validity (Linn, 1979, 1980). This recent work reflects a broadening of the concept of construct validity away from an exclusive focus on psychological constructs. The current effort involves consideration as to whether the types of items selected are the most representative (best) way to measure a particular skill or competency. Put another way, the question is, what is this test really measuring (Messick, 1981)?

For example, one may have set out to design a test of understanding fraction concepts. To attempt to demonstrate construct validity for the new test, test scores might be correlated with scores obtained from another well-established measure of understanding fraction concepts as well as a whole number computation test. The finding of high correlations between scores on the new test and scores on the computation test and correspondingly lower correlations with scores on the established measure of fraction concepts would weaken a claim for construct validity for the new test. The new test might be a valid measurement of computation of fractional numbers, but not a test of understanding fraction concepts.

This example is only suggestive of the variety of analysis processes available to seek support for construct validity. The techniques and approaches to seeking construct validity are quite diverse (Cronbach & Meehl, 1955). The very recognition of the importance of construct validity only serves to focus attention on the critical choices to be considered in selecting an appropriate measurement tactic for evaluating each instructional outcome.

Decision validity in most settings remains the ultimate criterion of interest in evaluating a domain-referenced test (Hambleton, 1980b). Most domain-referenced tests used by the classroom teacher result in an instructional decision—to advance the student to a new topic or unit or to retain the student in the current topic or unit for additional practice or remediation. Opportunities seldom are presented to conduct studies supporting the validity of decisions reached as a result of scores obtained on domain-referenced tests. This should not be interpreted as suggesting that those studies should not be attempted whenever possible or practical.

Typically, the teacher who is teaching within a mastery paradigm would make instructional decisions as a result of the scores obtained on the domain-referenced tests in comparison with a standard of performance (e.g., 80 percent correct). However, there may be an opportunity created as a result of an administrative necessity (to start a larger group of students in a new unit simultaneously) to conduct a natural experiment. The performance of students who failed to meet the standard on the last domain-referenced test can be contrasted with the performance of students who exceeded the standard. If the two groups did not significantly differ in their performance in the new unit, the claim for validity would be substantially impaired.

### Commercial Domain-Referenced Tests

The increased interest in domain-referenced measurement has given impetus to the development of a number of excellent criterion-referenced (domain-referenced) tests by commercial test publishers. Some of these tests are independent of an instructional program, while others are closely linked to a commercially available instructional system. Often those tests that are independent of an instructional system will provide excellent suggestions linking the assessment objectives to a variety of widely disseminated instructional materials. Goodstein (1984) includes a review of many such achievement tests.

Several of these domain-referenced achievement tests also publish data of representative pupil performance to allow normative comparisons. However, the distinguishing characteristics of these tests are not the presence or absence of norms but rather their clear specification of the measurement domain and the use of a sufficient number of test items to reliably and validly assess each objective.

The greater availability of high quality commercially developed domain-referenced tests and inventories will greatly assist the teacher who wishes to implement a domain-referenced instructional planning system. The teacher should be able to supplement the commercial test to tailor the assessment to the specific instructional program used in the classroom. This would relieve the teacher of the burden of creating an entire test battery of well-crafted items. More attention could be placed on creating items to supplement the commercial tests that require alternative response modes or that measure unique content. Alternatively, the commercial test could provide for cross-validation of the results obtained from teacher-developed tests (Merwin, 1982). Commercially developed tests linked with teacher-developed tests within a domain-referenced instructional planning system offer a significant opportunity for improving instructional planning and decision making.

## SELECTING A COMMERCIALLY DEVELOPED TEST

The primary criterion for the selection of a commercially developed achievement test (domain-referenced or norm-referenced) is the congruence between the objectives assessed by the test and the objectives that comprise the instructional program. This fit should include a similarity between the measurement tactics used by the test publisher to assess the content as well as a similarity of content emphasis.

Any test that is a candidate for selection should be accompanied by a complete test manual that would include the following types of information:

(1) Uses for which the test is recommended.
(2) Qualifications needed to administer and interpret the test.
(3) Validity: Evidence of validity for each recommended use.
(4) Reliability: Evidence of reliability for recommended uses and an indication of equivalence of any equivalent forms provided.
(5) Clear directions for administration and scoring the test.
(6) (For norm-referenced tests) Adequate norms (including a description of procedures used in obtaining them) or other bases for interpreting the scores. (Gronlund, 1981)

Any commercially developed test should conform to the standards for educational and psychological tests developed by a joint committee of the National Council on Measurement in Education, the American Educational Research Association, and the American Psychological Association (American Psychological Association, 1974). Those standards and guidelines cover the development, evaluation, interpretation, use, and reporting of information on psychological tests and assessment methods. An excellent commentary on those standards is available from the National Council on Measurement in Education (Brown, 1980).

The Standards suggest the following most relevant principles in the selection of an educational or psychological test:

(1) The test manual should state explicitly the purposes and applications for which the test is recommended.
(2) The test manual should describe clearly the psychological, educational, or other reasoning underlying the test and the nature of the characteristics it is intended to measure.
(3) A test manual should describe fully the development of the test: the rationale, specifications followed in writing items or selecting observations, and procedures and results of items analysis or other research.
(4) Evidence of validity and reliability, along with other relevant research data, should be presented in support of any claims being made.

(5) The test, the manual, the record forms, and other accompanying material should help users make correct interpretations of the test results and should warn against common misuses (Brown, 1980).

Berk (1981) observes that it is a common misperception that criterion-referenced (domain-referenced) tests are informal measures consisting of a collection of items and an arbitrarily set standard for mastery such as 80 percent and lacking any technical properties such as reliability or validity. Berk admonishes that any criterion-referenced test that is used for important individual decisions should be developed with the same rigor and precision as its norm-referenced counterpart. Hambleton and Eignor (1978) have published a rating scheme that supplements the Standards to guide the evaluation and selection of domain-referenced tests.

Additional evaluative information concerning commercially developed tests may be found in test publishers' catalogs (the claims therein to be viewed cautiously), *The Eighth Mental Measurements Yearbook* (Buros, 1978), the Educational Resources Information System (ERIC) Clearinghouse for Tests, Measurement and Evaluation located at the Educational Testing Service in Princeton, New Jersey, and professional journals that feature test reviews and validity studies (*Journal of Educational Measurement, Journal of School Psychology, Journal of Learning Disabilities,* etc.).

Regardless of the quality of the reviews of a particular achievement test or the technical completeness of the test manual, there is no substitute for a careful examination of the actual test items. Gronlund (1981) suggests that the best method for accomplishing this examination is to attempt to answer each item as if one was actually taking the test. Classifying each item by content and/or measurement tactic to construct a table of test specifications is also recommended. As Gronlund observes: "Although time-consuming, there is no better means of determining the extent to which a test is appropriate for measuring the knowledges, skills, and understandings emphasized in the instructional program" (1981, p. 283).

**REFERENCES**

Alderman, D.L., Swinton, S.S., & Braswell, J.S. (1979). Assessing basic arithmetic skills and understanding across curricula: Computer-assisted instruction and compensatory education. *The Journal of Children's Mathematical Behavior, 2,* 3–28.

Allen, M.J., & Yen, W.M. (1979). *Introduction to measurement theory.* Belmont, CA: Wadsworth.

American Psychological Association. (1974). *Standards for psychological and educational tests.* Washington, DC: Author.

Berk, R.A. (1980). Item analysis. In R.A. Berk (Ed.), *Criterion-referenced measurement: The state of the art* (pp. 49–79). Baltimore, MD: The Johns Hopkins University Press.

————. (1981, May). *Identification of children with learning disabilities: A critical review of methodological issues.* Paper presented at the Johns Hopkins University Colloquium on Gifted/Learning Disabled Children, Baltimore, MD.

Brennan, R.L. (1980). Applications of generalizability theory. In R.A. Berk (Ed.), *Criterion-referenced measurement: The state of the art* (pp. 186–232). Baltimore, MD: The Johns Hopkins University Press.

Brown, F.G. (1980). *Guidelines for test use: A commentary on the Standards for Educational and Psychological Tests.* Washington, DC: National Council on Measurement in Education.

Buros, O.K. (Ed.). (1978). *The eighth mental measurements yearbook.* Highland Park, NJ: Gryphon Press.

Cole, N.S. (1982, March). *Grade equivalent scores: To GE or not to GE.* Division D Vice Presidential Address, American Educational Research Association Annual Meeting, New York City.

Cronbach, L.J. (1980). Validity on parole: How can we go straight? *New Directions for Testing and Measurement* (pp. 99–105). San Francisco, CA: Jossey-Bass.

Cronbach, L.J., & Meehl, P.E. (1955). Construct validity in psychological tests. *Psychological Bulletin, 52,* 281–302.

Goodstein, H.A. (1982). The reliability of criterion-referenced tests and special education: Assumed versus demonstrated. *Journal of Special Education, 16,* 37–48.

————. (1984). Assessment: Examination and utilization from pre-K through high school. In J.F. Cawley (Ed.), *Developmental mathematics for the learning disabled.* Rockville, MD: Aspen Systems.

Goodstein, H.A., Howell, H., & Williamson, K. (1982, August). *The reliability of criterion-referenced tests for special education and regular education students: The impact of item format and content sampling.* Nashville, TN: Peabody College of Vanderbilt University. Mimeograph.

Gronlund, N.E. (1981). *Measurement and evaluation in teaching.* New York: Macmillan.

Hambleton, R.K. (1980a). Contributions to criterion-referenced testing technology: An introduction. *Applied Psychological Measurement, 4,* 425–446.

Hambleton, R.K. (1980b). Test score validity and standard setting methods. In R.A. Berk (Ed.), *Criterion-referenced measurement: The state of the art* (pp. 80–124). Baltimore, MD: The Johns Hopkins University Press.

Hambleton, R.K., & Eignor, D.R. (1978). Guidelines for evaluating criterion-referenced tests and test manuals. *Journal of Educational Measurement, 15,* 321–327.

Horst, D.P., Tallmadge, G.K., & Wood, C.T. (1974, October). *Measuring achievement gains in educational projects* (RMC Report UR-243). Los Altos, CA: RMC Research Corporation.

Jones, R.I. (1973). Accountability in special education: Some problems. *Exceptional Children, 40,* 631–642.

Kapfer, M.B. (Ed.). (1978). *Behavioral objectives: The position on the pendulum.* Englewood Cliffs, NJ: Educational Technology Publications.

Linn, R.L. (1979). Issues of validity in measurement for competency-based programs. In M.A. Bunda & J.R. Sanders (Eds.), *Practices and problems in competency-based measurement* (pp. 108–123). Washington, DC: National Council on Measurement in Education.

_____. (1980). Issues of validity for criterion-referenced measures. *Applied Psychological Measurement, 4,* 547–561.

_____. (1981, April). *Criterion-referenced measurement: Psychometric problems.* Paper presented at the annual meeting of the American Educational Research Association, Los Angeles, CA.

Merwin, J.C. (1982). Standardized tests: One tool for decision making in the classroom. *Educational Measurement: Issues and Practice, 1,* 14–16.

Messick, S. (1981). Evidence and ethics in the evaluation of tests. *Educational Researcher, 10*(9), 9–20.

Millman, J. (1980). Computer-based item generation. In R.A. Berk (Ed.), *Criterion-referenced measurement: The state of the art* (pp. 32–44). Baltimore, MD: The Johns Hopkins University Press.

Nitko, A.J. (1980). Distinguishing the many varieties of criterion-referenced tests. *Review of Educational Research, 50,* 461–485.

Popham, W.J. (1978). *Criterion-referenced measurement.* Englewood Cliffs, NJ: Prentice-Hall.

Popham, W.J. (1980). Domain specification strategies. In R.A. Berk (Ed.), *Criterion-referenced measurement: The state of the art* (pp. 15–31). Baltimore, MD: The Johns Hopkins University Press.

Popham, W.J. (1981). *Modern educational measurement.* Englewood Cliffs, NJ: Prentice-Hall.

Popham, W.J., & Husek, T.R. (1969). Implications of criterion-referenced measurement. *Journal of Educational Measurement, 6,* 1–9.

Quelmallz, E.S. (1981, April). *Criterion-referenced measurement: From the cognitive psychology view.* Paper presented to the annual meeting of the American Educational Research Association, Los Angeles, CA.

Salvia, J., & Ysseldyke, J.E. (1981). *Assessment in special and remedial education* (2nd ed.). Boston: Houghton Mifflin.

Traub, R.E., & Rowley, G.L. (1980). Reliability of test scores and decisions. *Applied Psychological Measurement, 4,* 517–545.

Tyler, R.W., & White, S.H. (1979). *Testing, teaching and learning: Report on a conference on research in testing.* Washington, DC: DHEW/NIE.

Wilcox, R.R. (1980). Determining the length of a criterion-referenced test. *Applied Psychological Measurement, 4,* 425–446.

# Chapter 3

# Linking Assessment to Curriculum and Instruction

*Colleen S. Blankenship*

Assessment, curriculum, and instruction can be likened to threads which, woven together, produce a strong fabric. However, like threads in a piece of cloth, those of assessment, curriculum, and instruction can also become separated. When this occurs, the threads need to be carefully rewoven to ensure that (1) assessment is based on the curriculum used in the classroom, (2) behavior is assessed before, during, and following instruction, and (3) instructional decisions are based on pupil performance. Only in this way can teachers match curriculum and instruction to the individual needs and abilities of pupils.

To maintain the proper relationship among assessment, curriculum, and instruction care must be taken to select appropriate assessment methods. Often, assessment takes the form of administering achievement tests at the beginning and end of the year. Achievement tests provide little useful information for planning instructional programs or evaluating pupil progress (Eaton & Lovitt, 1972; Freeman, Kuhs, Knappen, & Porter, 1982; Jenkins & Pany, 1978). They are simply given too infrequently to be of much help in decision making. Items on achievement tests do not reflect the contents of any particular curriculum; therefore, the results cannot be used to evaluate a student's skills with respect to those presented in the text used in the classroom. Yet, it is precisely this kind of information that is needed to plan instructional programs and to evaluate pupil progress.

Textbook tests come closer to providing teachers with useful information because the items on these tests are drawn from the curriculum used for instruction. Although most series provide placement tests and chapter and unit post-tests, pretests are not always included. When they are, they frequently fail to measure prerequisite skills. Placement tests and end-of-chapter and unit tests provide only a limited amount of information because (1) they restrict assessment to behaviors that are easily measured by written responses, (2) they may fail to adequately measure important concepts and skills, (3) they are designed to be administered to an entire class, thus limiting opportunities to observe the behavior of individual students, and (4) they are given on one occasion and therefore scores may not reflect a student's typical performance.

Clearly, an alternative to current assessment methods is required that links assessment to curriculum and instruction. To be useful, assessment data should provide teachers with the necessary information to

1. Place students into an appropriate curriculum
2. Determine necessary curricular modifications
3. Select potentially effective instructional techniques
4. Continuously evaluate pupil performance as pupils progress through the curriculum
5. Determine the effectiveness of their instructional interventions
6. Communicate progress to students, parents, and other school personnel.

An alternative to the traditional testing approach is presented in this chapter. Although the strategies included here can be applied to any academic subject, the focus is on the assessment of mathematical performance. Following an overview of the assessment process, suggestions for designing assessments for the purposes of planning mathematics instruction and evaluating pupil progress are discussed.

## OVERVIEW OF THE ASSESSMENT PROCESS

Educational assessment is the process of systematically measuring and evaluating pupil performance in order to make instructional decisions. Assessment requires planning to ensure that the information obtained will be of assistance in making instructional decisions. Planning for assessment begins by asking the following questions:

1. What decision needs to be made?
2. What information is needed to make the decision?
3. How can the desired information be obtained?
4. How will conclusions be drawn based on the information obtained?

To illustrate how these simple questions can be used to develop mathematics assessments, we will begin by examining the types of decisions that need to be made. Later in the chapter procedures will be discussed for collecting assessment information and making decisions based on the data obtained.

## Types of Decisions

Teachers make a variety of instructional decisions during the year. Different decisions are required prior to, during, and following instruction. The critical decisions that must be made at each step in the instructional process are as follows:

1. Is the material presented in each chapter or unit of the text appropriate for all students?
2. How will instruction be provided?
3. Are students mastering the skills taught?
4. Are all students maintaining their skills?
5. Can students apply their skills to solve related problems?

Strategies for obtaining the necessary information to make each decision are presented in the following section.

## Strategies for Obtaining Information

An overview will present the general purposes of two strategies. Then, attention will be focused on the appropriate use of each strategy to make the previously discussed decisions.

The first strategy, curriculum-based assessment (CBA) (Blankenship & Lilly, 1981; Idol-Maestas, 1983), allows teachers to assess student performance on a variety of objectives drawn from the text used in the classroom. CBAs are given in a prepost-test fashion. By periodically readministering a CBA during the year, teachers can assess students' long-term maintenance.

Based on the results of a CBA, a teacher identifies one or more specific objectives an individual student needs to learn. To measure performance on the targeted objectives the second strategy, direct and frequent measurement, can be used. Direct means "the behavior of concern is the one measured" (Haring, Lovitt, Eaton, & Hansen, 1978, p. 8). For example, if the desired behavior is to have a student measure with a ruler, a student would be given a ruler and asked to measure the lengths of different objects. Direct measures are collected daily or at least frequently. Typically, performance is graphed, thus providing teachers with a visual display of pupil progress.

Curriculum-based assessment applies equally well to all students in a class as it assists teachers in planning instructional programs, evaluating mastery, and assessing long-term maintenance. For students with learning problems, assessment needs to be continuous in order to provide teachers with sufficient information to guide daily instruction. Direct and frequent measurement provides a teacher with constant feedback concerning an individual pupil's progress, thereby allowing the teacher to quickly change techniques when academic gains are not being made. Both strategies provide useful information to assist teachers in making the decisions mentioned above.

### *Is the material presented in each chapter or unit of the text appropriate for all students?*

Mathematics instruction is typically provided to an entire class using the lecture-discussion approach. Typically, a single textbook is used, consisting of five or six units that are further divided into chapters. Because students vary with respect to their ability to acquire new skills and to retain previously mastered skills, instructional content must often be modified. At the beginning of the year, and prior to introducing each new topic, teachers must determine whether the contents of a particular chapter are appropriate for all students.

Although the standard curriculum is likely to be appropriate for most students, modifications must be made for students who lack prerequisite concepts or skills and for those who have already mastered the material presented in a particular chapter. To make this decision, the following types of information are needed:

1. Which students have already mastered certain concepts or skills targeted for instruction?
2. Which students possess sufficient knowledge of prerequisite concepts and skills and are therefore ready to begin instruction on topics presented in the chapter or unit?
3. Which students lack mastery of prerequisite concepts or skills?

Curriculum-based assessment is the appropriate strategy to use in this case. By administering a CBA prior to instruction, teachers can readily pinpoint skills students need to learn. Attention then shifts to identifying potentially effective methods of teaching the chosen content.

### *How will instruction be provided?*

Determining how a skill will be taught actually involves making two related decisions: (1) deciding how students will be grouped for instruction and (2) identifying potentially effective teaching techniques. Although instruction is typically provided to an entire class of students using the lecture-discussion approach, other instructional arrangements are often more appropriate for students with learning problems. To determine whether the large-group lecture-discussion approach is appropriate for all students, a teacher needs to know

1. Which students can *read* the directions and explanations provided in the text
2. Which students can *attend* to demonstrations and participate in class discussions
3. Which students can *work independently* and complete their assignments on time

By observing students during the first few weeks of the year, teachers can determine whether particular students may profit from receiving instruction in small groups or on an individualized basis.

Instructional delivery systems that allow teachers greater flexibility in matching instructional techniques to the needs of individual pupils include small group, peer tutoring, computer-assisted instruction, and one-to-one instruction. Teachers can select from a variety of techniques, including verbal instruction, demonstration, modeling, drill-and-practice, prompts and cues, feedback, reinforcement, and contingencies for errors (Blankenship, 1981; Haring, Lovitt, Eaton, & Hansen, 1978). By collecting direct and frequent measures of performance under various instructional conditions, teachers can evaluate the effects of different teaching techniques on the performance of individual students. Potentially effective techniques can be identified by inspecting a student's charted data to determine the types of techniques that have been effective in teaching similar skills in the past.

### Are students mastering the skills taught?

During instruction attention focuses on determining the extent to which students are mastering the material being taught. To make sound decisions during instruction, a teacher needs to know

1. Which students have demonstrated mastery and are therefore ready to begin instruction on a new topic
2. Which students are making sufficient progress but require more practice or continued instruction to achieve mastery
3. Which students are making insufficient progress, thereby requiring the teacher to modify some aspect of instruction

Both strategies can be used to assess skill mastery. CBAs are given *following* instruction; hence, CBA results indicate whether a student mastered a skill. Direct and frequent measurement provides continuous data on pupil progress, thus allowing teachers to monitor performance *during* instruction and adjust instruction should performance deteriorate or mastery be achieved.

### Are all students maintaining their skills?

Maintenance of skills is an area of concern to teachers. To ensure that students are retaining what they have learned, it is important to occasionally measure performance on previously instructed skills. In this way, teachers can determine if students are ready to learn more advanced topics that require mastery of previously taught skills, or if reteaching is needed.

Both strategies provide useful information for assessing maintenance of skills over time. If a teacher wishes to assess maintenance of a variety of previously taught skills, all or portions of a CBA could be administered periodically throughout the year. If a teacher wishes to evaluate maintenance of a specific skill over time, direct and frequent measurement would be the strategy of choice.

### Can students apply their skills to solve related problems?

Whereas measures of student performance are frequently collected following instruction to determine levels of skills mastery, less emphasis is usually placed on measuring students' abilities to generalize. Some students have difficulty applying previously acquired skills to new situations. For example, after mastering renaming from ones to tens in addition, some students may be unable to apply their newly acquired skill to solve more complex problems. Direct and frequent measurement is used to assess generalization. While instruction is focused on a particular skill, such as counting by twos, performance on similar tasks, such as counting by fives or tens can be measured occasionally. In this way teachers can determine the extent to which students are able to apply their knowledge to solve related problems.

Suggestions for developing and using CBAs are provided in the next section. Examples are presented to show how CBAs can be developed by adapting chapter tests. Procedures for interpreting the results of CBAs and making decisions are illustrated through the use of examples. Guidelines for using direct and frequent measurement are then discussed with examples provided to show how decisions are made based on charted data.

## DEVELOPING AND USING CURRICULUM-BASED ASSESSMENTS

A CBA may be developed for each chapter in a mathematics text. CBAs, like criterion-referenced tests, compare the performance of individual students with a given standard or level of performance. Because CBAs are teacher-made, it is the teacher who selects the skills to be assessed and determines methods for evaluating pupil performance. Hence, CBAs provide teachers with an opportunity to structure the assessment so that the results will give them the information they deem to be most important for planning instructional programs.

The results of a CBA can be used to pinpoint precisely which skills individual students have and have not mastered. When given prior to instruction, the results of a CBA can be used to form instructional groups and, when necessary, plan individualized programs. By periodically re-administering a CBA, teachers can assess pupils' long-term maintenance.

To decide whether it is necessary to develop a CBA, a teacher may ask the following questions:

1. Does the chapter test assess the important concepts and skills I intend to teach?
2. Am I satisfied with the types of skills included on the chapter test and the way performance is measured?

If a teacher can answer both questions in the affirmative, a CBA is not needed. More typically, however, the answer to one or both questions is no. In either case, development of a CBA is justified.

### Suggestions for Developing CBAs

Remembering that the aim is to link assessment to curriculum and instruction, one begins by examining the extent to which items on the chapter test reflect the contents of the chapter. Teachers' manuals usually contain lists of objectives for each chapter that are keyed to test items. These reference charts can be useful in determining whether the test covers the entire range of topics presented in a particular chapter. By matching the items on the test to the objectives listed for the chapter, teachers can determine the extent of agreement between the two.

Even though the test items may perfectly match the contents of a chapter, few teachers rigidly adhere to the activities provided in texts. Often, teachers incorporate other information they deem to be appropriate or emphasize certain topics more than others. Hence, a teacher's instructional objectives may differ from the objectives listed in the text. To ensure that the skills presented on the CBA match the teacher's instructional objectives, it is often necessary to revise the chapter test.

To adapt a chapter test to better match one's instructional objectives, a teacher might proceed as follows. First, examine the text's objectives and determine how those objectives are assessed on the chapter test. When examining the test, note whether (1) all objectives listed in the text are assessed, (2) items on the test directly measure the behaviors of interest, (3) prerequisite concepts and skills are included, and (4) a sufficient number of items are presented to adequately assess students' abilities.

To illustrate the process of revising a chapter test, a sample set of objectives and the corresponding test items for a chapter on numeration are shown in Table 3-1. Although the sample test is taken from a third grade text, the same procedures can be used to adapt tests in higher grade level texts.

After evaluating the chapter test shown in Table 3-1, a teacher might develop a CBA along the lines shown in Table 3-2. The teacher's rationale for revising the chapter test might be as follows:

Place Value
: Items 1 and 2 on the chapter test are essentially copying tasks. These items were deleted and a new task (objective 5) was developed. To measure understanding of place value, the teacher added skills such as naming and writing numbers given their physical representations. A task similar to test items 3 through 11 on the chapter test was included on the CBA.

Comparison
: The task for objective 17 on the chapter test requires students to use the correct symbols for greater than and lesser than. If a student errs on this task, the teacher could not determine whether the student's error was due to confusion over the direction of the symbols or not knowing which number is greater than the other. The teacher decided to assess knowledge of greater than and less than separately from use of the appropriate symbols.

Order
: The only change made was that oral counting was included to aid the teacher in determining whether a student who was unable to write a numerical sequence did in fact know how to count.

**Table 3-1** Sample Chapter Objectives and Test Items

|  | *Objectives* | *Text Pages* | *Sample Test Items* |
|---|---|---|---|
| Place Value | 16. Write numbers through 999, and give the place value for any digit in a number through 999. | 62–63, 64–65, 66–67, 68–69 | 1–2. Give the standard form for each number:<br><br>\| hundreds \| tens \| ones \|<br>\| 4 \| 2 \| 6 \|<br><br>3–11. What digit is in the $\begin{cases} \text{ones} \\ \text{tens} \\ \text{hundreds} \end{cases}$ place?<br>367  942  138 |
| Comparison | 17. Compare numbers, less than 1000, using < or >. | 70–71 | 12–15. Replace the ○. Use < or >.<br>47  ○  56 |
| Order | 18. Count and order numbers, less than 1000. | 72–73 74–75 | Give the numbers in order. Begin with the least number.<br>16–18. 96    91    95<br>19–21. Count by $\begin{cases} \text{twos} \\ \text{fives} \\ \text{tens} \end{cases}$ |
| Money | 19. Count money using dollars, dimes, and pennies; and record the amount, using the dollar sign and the cent point. | 76–77 |  |
| Money | 20. Count money using dollars, half dollars, quarters, dimes, nickels, and pennies; and record the amount, using the dollar sign and the cent point. | 78–79 | 22–24. Use $ and . to show each amount:<br>2 dollars, 3 dimes, 5 pennies. |
| Logic | 21. Choose a sensible answer to a word problem. | 82 | 25. Choose the best answer.<br>May is 6 years old. How old is her younger sister?<br>(2, 20, 200) |

Adapted with permission from *Scott, Foresman Mathematics, Teacher's Edition, Book 3* (1980). Palo Alto, CA: Scott, Foresman, p. 61B.

**Table 3-2** Teacher's Plan for Developing the CBA

*Teacher's Instructional Objectives*

| | Condition | Behavior | Criteria | Sample Tasks |
|---|---|---|---|---|
| Place Value | 1. Given: Single sticks & bundles of ten & one hundred sticks for values between 0 and 999 | The student will: Say name of number shown. | 3 out of 3 correct for 2 days | hundreds   tens   ones |
| | 2. Verbal directions to display a number between 0 and 999 | Place sticks & bundles on place value board. | " | hundreds   tens   ones |
| | 3. Verbal directions to write the value of the sticks & bundles shown | Write the number shown. | " | hundreds   tens   ones |

**4.**
A written number from 0–999 | Circle the digit in the { ones, tens, hundreds. | " | Circle the digit in the { ones, tens, hundreds place.

a. 423   b. 648   c. 76

**5.**
Ones, tens, & hundreds in random order | Write number. | 3 out of 3 correct | What number can you make?

| 2 tens | 5 hundreds | 8 ones |
| 5 ones | 0 tens | 7 hundreds |
| 3 hundreds | 4 ones | 3 tens |

____

**Comparison**

**6.**
Pairs of numbers between 0 and 999 | Circle the greater number. | " | Circle the greater number in each pair

42   91

"   " | Circle the lesser number. | " | Circle the lesser number in each pair

87   74

**7.**
Pairs of numbers between 0 and 999 | Use the symbols > or <. | " | 47 ○ 56

**Order**

**8.**
A series of three or four numbers between 0 and 999 | Write the numbers in order. | " | 96   91   95 ____

**Table 3-2** continued

| | | | | |
|---|---|---|---|---|
| | 9.<br>Verbal directions to count by twos, fives, tens, beginning and ending with numbers between 0 and 999 | Orally count. | " " | 3 out of 3 correct |
| | 10.<br>Written directions to count by twos, fives, and tens, beginning and ending with numbers between 0 and 999 | Write numbers in order. | | 3 out of 3 correct |
| Money | 11.<br>A penny, nickel, dime, quarter, half-dollar, and dollar shown separately on a card | Say name of coin. | *Draw a penny | 5 out of 5 correct for 2 days |

*for fourth page!*

| | Skill | Task | Criterion | Example |
|---|---|---|---|---|
| 12. | Combinations of coins and one dollar bills | Count amount shown. | 3 out of 3 correct for 2 days | *Draw dollars & coins |
| 13. | Combination of coins and one dollar bills | Write amount shown. | " | *Draw dollars & coins |
| 14. Logic | Written questions containing numerical information | Circle the most sensible answer. | " | Fred is 4 feet, 2 inches tall. His brother is taller. How tall is Fred's brother?<br>a. 3 feet, 9 inches<br>b. 5 feet, 6 inches<br>c. 15 feet, 8 inches |

Based on *Scott, Foresman Mathematics, Teacher's Edition, Book 3* (1980). Palo Alto, CA: Scott, Foresman, p. 83.

Money          The chapter test did not directly assess counting money. The teacher decided to measure the skill using real money. Identification of coins was also assessed because in the teacher's experience, students often had difficulty identifying quarters and half dollars.

Logic          Only one item was included on the chapter test to assess ability to give a sensible answer to a word problem. Therefore, the teacher developed a few more problems to assess this skill.

Based on the plan shown in Table 3-2 for developing the CBA, the teacher would then develop the assessment materials. This is relatively easy because in writing the objectives, the teacher has already decided on the type of materials needed to assess each objective. Because the teacher intends to assess performance on two occasions, to ensure the reliability of the data obtained, two alternative forms will be developed.

## Administering the CBA

The next step involves determining procedures for administering the assessment. Although many of the tasks can be assessed in large groups, other tasks such as "counting coins" must be given on an individual basis. To make administering the CBA as efficient as possible, the teacher may enlist the aid of class members. For example, to test identification of coins (objective 11), the teacher may provide student examiners with cards showing a coin on one side and the name of the coin on the other side. If provided with a simple recording sheet, the student examiners could easily record the desired information for the teacher. Student involvement in assessment is desirable. By making students partners in the assessment process, a teacher can stress that the purpose is to determine exactly what they do and do not know so that the teacher can focus instruction on the skills they need to learn. In addition, student participation in assessment can serve to clarify goals and heighten student interest in achieving them.

## Recording Results

The last step consists of developing a method of recording the results of the CBA. Performance may be recorded using a form similar to the one shown in Exhibit 3-1. By recording performance in the manner shown, a teacher can quickly scan the scores for the entire class, noting the skill levels of individual students.

**Exhibit 3-1  CBA Recording Sheet**

| Student | Condition | Date | Place Value | | | | | Comparison | | Order | | | Money | | | Logic |
|---|---|---|---|---|---|---|---|---|---|---|---|---|---|---|---|---|
| | | | Say | Show | Write | Circle | Write | Circle | Symbols | Write | Count Oral | Count Written | Name | Count | Write | Sensible Ans. |
| | | | 1 | 2 | 3 | 4 | 5 | 6 | 7 | 8 | 9 | 10 | 11 | 12 | 13 | 14 |
| Sue | Prior to Instruction | | 0/3 | 0/3 | 0/3 | 2/1 | 0/3 | 3/0 | 1/2 | 3/0 | 3/0 | 2/1 | 3/2 | 0/3 | 0/3 | 3/0 |
| | | | 0/3 | 0/3 | 0/3 | 3/0 | 0/3 | 3/0 | 0/3 | 3/0 | 3/0 | 3/0 | 3/2 | 0/3 | 0/3 | 3/0 |
| | Following Instruction | | | | | | | | | | | | | | | |
| | Maintenance | | | | | | | | | | | | | | | |
| Joe | Prior to Instruction | | 3/0 | 3/0 | 3/0 | 3/0 | 3/0 | 3/0 | 0/3 | 2/1 | 3/0 | 2/1 | 5/0 | 3/0 | 3/0 | 3/0 |
| | | | 3/0 | 3/0 | 3/0 | 3/0 | 3/0 | 3/0 | 0/3 | 3/0 | 3/0 | 3/0 | 5/0 | 3/0 | 3/0 | 3/0 |

## Using CBA Data To Make Decisions

As we have noted, CBA data can be used to determine entry-level skills prior to instruction, skill mastery following instruction, and long-term maintenance. To demonstrate how decisions are made based on the results of a CBA, let's begin by examining the hypothetical data shown in Exhibit 3-1.

By comparing Sue's performance to the criterion levels noted in the teacher's instructional objectives shown in Table 3-2 and circling the scores below the criterion, it is easy to pinpoint the skills she needs to learn. Sue's data indicate that she needs to learn about place value, use of the symbols < and >, ordering written numbers, and all of the money skills. Contrasting Sue's performance with Joe's, it is apparent that Joe has a good understanding of place value; however, he needs to learn the appropriate use of the symbols for greater than and less than. Joe also had difficulty ordering written numbers and producing a written count. Like Sue, he made few errors on the other order tasks, which may suggest carelessness.

By analyzing student's scores in this manner, teachers can easily determine which students will require instruction to master particular skills. Students who fail to perform at the criterion level may be grouped together for instruction. Students who meet criteria may still be included in a large group discussion of the topic; however, they may receive shortened assignments. Provided that they perform as well as they did on the CBA, there is no reason to give them extended practice on skills they have already mastered. Instead, time might be more profitably spent focusing on enrichment activities or on other skills they need to learn.

CBA results can also be used to determine mastery of skills following instruction. Inspecting Sue's data shown in Exhibit 3-2, it is apparent that she acquired a number of new skills. Her errors on objectives 2 and 13 may indicate careless mistakes; however, some additional practice on these skills may be warranted. With respect to long-term maintenance, Sue was able to retain most of the skills she learned. Based on her scores on objectives 7 and 13 during maintenance, it appears that she will require some remedial instruction on these skills.

In addition to assisting teachers in decision making, CBA data also serve another important function. The results of a CBA can be used to communicate to both students and parents exactly which skills have been acquired and which need to be learned. Teachers who use CBAs often comment that the information is invaluable at parent-teacher conferences.

**Exhibit 3-2** Results of CBA for Sue

| Student | Condition | Date | Place Value | | | | | Comparison | | | Order | | Money | | | Logic |
|---|---|---|---|---|---|---|---|---|---|---|---|---|---|---|---|---|
| | | | Say | Show | Write | Circle | Write | Circle | Symbols | Write | Count Oral | Count Written | Name | Count | Write | Sensible Ans. |
| | | | 1 | 2 | 3 | 4 | 5 | 6 | 7 | 8 | 9 | 10 | 11 | 12 | 13 | 14 |
| Sue | Prior to Instruction | 9/1 | 0/3 | 0/3 | 0/3 | 2/1 | 0/3 | 3/0 | 1/2 | 3/0 | 3/0 | 2/1 | 3/2 | 0/3 | 0/3 | 3/0 |
| | | 9/2 | 0/3 | 0/3 | 0/3 | 3/0 | 0/3 | 3/0 | 0/3 | 3/0 | 3/0 | 3/0 | 3/2 | 0/3 | 0/3 | 3/0 |
| | Following Instruction | 9/16 | 3/0 | 2/1 | 3/0 | 3/0 | 3/0 | 3/0 | 3/0 | 3/0 | 3/0 | 3/0 | 5/0 | 3/0 | 3/0 | 3/0 |
| | | 9/17 | 3/0 | 3/0 | 3/0 | 3/0 | 3/0 | 3/0 | 3/0 | 3/0 | 3/0 | 3/0 | 5/0 | 3/0 | 2/1 | 3/0 |
| | Maintenance | 10/15 | 3/0 | 3/0 | 3/0 | 3/0 | 3/0 | 3/0 | 1/2 | 3/0 | 3/0 | 3/0 | 5/0 | 3/0 | 2/1 | 3/0 |
| | | 10/16 | 3/0 | 3/0 | 3/0 | 3/0 | 3/0 | 3/0 | 1/2 | 3/0 | 3/0 | 3/0 | 5/0 | 3/0 | 2/1 | 3/0 |

## DIRECT AND FREQUENT MEASUREMENT

Although a CBA can be used to assess performance before and following instruction, other methods must be used to monitor progress during instruction. Teachers commonly rely on inspecting students' daily work to gauge pupil progress. Scores on daily assignments are typically not recorded, nor are careful records kept indicating the effectiveness of specific instructional techniques on the performance of individual students. Information of this type is of great assistance in planning instructional programs for students with learning problems.

As we have noted, direct and frequent measurement allows teachers to continuously monitor pupil progress and to evaluate the effects of their teaching techniques. Only the basics of direct and frequent measurement will be presented here. A number of texts devoted to this topic provide a more detailed explanation (Blankenship & Lilly, 1981; Haring, Lovitt, Eaton, & Hansen, 1978; Idol-Maestas, 1983).

Based on the results of a CBA, a teacher may target one or more objectives that an individual student needs to master. Prior to instruction on each objective, baseline data are collected. Baseline data establish a student's entry level and provide a standard by which teachers can evaluate the effectiveness of later interventions. Performance is usually recorded on a graph, which provides teachers with a visual display of progress over time. Graphs provide an easy method of determining whether a student is or is not making sufficient progress toward mastering an instructional objective. If during instruction the student's graph reveals that little progress is being made, another teaching technique can be applied. Once mastery is achieved, data collection continues on a less frequent basis to ensure that the student maintains his or her accuracy at an acceptable level. As a student approaches mastery, performance on related skills can be occasionally measured to determine the student's ability to generalize his or her skills to solve similar types of problems.

To illustrate the ease with which decisions can be made based on charted measures of performance, let's examine the hypothetical data shown in Exhibit 3-3. The data indicate the number of subtraction renaming problems answered correctly by four students. During baseline, all students were performing at low levels of accuracy, indicating the need for specific instruction on this computational skill. Meeting with these students in a small group, the teacher required the students to display problems using sticks on a place value board and simultaneously record their answers. The students then completed a worksheet containing 25 subtraction renaming problems. Within three days, it was apparent that Student 1 was making good progress. Based on his performance, the teacher decided to

**Exhibit 3-3** Hypothetical Pupil Progress Data

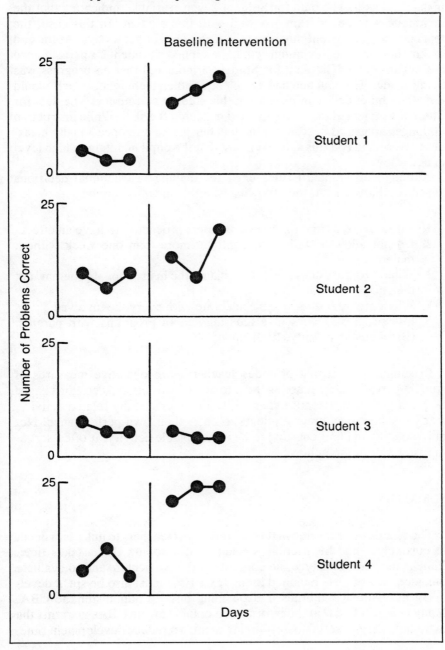

continue instruction as it appeared likely that the student would soon master the skill. The data for Student 2 were variable, indicating that the technique was not working as well with this student. In this case, the teacher decided to continue using the technique for a few days. At the end of that time, another technique would be applied if Student 2's performance did not improve. The data for Student 3 indicated that no progress was being made. The teacher had to select another technique, which would hopefully be effective in increasing this student's accuracy. The data for Student 4 indicated that the pupil had mastered the skill. While instruction no longer appeared necessary, the teacher planned to occasionally measure performance on this skill to ensure that the pupil maintains a high level of accuracy.

Although no standard rules exist for making instructional decisions based on charted data, the following general guidelines apply:

1. Allow enough time for an instructional procedure to have an effect.
2. Do not allow a student to continue more than one week without making progress.
3. When progress does not occur, blame the instructional program, not the student.
4. When progress does occur, celebrate with everyone involved.
5. Use progress charts in discussing school programs with parents. (Blankenship & Lilly, 1981, pp. 45–46)

In summary, charting provides teachers with objective measures of student performance, enabling them to make instructional decisions based on pupil progress. Because charting is a mathematically related activity, many teachers encourage students to chart their own performance. Not only do students find charting to be an enjoyable activity, it often serves to foster a desire to achieve.

## SUMMARY

The strategies presented in this chapter allow teachers to link assessment to curriculum and instruction. Certainly, developing CBAs takes time. Time is needed to analyze the contents of the curriculum and to evaluate the adequacy of tests included in the text. Time must also be spent developing assessment materials and planning how to administer the CBA. Many teachers find that the information obtained from CBAs warrants the extra time they devoted to developing them. To reduce development time, teachers using the same level text have worked together to produce CBAs for different chapters. The aid of student teachers has been enlisted.

As with anything new, it's best to approach developing CBAs one step at a time. Rather than developing one for each chapter, it is a good idea to start small and concentrate on a chapter that students typically have difficulty mastering. Then, give the CBA and evaluate the extent to which it provides useful information for planning instructional programs and evaluating progress.

The same cautious approach should be applied to charting pupil progress data. It is not necessary to chart each student's progress on every instructional objective taught. Direct and frequent measurement is a tool that teachers can use when it is necessary to closely monitor pupil progress. Start by charting the performance of one student on a skill that the pupil is having difficulty mastering. If after a few days of practice, performance remains at a low level, begin instruction. Continue to record pupil progress during instruction. Often, teachers are surprised by the rapid improvement that results once they precisely pinpoint a student's difficulty and provide appropriate instruction, practice, and reinforcement.

---

**REFERENCES**

Blankenship, C., & Lilly, M.S. (1981). *Mainstreaming students with learning and behavior problems: Techniques for the classroom teacher.* New York: Holt, Rinehart & Winston.

Eaton, M., & Lovitt, T.C. (1972). Achievement tests vs. direct and daily measurement. In G. Semb (Ed.), *Behavior analysis and education—1972.* Lawrence, KS: University of Kansas Press.

Freeman, D.J., Kuhs, T.M., Knappen, L.B., & Porter, A.C. (1982). A closer look at standardized tests. *The Arithmetic Teacher, 29,* 50–54.

Haring, N.G., Lovitt, T.C., Eaton, M.D., & Hansen, C.L. (1978). *The fourth R: Research in the classroom.* Columbus, OH: Charles E. Merrill.

Idol-Maestas, L. (1983). *Special educator's consultation handbook.* Rockville, MD: Aspen Systems.

Jenkins, J.R., & Pany, D. (1978). Standardized achievement tests: How useful for special education? *Exceptional Children, 44,* 448–453.

*Scott, Foresman Mathematics, Teacher's Edition, Book 3* (1980). Palo Alto, CA: Scott, Foresman.

# Chapter 4

# Assessment Techniques and Practices in the Early Years

*Anne M. Fitzmaurice Hayes*

The very qualities that make young children so endearing and delightful to observe also present major challenges to the successful assessment of cognitive development or academic achievement. The patterns of development in the young child and the necessary attributes of good measurement instruments make strange, if not wholly incompatible, bedfellows. Assessment in areas related to mathematics concepts and skills is by no means exempt from the consequent difficulties.

In this chapter we will examine the interrelationships between the two universes of the traits of the preschool child and the requirements of good measurement procedures. We will attempt to describe the mathematical development of the young child and particularly that of the learning-disabled child. After a brief discussion of mathematics assessment instruments, the chapter will conclude with a suggestion for an approach to the assessment of young learning-disabled children in mathematics.

## YOUNG CHILDREN AND ASSESSMENT—SOME PROBLEMS

> Grownups never understand anything by themselves, and it is tiresome for children to be always and forever explaining things to them. (St.-Exupéry, *The Little Prince,* 1943)

St. Exupéry's child grows weary of explaining things to grownups. His young person reflects a growing, if not grown, body of thought that recognizes the young child as someone other than a small adult. There seem to be qualitative differences between the perspectives of the young child and those of the adult. These differences originate from both the cognitive and affective characteristics of the preschool child.

The cognitive characteristics of the young child include several that pose problems in an assessment situation. The preschooler sees the environment from a limited viewpoint, his or her own. The four-year-old child standing directly in front of the television set is not necessarily selfish; his or her thinking seems to be, "I can see the screen clearly, so everyone else can also." Young children also seem to attend to only one or another dimension of a stimulus or a changing situation. These tendencies may result in misleading responses to test items.

Another source of problems for the test developer lies in the relatively rapid pace with which changes can take place with respect to the young child's thinking. A child's responses today may not match those given one month from now. Young children often reflect on these alterations in their thinking. "When I was little I used to think that. . . ." is a clause frequently overheard by the adult sensitive to the conversations of preschoolers. Such changes suggest a need for caution in interpreting test responses as static indicators of developmental level.

The language development of the young child offers many challenges to the task of assessment. Emerging language skills, both in vocabulary and syntax, can be a source of delight and frustration to an observer. The young child can use words, apparently in a knowledgeable fashion, without accurate understanding. On the other hand, a child may be unfamiliar with terms used by an examiner, even though he or she may understand the concepts in question. Care must be exercised that communication in both directions is taking place.

Last, and most obvious in this list of cognitive considerations, is the limited repertoire of test-taking skills possessed by the young child. This individual has little or no reading and writing skills. Task completion is seldom a goal; process is far more important. Time constraints do not ordinarily exist in the mind of the preschooler. Attention to tasks imposed from without is often quite limited. These factors pose concerns for both the examiner and the test developer.

Of necessity related to cognitive characteristics but meriting separate mention are the social and emotional attributes of the young child, for these too can affect a preschooler's responses in a test situation. For example, the physical condition of a preschool child often outweighs any other concerns the child may have. Hunger, fatigue, pent-up energy, a recent trauma such as a fall—any one factor or a combination of such factors can cause a child to put aside all other considerations until the physical need is met. In some cases the need can be easily recognized and satisfied. The child who knows that he or she is hungry can and usually does express the need for food. Few young children, however, will easily admit to fatigue as such. A high degree of sensitivity to the physical needs of the young child is required in any testing situation.

The young child often tends to combine affective responses with cognitive ones. The gifted four-year-old hauled off to an art lesson when he or she would rather be playing can well and unwittingly perform in such a way as to make parent and teacher wonder if there is any talent worth cultivating. Likewise the performance of young children in a test situation seems to be more influenced by affective considerations (a strange environment, unfamiliar materials, a stranger doing the testing) than that of older children.

Young children are sometimes less aware of social cues and social reinforcers than older children are. One is reminded in this context of the kindergarten child, who, early in the school year, came home from school one day somewhat chastened. When telling his mother of the circumstances contributing to his mood, he said, speaking of his teacher, "I thought her was glad, Mom, but her was mad." The child had misinterpreted the cues he received, to his eventual dismay. The young child may not always pick up on facial and tonal hints; the older child tends to be more receptive to both. The young child may not respond to the examiner's praise for doing a task, or to a polite request to begin a task. Task-induced reinforcement is generally more binding. The young child asserting his or her independence may well refuse to do any task, just for the sake of refusing. Such behavior can be and often is quite normal from a developmental standpoint; it can be quite stymying to the accomplishment of academic evaluation.

These cognitive, affective, and social characteristics of the young child that influence test-taking behaviors must be taken into consideration by the examiner. They also have grave implications for anyone setting out to develop measures of academic attainment on the part of young children, for they have special application to the issues of validity and reliability.

## VALIDITY AND RELIABILITY

In the field of standardized testing, reliability has traditionally been allied to the notion of consistency. Someone has remarked that consistency is the last refuge of the unimaginative. Most young children are anything but unimaginative. Patterns of behavior exist. Day-to-day responses can and do vary. Time-honored approaches to the derivation of reliability coefficients by way of test-retest or parallel forms methods seem to have inherent limitations where the preschool child is concerned. Measures of internal consistency are somewhat reliant on reasonably sized tests of similar items, all of which require a limited number of easily judged, quantifiable responses. As might be expected, reliability coefficients for tests designed specifically for young children are typically lower than desirable.

The issue of validity raises even more serious questions, especially with respect to mathematics assessment. The question of whether or not a test measures what it claims to measure presupposes a knowledge of what is to be measured. Without that knowledge, proper interpretation of test results is at best risky.

With respect to the mathematics development of the young child, Gelman and Gallistel (1978) have made some pertinent comments:

> Whatever the theoretical framework, the overriding tendency is to treat the preschooler's cognitive capacities, or lack thereof, in the light of those possessed by the older child. Knowing what the older child can do, we formulate a theoretical account of his capacities, and slip into the position that such capacities are absent in the preschooler. (p. 3)

> We are ignorant of the cognitive structures that enable preschoolers to assimilate their experience . . . the more evidence we have about the preschooler's quantitative knowledge, the easier our job of explanation will be. (p. 9)

The problem is clear and the situation has improved only slightly since these comments were made. Ideally, the task of mathematics assessment of the young child would be the determination of the degree to which he or she possesses the skills and concepts he or she ought to possess, but we know relatively little about what mathematics concepts and skills the preschool child can be expected to have. One can also argue that we have little evidence about what preschool capabilities in mathematics predict about successful mathematics learning in school. Only as our knowledge in each of these areas expands can we improve the quality of evaluation instruments.

At present we seem to be dependent on the results of research into the quantitative concepts of young children for guidelines in the development of an approach to the task of assessment. For this reason an examination of the development of mathematical skills and concepts during the early years seems justified in a chapter devoted to the topic of mathematics assessment during those same years.

## THE EVOLUTION OF PREMATHEMATICS SKILLS

Children acquire many mathematics skills and understandings as part of their cognitive development during their early years. Much of this growth is spatial in nature; much of it represents the rudiments of logical thinking and forms the basis for understanding number. Both areas are important for success in comprehending the language we use to embrace the quantitative aspects of our environment.

## Understanding Space

A look at any checklist used for evaluating the competencies of primary grade children soon convinces one of the multitude of understandings about space and location in space the young child is expected to acquire. Terms denoting position abound: *above, below, in front of, behind, top, bottom, left, right, inside, outside, on, between, under, over,* and so on. Size words and the names of shapes also require recognition.

Children become involved with such understandings from infancy onwards. Initial awareness seems to be centered on degrees of proximity of other persons and objects to self, then to each other; the baby quickly proceeds to become cognizant of separateness. As the child's perceptual capabilities and motor skills mature, so does discernment of space and position in space, both that of the child and the objects in his or her environment.

Geometry is the branch of mathematics that has as its main object the study of space and position in space. Some idea of how a child progresses in laying the foundations for the investigation of geometry can be obtained from following a young child's experience with such common shapes as squares, triangles, and circles.

Copeland (1974), following Piaget's lead, tells us that when asked to copy a drawing of a triangle, the preschooler is likely to draw shapes like those illustrated in Figure 4-1. Very seldom, however, would one find a child above the age of three who would draw an open figure in response to the same request. Most three-year-old children have already learned to distinguish between open figures and closed figures. Within a short time, children also discriminate between simple closed figures and closed figures that are not simple. For examples, see Figure 4-2.

The young child also begins to comprehend some basic topological relationships. We mentioned the awareness of proximity and separation. The recognition of open/closed prepares the way for a grasp of the concepts inside, outside, and on. Cognizance of betweenness and the related ability to recognize and reproduce ordered arrangements follow. By the end of the primary grades most children can reproduce the order of colored beads on a string, even when the string is arranged in a circular fashion. Not only can they do that, but upon request most children can reverse the order of the beads. Only after at least the rudiments of these topological

**Figure 4-1**  Sample Drawings of a Triangle, Produced by a Three-Year-Old Child

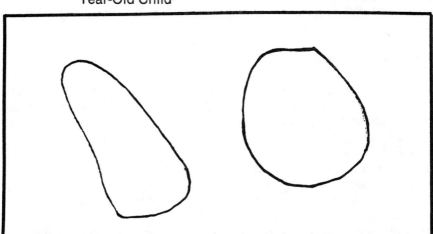

relationships are mastered does the child tackle Euclidean characteristics of and relationships between shapes: number of sides, size of angles, length, congruence, similarity, and so on.

Closely related to geometry is the area of measurement, with which young children also have experience. The language of size and comparison becomes familiar at a very young age: *big(ger), little(r), small(er), large(r), more, less, tall(er), short(er), long(er),* and so on. The comparative forms are important, because measurement by comparison seems to be the young person's favorite strategy. In fact, as Piaget detected, young children refuse to acknowledge absolutes when it comes to such characteristics of objects as length, volume, area, and the like. Thus, in the well-known Piagetian task, the preschooler will acknowlege the sameness of the length of two sticks arranged like this: _____. That same child, however, after observing the position of one stick being changed so that the arrangement is this: _____, will maintain that the two sticks are no longer of the same length. One is now longer than the other.

Just when children become aware that length remains constant in spite of a change in position is the subject of debate. Piaget (Piaget, Inhelder, & Szeminska, 1960) maintained that many children did not conserve length before the age of seven. Cruickshank, Fitzgerald, and Jensen (1980) assign the acquisition of conservation of length to ages three to five. The timing is perhaps not so important as the awareness that the young child's thinking

**Figure 4-2** Closed Curves That Are Simple and Closed Curves That Are Not Simple

about length, area, and volume undergoes radical changes during the preschool and primary grade years.

**Prelogic and Prenumber Understandings**

Remarkable is the young child's progress in developing spatial concepts; no less noteworthy is the parallel growth in prenumber skills and understandings. These developments pave the way for success in working with numbers and in the use of logic.

These abilities develop slowly. We will examine them in the order in which they seem to appear, but in actuality they develop, as it were, alongside each other. Figure 4-3 illustrates this mutual growth.

**Classification**

Classification is one of the most basic intellectual skills in which we as human beings engage. Through classification we introduce some order into the myriad of experiences to which we are always subject. An infant classifies initial events as pleasant or unpleasant. As the baby grows, classification schemes become more sophisticated.

A young person's progress in classification can be gauged by examining his or her approach to sorting tasks. The two-year-old child is likely to sort a pile of items in the simplest way possible, by merely heaping items together, with no thought for likenesses or differences. The three-year-old

**Figure 4-3** Parallel Development of Mathematical Understandings

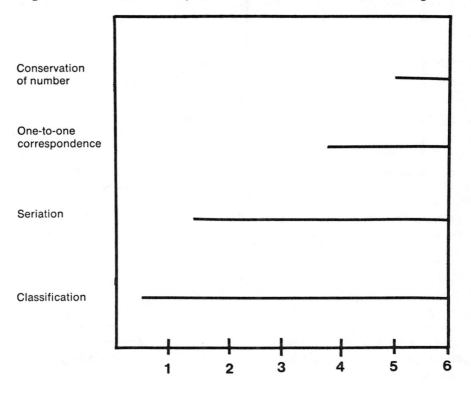

child, faced with a number of items, takes a unique approach to sorting them. He or she will usually line up the items in one way or another, according to a rule that may change several times in the course of the task.

The four-year-old child, given a sorting task, will usually consistently group items according to some common trait, but will usually fail to complete the sorting task. That is, given square shapes of three different colors, red, yellow, and blue, the child will group some blue ones together, some red ones together, and some yellow ones together, and declare the activity completed, even though there may be some pieces remaining in the original pile. The child does not understand that the sort must be exhaustive, as well as accurate. Some five-year-old children and most six-year-old children can complete the sorting task accurately and exhaustively.

A second indicator of growth in the area of classification is the type of attribute according to which a child can sort. Initially the child is confined to physical attributes: color, size, shape, texture, and the like. Classification according to function follows closely in sequence. At a much later time, during the primary grades at the earliest, classification of ideas becomes possible. Examples of this skill include classifying sets according to the number of items in the sets and outlining written material.

A final word about classification concerns the number of attributes on which the child can focus. Initially, children attend to only one attribute at a time. As they progress, they can keep in mind two and even three attributes at the same time.

## Seriation

To classify is to be able to recognize similarities between or among different objects. Seriation requires that the child be able to discern differences between or among objects along one dimension or another: length, width, pitch, texture, and so on. As was the case with classification, seriation activities range from the very basic to the very complex.

Initial steps in the development of seriation abilities involve comparing two items or quantities in terms of more, less, longer, shorter, greater number, fewer number, or similar dimensions. The child then moves on to sets of items on which an ordering relationship can be imposed, for example, three or four sticks, each of which differs from the others in length.

The seriation task becomes more difficult as the number of items to be ordered becomes greater. When first faced with a set of several sticks of different lengths, the four- or five-year-old child is likely to place the first and last sticks correctly but mix up some of the sticks in between. As the child gains experience, he or she will begin to realize the necessity of comparing each stick with the one before it and the one after it if the entire set is to be ordered properly.

The method a child uses when ordering the member of a set undergoes change as seriation skills increase. For the three-year-old child, the procedure may resemble that of classification more than seriation. That is, given several sticks of different lengths to be ordered, the child may merely make three groups of sticks: small, medium, and large. Gradually, as time goes on, the child will use a trial-and-error approach to lay out the sticks in the appropriate order. Copeland (1974) maintained that not before the age of seven can most children perform the task in an organized manner, first selecting from the group the smallest (largest) stick, then the next smallest (largest), and so on, until all sticks have been placed.

At about the same time, during the primary grade years, the child gains proficiency in ordering sets of items according to number, and finally, ordering numbers themselves. The child's language of seriation can then include both the cardinal numbers and the ordinal numbers.

In addition to ordering sets according to number, the seriation task can have as its purpose the ordering of sets according to the class inclusion relationship. Think of tea roses, flowers, plants, and roses. The class inclusion relationship for these sets is illustrated in Figure 4-4. A sequence based on this relationship is, clearly, tea roses, roses, flowers, plants. According to Piaget (Piaget, Inhelder, & Szeminska, 1960), the ability to understand such relationships does not develop until the age of seven or eight years in most children. Many researchers have concluded that the understanding comes even later (Winer, 1980).

Ordering relationships (is more than, is taller than, is contained in, and so on) are of a special kind because they have a special property, called transitivity. To better understand transitivity, let us examine a nontransitive relation, for example, "is a friend of." Suppose Mary is a friend of Amy and Amy is a friend of Sue. That Mary and Sue are friends does not necessarily follow; they may not even know each other. "Is a friend of" is not a transitive relationship. Hence, there is no necessary ordering of the three girls on the basis of "is a friend of."

On the other hand, suppose the relationship becomes "is wealthier than." If Mary is wealthier than Amy and Amy is wealthier than Sue, then, of necessity, Mary is wealthier than Sue, and a corresponding sequence, based on degrees of wealth, can be derived. Such is the connection between ordering relationships and the transitive property. The child with a working knowledge of one will have a working knowledge of the other.

**Figure 4-4** Class Inclusion

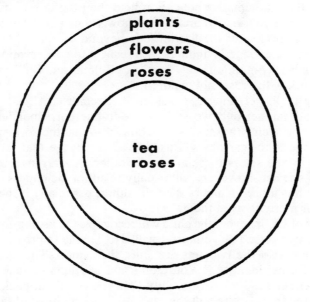

**Figure 4-5** Examples of Equivalent Sets and Nonequivalent Sets

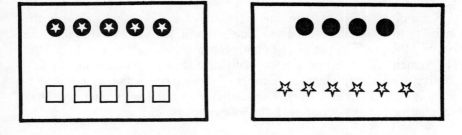

## Equivalence

Another important relationship that can be defined on sets is that of equivalence. To test for equivalence we try to establish a one-to-one correspondence between the members of one set and the members of the other. The first pairs of sets in Figure 4-5 are equivalent because such a correspondence exists. The second pairs of sets are not equivalent.

Young children only gradually come to recognize one-to-one correspondence, and the lasting equivalence between any two sets for which such a correspondence can be demonstrated. Few topics have received more attention in the mathematics education field than the questions of when and how children conserve number, and how we can best tap the ability to conserve. A review of the literature is beyond our present purposes. We will summarize Piaget's findings with respect to conservation of number, and then briefly mention a few results of Gelman and Gallistel's (1978) extensive work with preschool children.

According to Piaget (Piaget, Inhelder, & Szeminska, 1960), the four-year-old child can set out two sets in one-to-one correspondence, with guidance. Upon seeing two such sets arranged so that the correspondence is obvious, the four-year-old will usually acknowledge that there are as many items in one set as there are in the other. A rearrangement of the members of one set, however, will usually result in the child's claim that one set now has more members than the other, especially if the two sets have eight or more items in them.

By the age of six or seven, the child will recognize the lasting equivalence between the two sets. The youngster will also be able to provide a reason for maintaining that the two sets are still "the same." The reason takes one of two forms: identity ("You didn't add anything or take anything away from either set") or reversibility ("If you put them back like they were you'll see that they're still the same"). The supplying of the reasons marks the true conserver. Traditional Piagetian doctrine teaches that meaningful work with numbers can follow only upon the achievement of conservation of number.

According to Piaget, one characteristic of the preschool child is the inability to conserve. Hence any true sense of number would seem to be beyond the grasp of the young child. Nonetheless, Gelman and Gallistel (1978) maintained that preschoolers do have some understanding of quantitative invariance, when the number of items in the sets under consideration is small (five or fewer). The studies they cited are numerous. They summarized their findings with the following remarks:

> . . . the child's numerical reasoning principles recognize that between any two numerosities an equivalence relation may or may not hold. The practical decision about whether it holds or not rests on counting. If counting yields identical representations for the numerosities of the two sets, the sets are judged to satisfy the equivalence relationship. (p. 164)

### Counting

It would seem, then, that the young child relies on counting to make judgments about equivalence. Since the preschooler's counting skills are very limited, the child best determines equivalence or nonequivalence between sets that have only a few members.

Gelman (1972) went even further. She demonstrated the use of operators (addition, subtraction, identity) by young children to explain change or no change with respect to the number of items in previously observed sets. As with the strategy for determining equivalence or nonequivalence, for the above processes the child also depends on counting.

The young child, then, although lacking fully mature concepts, nonetheless seems to have a working knowledge of small numbers and a means to quantify combined or separated quantities. As the child's store of counting numbers increases, so do the skills needed for working with these numbers.

What is the counting process all about? The successful counter is one who can coordinate a number of counting behaviors, or principles. Gelman and Gallistel (1978) listed these as

1. the one-one principle
2. the stable order principle
3. the cardinal principle
4. the abstraction principle
5. the order irrelevance principle

Adults are frequently amused, or frustrated, when watching a preschooler count items in an array. The child may skip some items altogether and count other items twice. This behavior indicates the absence of the one-one principle. Accurate counting demands that each item being counted must be tagged once and only once. By the age of four many children have learned this principle (Schaeffer, Eggleston, & Scott, 1974).

The child who does not know a sequence of number names in a stable order will have difficulty counting in any meaningful fashion. The attainment of the correct sequence seems to be a function of age and exposure to the number names. The first 13 number names are acquired largely by rote memory. From then on the child can, and usually does, discover rules to aid the learning task. Many kindergarten children have learned the number names to 20 in the correct sequence.

The cardinal principle states that when counting the members of a set, the last number named is the number of the set. Awareness of this principle seems to develop later than facility with the one-one principle and the stable order principle (Schaeffer, Eggleston, & Scott, 1974), but many preschool children attain all three of these "how to count" principles.

The abstraction principle holds that any collection of entities can be counted. Young children confine counting largely to collections of objects, although movements and sounds quickly become countable. Little research has concerned itself with the ages at which children recognize various other entities as countable.

The observant adult who happens to be present at the right time might see a young child count the members of a set arranged in a linear fashion from left to right and from right to left. At a certain point in development, the child will appear surprised that the outcome is the same both times, or will evidence no dismay if one count is different from the other. Such a child has not yet grasped the order irrelevance principle: the order in which the members of a group are counted does not matter. The establishment of this principle marks an important step, for it signifies an awareness that number as such is different from things.

The preschool and primary grade child is busy with the learning and consolidation of all five counting principles, at one level or another. Add that area of development to those previously discussed and we see that, far from being a time of inactivity, mathematically speaking, the first seven or eight years of life mark a time of major achievements in learning about quantity. Once good number concepts are in place, the work of building skills in addition and subtraction is undertaken. All of the material that has been discussed here can form the subject of assessment in mathematics during the early years.

## THE MATHEMATICS DEVELOPMENT OF THE YOUNG LEARNING-DISABLED CHILD

The treatment of the question of what impact learning disabilities would have on normal development in the early stages of understanding mathematics is difficult for several reasons. First of all, the recognized difficulty in defining learning disabilities and the resulting heterogeneity in the group of children labeled as learning disabled defies any precise analysis of developmental impact, except, perhaps, for subgroups of the population.

A second but related factor is the interaction between child and environment. Adelman (1971) noted that "learning problems result not only from the characteristics of the youngster, but also from the characteristics of the classroom situation to which he is assigned" (p. 529). For the preschool child, the classroom situation must be translated as the home, day-care setting, or preschool surroundings. The primary grade classroom environment also can and does differ from school system to school system. Some environments may be more conducive than others to offsetting the negative effects of learning disabilities on cognitive growth.

A third element of difficulty stems from the present state of the art in detecting learning disabilities in young children. Traditionally, a diagnosis of learning disabilities followed referral because of academic failure, achievement discrepancies, or behavior disorders within the classroom setting. Efforts at selecting "high risk" children during kindergarten screening have left much to be desired in the way of predictive value, especially when detected disabilities are not severe in nature (Keogh & Becker, 1973; Beers & Beers, 1980). Since locating populations of young learning-disabled children is difficult, studies measuring their mathematical development are hard to find.

The final reason to be cited here is actually a specific case of the first one given, but it merits special mention. Some children seem to have a severe learning disability in mathematics, or specific areas of mathematics, for example, arithmetic computation. These same children may not have a similar difficulty in the area of reading. The reverse, of course, is also true. In the mathematics-disabled group we have an instance of a severe impact of the disability on successful performance in mathematics. Is the impact as great on the early development of mathematics concepts?

Keeping the difficulties in mind, we will attempt to provide some indication of what the implications of the presence of a learning disability may be for the successful passage through the various stages of development characterizing the preschool or primary grade youngster. A first distinction to be recognized is that between cognitive development as measured by tasks such as the traditional Piagetian activities designed to detect conservation and mathematics achievement as measured by standardized tests, for example, the *KeyMATH Diagnostic Test* (Connolly, 1972). A second distinction to be recalled is that between concept and skill.

With the above in mind, the following conclusions can be supported:

1. In general, learning-disabled children, even those as young as seven or eight years of age, do not score as high as their normal peers on standardized tests of mathematics achievement (Cawley, Fitzmaurice, Shaw, Kahn, & Bates, 1979; Fincham & Meltzer, 1976).
2. Learning disabled children labeled as dyslexic or perceptually handicapped seem to perform as well as their normal counterparts on Piagetian tasks measuring attainment of conservation (Fincham & Meltzer, 1976; Meltzer, 1978; Fincham, 1979).
3. There is some evidence that children who are learning disabled in mathematics do not perform as well as their normal peers on Piagetian tasks measuring attainment of conservation (Saxe & Shaheen, 1981).

4. Mathematics achievement as measured by standardized tests seems to be related to verbal ability as well as spatial ability.

From these findings the following set of principles emerges:

1. Mathematics assessment for the young learning-disabled child should systematically embrace many areas of mathematics, those that tap nonverbal abilities as well as those that tap language skills.
2. Mathematics assessment for young learning-disabled children should be concept oriented, rather than skill oriented.
3. Mathematics assessment for young learning-disabled children should be based on a systematic set of interactions between examiner and child so that each area of strength available to the child can be utilized.
4. The mathematics assessment of the young learning-disabled child should be directed to the ascertainment of developmental status as well as achievement status. This evaluation should also highlight capabilities, as well as disabilities.

The last point serves as the justification for the approach to a process of evaluation suggested in the following pages. One who is concerned with the mathematics assessment of the preschool or primary grade child who may be learning disabled must, of necessity, participate in Gelman and Gallistel's search for what the child can do, for what understandings the child does, in fact, possess.

## ASSESSMENT INSTRUMENTS

The tenets governing mathematics assessment of young learning-disabled children and the groundwork underlying those tenets were a necessary prelude to an examination, however brief, of existing instruments. The examination will center on selected assessment instruments, with particular attention to the purpose of the instruments and the content of the items designed to measure some aspect of knowledge of mathematics.

Of necessity, the number of instruments selected is limited. For the most part, those selected represent recent contributions to the field. One would hope, therefore, that these instruments reflect the present state of the art, as it were, in mathematics assessment for young children.

Of the instruments under discussion, most include mathematics as a subtest of a larger set of tests measuring overall readiness for school or academic achievement. Hence statements of purpose often refer to the larger picture of readiness or achievement.

The *Beginning Education Assessment* of the Scott, Foresman Achievement Series (Cawley, Cawley, Cherkes, & Fitzmaurice, 1980) contains a mathematics component designed to supply teachers with a quick way to obtain some idea of a child's developmental level with respect to mathematics. The 15-item scale, concentrated on the areas of open/closed, shape, inside/outside/on, size, number, and arithmetic, is intended to provide a measure of a young child's current focus of attention. That focus of attention, it is claimed, can be used in most cases as an indicator of a young child's developmental stage.

The *Brigance K and 1 Screen* (Brigance, 1982) has as its purpose the screening of kindergarten and first grade students by way of a criterion-referenced instrument. It consists of assessments from both the *Brigance Inventory of Early Development* (Birth–7 years) and the *Brigance Inventory of Basic Skills* (K–6th). Specifically, items focus on rote counting, numeral comprehension, numerals in sequence, more/less, one-one matching, joining sets, writing numerals, and naming differences. The manual contains a matrix cross-referencing the content of the *Brigance K and 1 Screen* to its parent instruments, so that when a more comprehensive assessment is in order, other items may be selected for that purpose.

The *Diagnostic Achievement Battery* (DAB) (Newcomer & Curtis, 1984) is designed to measure competency in spoken language, written language, and applied mathematics, in response to the needs created by P.L. 94-142. As a battery of tests, the DAB is supposed to identify those students with a lag in development in the areas mentioned above and provide a picture of component strengths and weaknesses that individual students may possess. The battery is also intended to provide a tracking device to measure students' progress as a result of special intervention strategies. The math portion of the DAB is composed of both a math reasoning component and a math calculations portion. The content of the math reasoning section includes counting objects (up to ten items), recognition of numerals, matching sets by number, longer/shorter, adding single-digit numbers, finding differences between single-digit numbers. The written calculations section contains examples of varying degrees of difficulty across the four operations of arithmetic. The DAB has as its target population children of ages 6 to 14.

The *Test of Early Mathematical Ability* (TEMA) (Ginsburg, 1983), designed for children of ages 4.0 to 8.11, claims as its purposes a set of objectives identical to those of the DAB but with special reference to the area of mathematics. The instrument is divided into two parts, one examining the informal mathematics of the child, the other looking at the formal mathematics the child has achieved. The former section includes items involving number comparison, counting, and calculation. The latter part purports to measure understanding of convention, number facts, and base ten concepts.

The *Basic School Skills Inventory—Diagnostic* (BSSI-D) (Hammill & Leigh, 1983), developed to aid teachers and other school personnel to examine the abilities of young children (ages 4–6), also contains a mathematics component. The content includes numeral recognition, printing numerals, counting quantitative relationships, equivalence, seriation, and simple arithmetic computations.

The last instrument to be mentioned here is the *Lollipop Test* (Chew, 1981). Conceived as an alternative to the *Metropolitan Readiness Test* (1976), the *Lollipop Test* can be administered and scored in no more than 20 minutes. The mathematics portion includes counting, number identification, and shape identification.

Finally, although not an assessment instrument as such, Copeland's *Diagnostic and Learning Activities in Mathematics for Children* (1980) may be mentioned in this context. It consists of activities designed to determine the quality or stage of a child's thinking. There are 32 activities, grouped in four basic areas: space, number, logical classification, and measurement. Each activity is keyed to the age level(s) for which it is appropriate. Levels of performance for each task are described, and teaching implications are presented briefly and clearly.

Such then is a sampling of the present state of the art in the mathematics assessment of young children. Two facts become apparent: emphasis on number skills and understanding  predominates, and quite often, in the cause of efficiency and economy, even that area receives only a cursory glance. The immense amount of mathematics the young child has encountered and mastered has little chance to come to light under such circumstances.


## AN APPROACH TO AN ALTERNATIVE

A set of activities such as the following is intended to provide an examiner with an insight into what a child can do and where he or she might be headed from there. The format in which the set is presented reflects a modified Interactive Unit as described by Cawley (1984). The Interactive Unit lends itself to the purpose of assessment because of its allowance for structuring the forms of interaction between evaluator and child. The set of activities outlined below would represent only one of many such units to be administered to a child over a period of time. The information gathered would include not only a comprehensive picture of how much mathematics a child knew, but also which forms of interaction between examiner and child yielded most success for the child. With such knowledge, an instructor could undertake efficient and effective instruction.

Topic:      Open and closed
Question:  Can the child distinguish between open figures and closed figures?
Materials:  Models and pictures of open figures and closed figures. Examples are illustrated in Figure 4-6.

1. Show the child a sheet like that of Figure 4-6. Ask the child to point to the figure in each row most like the first one.

**Figure 4-6** Sample Activity Sheet for Open/Closed

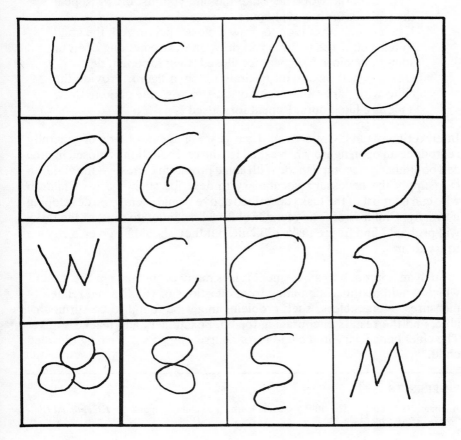

2. Point to each item in the first row of the worksheet. Ask the child to say "open" if the figure looks open and "closed" if the figure looks closed.
3. Provide the child with paper and crayon or pencil. Point to the first four figures in the first column of the worksheet, one at a time. Ask the child to draw each figure.
4. Cover up all but the first row of the worksheet. Ask the child to point to an open figure. Repeat for closed. Repeat for row 4.
5. Ask the child to tell you in his or her own words what "open" means. Repeat for "closed."
6. Ask the child to draw an open figure. Repeat for closed.
7. Cover up all but the first row of the worksheet. Use pencil or crayon to draw an open figure. Ask the child to point to a picture on the worksheet like the one you just drew. Repeat the activity for a closed figure.
8. Use a pencil or crayon to draw a closed figure. Ask the child to tell you if the picture you drew shows something open or something closed. Repeat for closed, then for open.
9. Use a pencil or crayon to draw an open figure. Provide the child with paper and pencil or crayon. Ask the child to draw a picture like yours. Repeat for closed.

Interpreting results: Children of three years of age or older can generally reproduce an open figure when asked to; the reproduction of closed figures can be similarly accomplished. With some prompting, most young children can supply the necessary vocabulary to describe such figures. Children who can do most of the tasks described above would seem to be developing normally. Children of four years or older who cannot do most of the tasks will probably find future tasks difficult, but they should be given a chance to try them.

Such an approach to assessment raises many problems, not the least of which would be those stemming from questions of validity and reliability measures. Nonetheless, such problems might be found to be surmountable, and the results encouraging for both examiners and teachers alike. The chief beneficiary in the end is, of course, the young learning-disabled child.

**REFERENCES**

Adelman, H.S. (1971). The not so specific learning disability population. *Exceptional Children*, 37(6), 528–533.

Beers, C.S., & Beers, J.W. (1980). Early identification of learning disabilities: Facts and fallacies. *The Elementary School Journal, 81*(2).

Brigance, A. (1977). *Brigance diagnostic inventory of basic skills.* Woburn, MA: Curriculum Associates.

_____ . (1978). *Brigance diagnostic inventory of early development.* Woburn, MA: Curriculum Associates.

_____ . (1982). *Brigance K & 1 screen for kindergarten and first grade.* Woburn, MA: Curriculum Associates.

Cawley, J.F., Cawley, L., Cherkes, M., & Fitzmaurice, A.M. (1980). *Beginning education assessment.* Glenview, IL: Scott, Foresman.

Cawley, J.F., Fitzmaurice, A.M., Shaw, R., Kahn, H., & Bates, H. (1979). LD youth and mathematics: A review of characteristics. *Learning Disability Quarterly, 2*(1), 29–44.

Chew, A. (1981). *The lollypop test: A diagnostic screening test of school readiness.* Atlanta, GA: Humanics Limited.

Connolly, A. (1972). *KeyMATH diagnostic arithmetic test.* Circle Pines, MN: American Guidance Service.

Copeland, R. (1974). *How children learn mathematics.* New York: Macmillan.

_____ . (1980). *Diagnostic and learning activities in mathematics.* New York: Macmillan.

Cruickshank, D.E., Fitzgerald, D.L., & Jensen, L.R. (1980). *Young children learning mathematics.* Boston: Allyn & Bacon.

Fincham, F.D. (1979). Conservation and cognitive role-taking ability in learning disabled boys. *Journal of Learning Disabilities, 12*(1), 34–40.

Fincham, F.D., & Meltzer, L.J. (1976). Learning disabilities and arithmetic achievement. *South African Journal of Psychology, 6,* 80–86. Reprinted in *Journal of Learning Disabilities, 10*(8), 43–45 (1977).

Gelman, R. (1972). Logical capacity of very young children: Number invariance rules. *Child Development, 43,* 75–90.

Gelman, R., & Gallistel, C.R. (1978). *The child's understanding of number.* Cambridge, MA: Harvard University Press.

Ginsburg, H. (1983). *Test of early mathematics ability.* Austin, TX: Pro-Ed.

Hammill, D., & Leigh, J. (1983). *Basic school skills inventory-diagnostic.* Austin, TX: Pro-Ed.

Keogh, B.A., & Becker, L.D. (1973, September). Early detection of learning problems: Questions, cautions, and guidelines. *Exceptional Children, 39,* 5–11.

Meltzer, L.J. (1978). Abstract reasoning in a specific group of perceptually impaired children: Namely, the learning disabled. *Journal of Genetic Psychology, 132,* 185–195.

Newcomer, P., & Curtis, D. (1984). *Diagnostic achievement battery.* Austin, TX: Pro-Ed.

Piaget, J., Inhelder, B., & Szeminska, A. (1960). *The child's conception of geometry.* New York: Basic Books.

Saxe, G., & Shaheen, S. (1981). Piagetian theory and the atypical case: An analysis of the developmental Gerstmann Syndrome. *Journal of Learning Disabilities, 14*(3), 131–135.

Schaeffer, B., Eggleston, V.H., & Scott, J.L. (1974). Number development in young children. *Cognitive Psychology, 6,* 357–379.

St.-Exupéry, A. (1943). *The little prince.*

Winer, G.A. (1980). Class-inclusion reasoning in children: A review of the empirical literature. *Child Development, 51*(2), 309–328.

# Chapter 5

# Assessment Techniques and Practices in Grades 5–12

*Robert A. Shaw*

The purpose of this chapter is to develop a framework for assessment procedures for grades 5 through 12. To achieve this we will examine the current situation in assessment, speculate on what is possible, and suggest modifications in existing procedures to obtain our goals. The sequence of the framework will begin with the testing programs of a school system, continue to classroom situations, and end in a clinical setting. Implied in this sequence is a need for special training in assessment procedures, curriculum development, and diagnostic teaching. Specific examples will supply background information in these areas.

Within this chapter assessment will be considered as a subset of the total evaluation process and as a connecting link between initial measurement and diagnostic procedures. We will have to explore measurement as a comparative process involving norm-referenced tests to establish a baseline from which to work. In assessment we search for intraindividual differences across mathematical content and processes. To continue the procedure we must consider diagnosis that involves internal analysis across a limited content area in a search for strengths and weaknesses.

## BEGINNING FACTORS AND CURRENT CONDITIONS

When students enter the middle school in grade 5, we know that they possess a wide range of characteristics, attitudes, and abilities. Many will have been exposed to a continuous progress program in reading; however, few will have had such opportunities in mathematics. In addition, some will have one or more disabilities that have hindered their progress in learning mathematics. A first-phase approach in attempting to meet the needs of these learners is homogeneous grouping. Past achievement grades, data from norm-referenced tests, and anecdotal records are used for placement purposes. The placement may be into different class groups or within different groups in a given class in mathematics.

The mathematics program for the classes and groups is usually defined by a commercially produced curriculum or a school syllabus. Modifications may have to be made to better serve learners' needs by individual teachers after they have had considerable experience in teaching mathematics. The overall approach is that students enter into a defined developmental program under the assumption that they can progress through such a program.

To determine if progress in mathematics is being made, many school systems have established an evaluation plan, for example, using standardized tests in grades 4, 8, 11 or grades 3, 5, 7, and 9. In an attempt to ensure that school systems adopt and follow a given plan some state boards of education have made testing mandatory, especially ninth grade proficiency or eleventh grade competency testing. The purpose of this chapter is *not* to support or reject testing plans or programs but to attempt to use the information that is available to enhance learning.

Since tests are used as initial measures of achievement in mathematics prior to specific assessment procedures, we need to understand the data that are obtained from such tests. When we use data from a norm-referenced instrument, each individual score is compared with the scores of other learners of the same age or in the same grade. Percentiles or grade-level equivalence scores are often reported. Since many different combinations of right answers can produce the same equivalency score, we need to examine subscores on various portions of the instrument to derive indications of group and individual strengths and weaknesses. The subscores of an instrument reflect the measurement on selected content objectives, and we may be able to use such data as starting points for assessment procedures.

Domain-referenced tests are designed to reflect achievement in specific content areas, for example, operations with whole numbers or problem solving. Many state proficiency tests are designed in this manner. Results are sent to the schools showing the total school performance, performance of each class, and an individual's performance. Tables 5-1 to 5-3 represent actual data from a state assessment test. Table 5-1 contains data for 708 eighth graders. Categories 16, 17, and 18 represent domains of content or goal areas. Categories 1–15 represent specific sets of objectives.

Looking at the total district we note that the strengths appear in the objective areas of whole number operations and addition and subtraction of numbers in decimal form. Weaknesses occur in the areas of ordering number values and using percent. In the goal areas mathematical concepts is the lowest and computation is the highest with respect to achievement.

**Table 5-1** Assessment of Educational Progress in Mathematics

Objectives summary for district: 708 students. 8th Grade

| Objective | Items | Mean N Correct | Mean % Correct |
|---|---|---|---|
| 1. Understand fraction, decimal, percent | 4 | 2.4 | 60 |
| 2. Order decimal, fraction, whole numbers | 4 | 1.7 | 44 |
| 3. Add and subtract whole numbers | 4 | 3.7 | 92 |
| 4. Multiply and divide whole numbers | 6 | 5.1 | 85 |
| 5. Add and subtract decimals | 4 | 3.3 | 82 |
| 6. Multiply and divide decimals | 5 | 3.5 | 69 |
| 7. Add and subtract fractions and mixed numbers | 4 | 2.2 | 55 |
| 8. Multiply and divide fractions and mixed numbers | 5 | 2.8 | 55 |
| 9. Use percent | 4 | 1.9 | 47 |
| 10. Find area and perimeter | 3 | 1.6 | 54 |
| 11. Convert U.S. measure to an equivalent | 4 | 2.4 | 59 |
| 12. Metric units of measure | 5 | 3.1 | 62 |
| 13. Interpret data from tables and graphs | 4 | 2.5 | 63 |
| 14. Solve word problems | 10 | 5.9 | 59 |
| 15. Basic geometric concepts | 4 | 2.6 | 66 |
| 16. Goal area:   Math concepts | 8 | 4.1 | 52 |
| 17. Goal area:   Computation | 32 | 22.4 | 70 |
| 18. Goal area:   Measurement | 12 | 7.1 | 59 |

Statistics for total test score:
Average number correct  =  44.7
Standard deviation  =  14.32
Average percent correct  =  63.8

The data and the mathematics program need to be examined in the indicated areas of weaknesses to determine if there is a curriculum, an instructional, or a learning problem. Low scores are not always caused by lack of knowledge or low level of ability on the part of students.

Similar data are often provided for each class in a given school district and the same general guidelines and cautions (as with the total district) can be noted for the results within each class. However, an examination of individual performance within the objective areas can provide data on consistency of performance across the objective areas, areas of strength, and possible areas of weakness.

In the small class represented in Table 5-2 it becomes obvious as you examine the data under each objective that objective 3, addition and subtraction of whole numbers, is a strong area and (with all of the zero scores) objective 7, addition and subtraction of numbers in fraction and mixed number form, indicates an area of weakness. The range for percent

**Table 5-2** Assessment of Educational Progress in Mathematics

Student objective report for class: 11 students. 8th Grade

| Objective Number | 1 | 2 | 3 | 4 | 5 | 6 | 7 | 8 | 9 | 10 | 11 | 12 | 13 | 14 | 15 | All Items |
|---|---|---|---|---|---|---|---|---|---|---|---|---|---|---|---|---|
| Number of Items | 4 | 4 | 4 | 6 | 4 | 5 | 4 | 5 | 4 | 3 | 4 | 5 | 4 | 10 | 4 | 70 |
| Student | Percent of Items Answered Correctly | | | | | | | | | | | | | | | |
| Gaylen | 50 | 0 | 100 | 66 | 75 | 20 | 0 | 20 | 50 | 33 | 25 | 20 | 50 | 40 | 50 | 40 |
| Lisa | 25 | 50 | 50 | 83 | 25 | 40 | 0 | 60 | 0 | 0 | 0 | 60 | 50 | 10 | 75 | 36 |
| Ernst | 75 | 75 | 100 | 83 | 100 | 40 | 75 | 80 | 100 | 66 | 100 | 100 | 50 | 70 | 100 | 80 |
| Kim | 50 | 25 | 100 | 83 | 100 | 20 | 0 | 40 | 50 | 66 | 0 | 40 | 75 | 50 | 75 | 51 |
| Mark | 75 | 25 | 100 | 66 | 75 | 20 | 25 | 60 | 50 | 66 | 0 | 20 | 25 | 40 | 100 | 49 |
| Valerie | 25 | 25 | 100 | 83 | 100 | 20 | 0 | 60 | 25 | 66 | 75 | 40 | 50 | 60 | 50 | 53 |
| Deanne | 25 | 25 | 75 | 66 | 75 | 20 | 0 | 40 | 50 | 66 | 25 | 20 | 50 | 50 | 75 | 44 |
| Karen | 50 | 0 | 100 | 100 | 100 | 40 | 50 | 80 | 50 | 66 | 50 | 60 | 75 | 40 | 25 | 59 |
| Frank | 50 | 0 | 100 | 83 | 75 | 40 | 0 | 40 | 0 | 33 | 25 | 20 | 50 | 20 | 25 | 37 |
| Jackie | 50 | 25 | 75 | 50 | 75 | 0 | 0 | 20 | 25 | 66 | 25 | 40 | 100 | 30 | 75 | 41 |
| Margaret | 25 | 50 | 75 | 83 | 75 | 40 | 0 | 40 | 25 | 33 | 75 | 0 | 100 | 40 | 100 | 50 |

of items answered correctly is from a low of 36 to a high of 80. The score of 80 is 21 points higher than the next highest score, 59; therefore, with the exception of Ernst, the class is rather homogeneous with respect to achievement in mathematics. A more thorough examination of the data will expose the variations from learner to learner. The fact that Lisa got a higher score on multiplication and division of whole numbers than on addition and subtraction of whole numbers indicates an area to be examined with more examples of her work. Objectives 5 and 6 reflect the same trend for her work with decimals. Data from charts such as this provide a classroom teacher with starting points for a more detailed analysis.

An item-by-item analysis such as in Table 5-3 indicates what distractors on a multiple-choice test the students are selecting. Some wrong choices indicate a faulty algorithm is being used.

These data also give an instructor an opportunity to examine a given test and ask questions about the test or curriculum. For example, why did everyone in the class get the wrong answer for item 9 with, in most cases, the same wrong answer?

Data such as these are readily available in grades 5 through 12. There are external pressures on schools from state-mandated proficiency and/or competency tests, state and national assessment projects in mathematics, and tests suggested by colleges and universities for admission purposes. Testing programs within schools and school districts provide us with more summative (and sometimes, formative) data to determine where learners are in regard to achievement in mathematics at a given time, place, and under a given set of conditions.

The extent to which we use data such as these to plan instructional and assessment activities for individuals with learning disabilities will depend on several factors. First of all, we have to *want* to use the data and, second, we need to possess the knowledge to enable us to make maximum use of the data. The answer to the question of why schools test students should be to learn as much as possible about them in order to be able to match classroom teaching techniques to specific learner needs. We use published tests so that we can sample a wide range of topics at one time with materials that have been developed with considerable time and effort in order to produce valid and reliable instruments. However, we should remember that no amount of tests given students will *teach* them how to compute and solve problems. In addition, the manner in which tests are usually given, through the graphic, symbolic mode (paper-pencil) may not produce the same results for learning-disabled individuals as would a verbal *and* written test. The implications are that we must approach the use and results of such tests with caution and they should serve only as initial sources of information in the assessment procedure.

**Table 5-3** Assessment of Educational Progress in Mathematics

Student item profile for class: 11 students. 8th Grade

| Student | Number Correct | Q1 12345 | Q1 67890 | Q2 12345 | Q2 67890 | Q3 12345 | Q3 67890 | Q4 12345 | Q4 67890 | Q5 12345 | Q5 67890 | Q6 12345 | Q6 67890 | Q7 12345 | Q7 67890 |
|---|---|---|---|---|---|---|---|---|---|---|---|---|---|---|---|
| Gaylen | 28 | ----1 | 1--4- | --64- | 31002 | -3--2 | 3-12- | 443-- | 53-13 | 1-1-3 | 11323 | 4--3- | 213-1 | -3252 | -2-2- |
| Lisa | 25 | -0-40 | 17442 | -32-- | ----- | -3--2 | 3311- | 34026 | 30214 | 534-3 | -1320 | -1--1 | 3-120 | -3--- | -2123 |
| Ernst | 56 | ----- | ---4- | ----- | 3---2 | -5--- | --1-- | 3---- | ---51 | 5---- | -5--- | ----- | 2---3 | ----- | ----2 |
| Kim | 36 | --40 | 1--42 | ----- | 344-2 | ----2 | 3-12- | 243-6 | -4-53 | --2-- | -50-3 | -4--- | 412-1 | 233-2 | -2--- |
| Mark | 34 | --14- | 1--47 | ----- | 41--2 | -5--2 | 3--1- | 34320 | 401-4 | 5---- | -4--1 | -1-3- | 24220 | -12-2 | -2--3 |
| Valeri | 37 | ---31 | 1--43 | ----- | -44-- | -3-32 | 3-12- | -43-- | 5---1 | 1-4-1 | --34- | ----1 | 31-43 | -3352 | ---43 |
| Deanne | 31 | ----3 | 1-442 | --64- | 34-32 | 25--2 | 3-12- | 343-- | -4-1- | 4-44- | ---43 | -4--1 | 44244 | -32-2 | 1--2- |
| Karen | 41 | ---1- | 1--47 | ----- | 34--- | ----2 | ---2- | -43-- | -4113 | 1-4-- | 4--4- | 442-1 | 313-3 | -3-5- | ---2- |
| Frank | 26 | --1-1 | 1--45 | ----- | 342-- | ----2 | 3311- | 34066 | 50110 | 5-2-1 | 41-24 | 44343 | 44344 | -325- | ---2- |
| Jackie | 29 | -3141 | 13-47 | ---31 | 3142- | -3--2 | 3-11- | 243-- | 4411- | 532-3 | ---44 | ----1 | 24-4- | -3354 | -3--- |
| Margaret | 35 | --1-2 | 1--73 | 5---4 | 34--- | ----0 | 1-111 | 20--- | -035- | 434-3 | 11424 | ----1 | 4-22- | -13-2 | ----- |

Legend: – = Correct Response    0 = Omitted Response    Numeral = Incorrect Response

As a specific example, an investigation of B's score on a state ninth grade proficiency test indicates that he is at the 94th percentile; however, his grades in first year algebra indicate that he does not have the necessary mathematical background to study algebra successfully. Mathematical gaps exist in the areas of fractions, decimals, and percentages. This is a case in which results do not reflect true ability. It provides evidence that teachers of mathematics must be alert to deviations from predicted performance. Such deviations often appear in classroom performance and on teacher-made tests; therefore, we need to examine data from the classroom as another beginning source of information for a more detailed assessment.

## TEACHER-MADE QUIZZES AND TESTS

As we become experienced teachers our tests begin to represent a good sampling of the range of concepts and skills of the classroom. From well-constructed tests we can gain information concerning strengths and weaknesses of a class and individual learners within the class. To illustrate these conditions a sample review quiz was obtained from a teacher of algebra 1. It should be noted that students were aware of what the two one-word directions imply. Exhibit 5-1 is the quiz and Exhibit 5-2 is a set of final answers from 6 students of the 25 in the class. Based on an answer

**Exhibit 5-1** Quiz

Name _____

I. Multiply
  1. $5(7 - 3b)$ (1) _____
  2. $-3(v + 2)$ (2) _____
  3. $3x(7x + 1)$ (3) _____

II. Simplify
  4. $-5(6y)$ (4) _____
  5. $x(3y)(-7z)$ (5) _____
  6. $(-3ab)(-7ab^2)$ (6) _____
  7. $\dfrac{-36ab}{6ab}$ (7) _____
  8. $6y + 3 - 4y - 7$ (8) _____
  9. $4x - 5y + 2x - y$ (9) _____
  10. $-7a + 4b - 9a - 4b$ (10) _____
  11. $3(y + 4) - 4$ (11) _____
  12. $2(x - y) - 3(x + y)$ (12) _____
  13. $5(y + 4) - 3(2y + 1)$ (13) _____
  14. $x(x + 2) - x(x - 3)$ (14) _____

**Exhibit 5-2** Answers

|     | BOB | DON | MARY | PETE | BARB | SUE |
|-----|-----|-----|------|------|------|-----|
| 1)  | $35 - 15b$ | $35 - 3b$ | $35 - 15$ | $20$ | $35 - 15b$ | $8 - 15b$ |
| 2)  | $3v + 6$ | $-3v - 6$ | $3v + 6$ | $3v - 6$ | $-3x - 6$ | $-3v + 6$ |
| 3)  | $21x^2 + 1$ | $2x^2 + 3x$ | $21x + 3x$ | $21x^2 + 3x$ | $21x^2 + 3$ | $21x^2 + 3x$ |
| 4)  | $-30y$ | $y$ | $(-1)30y$ | $-30y$ | $30y$ | $-30$ |
| 5)  | $-21yzx$ | $-21xyz$ | $3yx(-7z)$ | $-21(xyz)$ | $-21xyz$ | $21xyz$ |
| 6)  | $10ab^2$ | $-10a^2b^3$ | $21a^2b^3$ | $-21a^2b^3$ | $21ab^2$ | $21a^2b^3$ |
| 7)  | $-6$ | $\dfrac{-6}{1}$ | $\dfrac{-6ab}{1ab}$ | $a \neq 0$ <br> $\dfrac{-6}{b \neq 0}$ | $-6ab$ | $6$ |
| 8)  | $2y - 4$ | $-(4 - 2y)$ | $10y - 10$ | $2y + 4$ | $2y - 4$ | $4 - 2y$ |
| 9)  | $6x - 6y$ | $6(x - y)$ | $6x + 6y$ | $2x - 4y$ | $-6(y - x)$ | $6x - 6$ |
| 10) | $-16a$ | $-16a^2$ | $-16a + 0 \cdot b$ | $-16a^2 - b^2$ | $-16a$ | $-16a$ |
| 11) | $3y + 8$ | $3y - 8$ | $3y - 1$ | $3y$ | $3y + 8$ | $3y - 8$ |
| 12) | $-1(x + y)$ | $-x - 5y$ | $x - 5y$ | $-x - 5y$ | $5x - 5y$ | $-(x + 5y)$ |
| 13) | $2(y+4)(2y+1)$ | $2(3y + 5)$ | $-y + 17$ | $y - 17$ | $-(y - 17)$ | $y + 17$ |
| 14) | $0$ | $-1$ | $5x$ | $0$ | $5x$ | $-5x$ |

being right or wrong with no partial credit the scores within the class ranged from 14 to 4 when each item received one point.

As answers are viewed for kinds of errors, tentative hypotheses can be developed for later verification. When we just determine whether an answer is correct or incorrect within a total class we miss this opportunity. Some of the errors appear to be careless errors, e.g., Mary's number 1; Barb's number 2. Many errors represent incomplete or faulty algorithms, e.g., Bob's number 6, Don's number 7, Mary's number 10. Some errors represent a basic lack of understanding, e.g., multiplication involving a negative value: Bob, Mary, Barb.

Mathematical gaps exist for these students and we can only speculate as to the causes; however, we should make every effort to remedy the situation. We need to explore the processing skills of the learners. How do they obtain the answers that appear in written form?

Before we can approach the assessment procedure in detail student profiles must be established and a plan of action developed.

## A PROCEDURAL SUGGESTION

Before students enter the fifth grade we have some idea of what they can and cannot do. The opportunity exists to develop individual student profiles containing demographic information, evidence of affective and cognitive behavior, and, perhaps, some predictive indicators of strengths and weaknesses. A teacher or selected school personnel should collect as much information about a learner as is necessary to plan for instructional activities. In order to assess how a given learner is developing, we need to have knowledge of what is "normal" with respect to emotional, social, health and physical, cognitive and skill development and how far he or she is deviating from what is normal. Content development and general knowledge and skills also contribute to the profile.

The first sources of evidence are those described at the beginning of this chapter, survey instruments that include norm-referenced, domain-referenced, and criterion-referenced instruments. From such instruments we attempt to identify strengths and weaknesses and determine priorities. Such information of strengths and weaknesses and patterns of behavior may be used for writing objectives, determining intra- and interclass groupings, identifying areas for individual help or involvement of a workmate, establishing guidelines for differentiated assignments and quizzes, and initiating clinical interviews for a more detailed diagnostic procedure.

As areas of difficulty emerge, assistance with homework becomes necessary. Tutoring and monitoring activities should be initiated to determine if the difficulty is a symptom of a large problem. Directed observations may be used to establish behavioral patterns. An instructor may begin to sequence the content in smaller steps and provide alternate ways for the student to receive the information, e.g., notes, outlines, tapes. Short analytical quizzes may serve to define areas of strengths and weaknesses in greater detail. Evidence to support the need for a more detailed assessment procedure and diagnostic-prescriptive teaching often comes from studies of error analysis. As with the assessment test, carelessness, faulty algorithms, and lack of understanding may be discovered.

Step 1 is for the school to establish a testing (assessment-evaluation) plan to determine where learners are in mathematics achievement. In the beginning grade of a given school it is essential to establish baseline data, to determine what objectives should be achieved when, and to monitor progress toward these objectives. For grades 5 through 12 we should evaluate at the beginning of grade 5 and monitor progress in grades 7, 9, and 11. Note that the idea of establishing diagnostic procedures should not be restricted to general mathematics courses. Such procedures are also needed in algebra and geometry as we attempt to provide a more comprehensive background in mathematics.

## A SPECIFIC EXAMPLE

From testing data and teacher observations it became evident that N, an eighth grader, was experiencing difficulty with her assignments in mathematics. Some of the symptoms that she had were little confidence in her ability to do mathematics, a developing low self-concept, and increasing computational and reasoning errors. N said on several occasions that she couldn't do mathematics and when many from her peer group began algebra 1 in grade 8 and she didn't, her anxiety level increased and her attitude toward mathematics deteriorated. The concern of her parents only served to enhance these trends.

Testing data were collected from N's records and used to form questions for an interview and assessment procedures. It was discovered that much of N's knowledge in mathematics was on a superficial level and she was having difficulty in understanding relationships. Information that was not available for immediate recall could not be organized. A *lack* of knowledge became evident in subtraction of whole numbers where zeroes were involved, a basic understanding of multiplication and division involving whole numbers, place value, fractions and decimal meaning and operations.

The task became one of attempting to "fill in" the mathematical gaps while maintaining classroom performance in other areas and stabilizing pressure from peers and parents. Tutoring, monitoring, and independent study in different modes were recommended. Activities in which N could experience success were used as starting points, e.g., speed addition involving whole numbers in both verbal and written form. Parents were asked to relieve the pressure and help N to build her confidence. A content outline of concepts and skills was developed: place value, rounding values, whole number subtraction involving estimation and verification, basic meaning of whole number multiplication, multiplication involving estimation and verification, basic meaning of division, division involving estimation and verification, operations with decimals, meaning of fractions, operations with fractions, meaning of percentage, operations involving percentage.

Initially, N had two two-hour tutoring sessions per week. Each session was started with a potentially successful activity from previous work. Concepts and skills to be reviewed were then presented in different modes, e.g., place value was demonstrated with place value blocks and the results were placed on a written table. Supervised practice followed and suggestions were made for more study in the area. The last 30 to 45 minutes of the tutoring session were spent working on class assignments.

Four months later N was involved with her class, working with the tutor to reinforce class activities, and looking forward to taking algebra in the ninth grade. One of N's disabilities appeared to be in establishing relationships (number properties) when they were implied verbally. When she was told that addition and subtraction were related and inverse operations of each other, she saw no meaning in the statement; therefore, she had to compensate by memorizing a lot of disjoint (in her view) information.

N represents a success story and illustrates what can be accomplished with careful analysis and patient effort. While many cases are more severe, with the variables of age, abilities and disabilities, basic knowledge, compensating skills, time and effort all playing a role, N's disability may be more typical of individuals involved in secondary mathematics programs, where students are forced to learn compensatory skills to succeed. The premise under which we should work in the total mathematics program for grades 5 through 12 should be to use assessment procedures to get learners back on track or at least give them a solid foundation in mathematics to enable them to function to the best of their abilities.

## INDIVIDUAL ASSESSMENT

From group data we have noted variations in the performance of individuals across topics and objectives. To assess an individual's needs we often have to go beyond group data. We need to be concerned with process as well as with product. How does a learner obtain an answer? How does a learner like to receive information? In what manner of responding is a learner most comfortable?

In grades 5 through 8 we have the opportunity to fill gaps in mathematical background with developmental teaching of concepts and skills; however, in grades 9 through 12 we are faced with diagnostic teaching as we attempt to find a content level and interactive mode in which a learner can function successfully. In either situation a starting point must be determined. Since the learner's written errors represent available sources of information, we will branch from these errors. We will work from the written responses toward the object mode in searching for a learner's successful level of functioning. Examples will be given from general mathematics, algebra, and geometry. As the level of mathematics becomes more complex the modes of functioning are, by nature, more toward the symbolic level; also, the older the learner the more attention should be given to functioning in the symbolic mode.

### Task 1: Developing and Using Short Analytical Inventories

To determine if the errors made by learners are systematic errors or careless errors, we must develop short inventories of three to five similar examples or exercises. This step in the assessment procedure is often called a reliability check. Are the errors representative of an individual's level of functioning?

- Sample error pattern 1:
$$\begin{array}{r} 452 \\ -278 \\ \hline 226 \end{array}$$

The learner is subtracting the smaller value from the larger value without regard to where the larger value is located, minuend or subtrahend. We recognize that this is a common error pattern; however, it is being used to demonstrate some guidelines for developing short analytical inventories. If numerical values are involved, all examples should be similar. Zeroes and fives should remain in the same relative position in the example. Any values greater than five should be replaced by another value greater than five and values less than five should be replaced by another value less than five. Appropriate examples to verify the student error made in sample error pattern 1 would be:

$$\begin{array}{r} 351 \\ -189 \end{array} \qquad \begin{array}{r} 453 \\ -197 \end{array} \qquad \begin{array}{r} 354 \\ -167 \end{array} \qquad \begin{array}{r} 451 \\ -268 \end{array}$$

- Sample error pattern 2: $\dfrac{y^2 + 3y + 2}{y + 2} = \dfrac{y(y + 3) + 2}{y + 2} = y + 3$

The learner is canceling addends instead of factors. This is a common error made in algebra and shows a lack of understanding of factors and factoring. Appropriate exercises to determine if this is a systematic error are:

$$\frac{x^2 + 4x + 4}{x + 2} \qquad \frac{y^2 + 3y + 3}{y + 3} \qquad \frac{x^2 + 2x + 2}{x + 2} \qquad \frac{y^2 + 5y + 5}{y + 5}$$

- Sample error pattern 3:

> Premise: If a quadrilateral is a square, then the quadrilateral is a parallelogram.
> Conclusion: If a quadrilateral is a parallelogram, then the quadrilateral is a square.

This is an example of faulty reasoning by assuming that if an implication is true, then the converse of the implication is also true. For an individual with a language dysfunction this task can be overwhelming. To compound our problem is the fact that sometimes the converse is indeed true. For example, implication: if a point lies on a line, then the line contains the point (true); its converse: if a line contains a point, then the point lies on the line (true). Models, patterns, *and* definitions become essential elements to help the learner remember the rules of reasoning.

   Since this error pattern represents a higher level concept, an inventory to check the extent of the error may contain different representations of the concept. The learner may be asked to state or write a counterexample if the converse is false.

Implication (in symbol form):   $p \Rightarrow q$   (true)
                              Is $q \Rightarrow p$   true?   **No**

Implication:  A trapezoid is a quadrilateral;
and converse:  therefore, a quadrilateral is a trapezoid.

                    True or *False*?

Implication:   $\square \Rightarrow \boxed{:}$      A square is a special
                              rectangle.
Converse:   $\square \Rightarrow \boxed{!}$      A rectangle is a
                              special square.
                    True or *False*?

• Sample error pattern 4:  $\dfrac{1}{4} + \dfrac{2}{3} = \dfrac{3}{7}$

Analytical inventory:  $\dfrac{1}{3} + \dfrac{3}{4} =$

$\dfrac{1}{2} + \dfrac{1}{5} =$

$\dfrac{2}{3} + \dfrac{1}{4} =$

$\dfrac{2}{4} + \dfrac{1}{3} =$

• Sample error pattern 5:   $\begin{array}{r} 4.25 \\ .5 \\ +3. \\ \hline \end{array}$   $\rightarrow$   $\begin{array}{r} 4.25 \\ .5 \\ +\phantom{.}3 \\ \hline .433 \end{array}$

| Analytical inventory | 7 | .3 | .21 | 4.00 | 4.15 |
| in structured form: | 3 | .4 | .40 | 0.30 | .50 |
| | +5 | +.7 | +.33 | +0.04 | +2.00 |

| | 3.15 | | 1.45 | | 2.35 |
| | .5 | | .5 | | .5 |
| | +1. | | +4. | | +3. |

Ask the learner to write the answers for the examples and tell you how he or she obtained the answers. If the learner makes no errors and no doubts emerge as to his or her degree of understanding of the concept, a review sheet of other examples should be developed and used for reinforcement purposes. If the learner makes one or two careless errors, then a drill activity for this concept will be appropriate. Drill activities may be in the form of a game, puzzle, or similar activities. If the learner makes more than two errors and/or some doubts emerge as to the level of understanding, then the diagnostic procedure must continue.

### Task 2: Determining the Level of Understanding of Example, Exercise, or Problem

Select each example in which the learner made an error. Read the example and ask the learner to tell you how he or she obtained the answer or how he or she thinks the answer is obtained if no answer was given. If the learner now obtains the correct answer for each example and is able to explain how each answer was obtained, go to a drill activity for the concept.

If the learner gives incorrect answer(s) and/or some doubts emerge as to the level of understanding, make one of the following decisions involving either alternative algorithms or task analysis.

If the errors of the learner are systematic errors, that is, the learner possesses an algorithm or generalization that can be modified slightly and reprogramming can occur, go to an alternative algorithm (sometimes this is called a low-stress algorithm) for this concept and/or skill.

- Sample alternative 1:    352        2 4 2
                          − 178      −1 7 8

- Sample alternative 2: For the algebra example (sample error pattern 2) the variables may be given a numerical value for verification in an attempt to convince the learner that he or she is using a faulty rule.

$$\frac{y^2 + 3y + 2}{y + 2} \stackrel{?}{=} y + 3$$

Let $y = 2$

$$\frac{2 \cdot 2 + 3 \cdot 2 + 2}{2 + 2} \stackrel{?}{=} 2 + 3$$

$$\frac{4 + 6 + 2}{4} \stackrel{?}{=} 5$$

$$\frac{12}{4} \stackrel{?}{=} 5$$

$$3 \neq 5$$

Therefore, the canceling procedure was invalid.

When the learner understands what is incorrect, a set of developmental exercises might be presented to generalize the concept and to get to the original exercise.

- Developmental exercises:

a. $\dfrac{4}{4} = \dfrac{1}{1} = 1$

b. $\dfrac{x}{x} = \dfrac{1}{1} = 1$

an indicated sum is a factor

c. $\dfrac{(x+4)}{(x+4)} = \dfrac{1}{1} = 1$

d. $\dfrac{3(x+4)}{(x+4)} = 3 \cdot \dfrac{1}{1} = 3$

e. $\dfrac{(x+2)\,(x+4)}{(x+2)} = \dfrac{(x+2)}{(x+2)} \cdot (x+4)$

$$= \dfrac{1}{1} \cdot (x+4)$$

$$= (x+4)$$

f. $\dfrac{x^2 + 6x + 8}{x + 2} = \dfrac{(x^2 + 6x + 8)}{(x + 2)}$

$= \dfrac{(x + 2)\,(x + 4)}{(x + 2)} = x + 4$

- Sample alternative 3:  For the geometry example (sample error pattern 3) the if . . . then situation may be examined by using a diagram of a family of quadrilaterals.

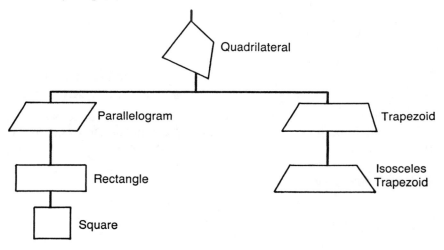

As the model is constructed more restrictions are placed on the figure. For example, four sides, opposite sides parallel, all right angles, all sides congruent. Each more restricted quadrilateral is a special case of the one above it, but this does not remain the case in reverse order. All squares are special rectangles, but all rectangles are not squares.

If a learner lacks a definite algorithm or procedure and developmental patterns and models fail to "activate" him or her toward the algorithm or generalization, we need to task analyze the concept to determine level of understanding. We must continue to analyze parts of an example or exercise for a given concept or skill. Selecting each numerical or word part and each symbol in turn, we read and explain the given symbol, using written examples if necessary. Every effort should be made to attempt to get the learner to function in the symbolic mode, especially if we are dealing with an older learner and the mathematics materials with which he or she is involved are symbolic in nature.

This stage of the assessment procedure can lead an instructor into a false sense of security because as we read, write, explain in detail, and demonstrate specific examples, learners often begin to function successfully within this detailed domain. The individual attention and the use of a variety of ways to present the information will serve to compensate for a dysfunction. The problem becomes one of *maintaining* the success level. Models, tables, graphs, charts, diagrams, or some similar device could become a memory-triggering device; therefore, they should be used whenever possible in the effort to maintain a set of concepts or skills. Tables of addition and multiplication facts are specific examples. This modeling stage may become a pictorial (iconic) stage in the diagnostic assessment of the abilities of the learners. The illustration of a family of quadrilaterals is an example of this. Sample exercises, problems, and proofs, although symbolic in nature, may also become models.

- Uniform motion problems from algebra 1.
  Example:   A bus left a terminal and traveled west at a constant rate of 50 miles per hour. Another bus left the terminal at the same time and traveled east at a constant rate of 55 miles per hour. In how many hours will the buses be 315 miles apart?

  Solution:   1. Let $t$ = the number of hours traveled.
  2. Make a sketch illustrating the given facts:
     Bus 1   50 miles/hour west
     Bus 2   55 miles/hour east
     Distance apart: 315 miles
     Each travels the same number of hours

  West  ⟵————— Terminal ————⟶  East
  $B_1$ ⟵ 50t ——————————————— 55t ⟶ $B_2$
  ⊢————————————— 315 miles —————————————⊣

  3. Arrange the facts in a chart.

  |       | r  | t | d   |
  |-------|----|---|-----|
  | $B_1$ | 50 | t | 50t |
  | $B_2$ | 55 | t | 55t |

  4. Write a mathematics sentence to show the relationships.

     $B_1$'s distance   plus $B_2$'s distance  = total distance
          50t          +         55t          =        315

5. Solve.
$$50t + 55t = 315$$
$$105t = 315$$
$$t = 3 \text{ hours}$$

6. Check the solution.
$B_1$ traveled 50t
$$50 \cdot 3 = 150 \text{ miles}$$
$B_2$ traveled 55t
$$55 \cdot 3 = 165 \text{ miles}$$
The sum of their distances = 315 miles
Answer of 3 hours is correct.

In this example a diagram, a chart, and sentences were used. This is a common practice in algebra 1. The detailed problem serves as a model for organizing similar problems. This multimodal organizational scheme should be beneficial to a learning-disabled individual.

Success at this point in the diagnostic assessment procedure should signal that we have an opportunity to advance to a higher level of understanding. If a learner fails to respond successfully, something other than just symbols must be used. The parts of situations must be demonstrated by pictures and objects.

### Task 3: Determine the Mode in Which Learners Function with Success

If it becomes necessary to continue the diagnostic assessment procedure into this stage, we will be searching for a beginning level from which developmental teaching can occur. We may have to make some concessions. For example, if we are dealing with a learner from grades 9 through 12 in the area of basic arithmetic operations, we may need to provide the learner with an aid to enable him or her to function successfully. The aid might be a calculator. We may also have difficulty in taking such an individual to a higher level of understanding of the concept.

In the pictorial stage behaviors we seek from learners include describing and identifying pictorial models of mathematical conditions. The instructor may choose to draw simple models in order to enhance learning. Place value blocks may be used for pictorial representations for numbers.

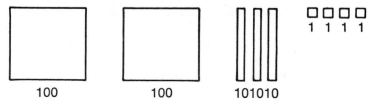

Adding numbers in pictorial form is a matter of showing a *joining* process and subtracting numbers in this form is a regrouping and separating process.

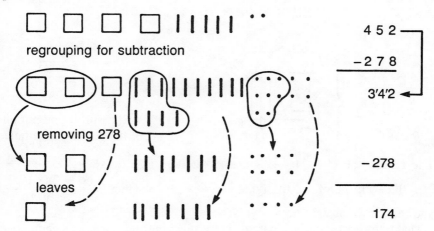

Likewise multiplication is a joining process and division is a separating-in-groups process.

For fractions the pictures are more familiar to learners.

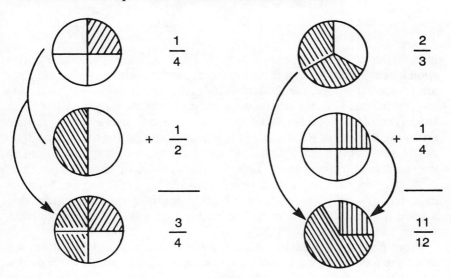

In algebra a factoring model may be drawn to demonstrate linear measure and square regions.

$x^2 + 4x + 4$    x: a square region x by x

4x: $4(1 \cdot x)$ regions

4: $4(1 \times 1)$ regions

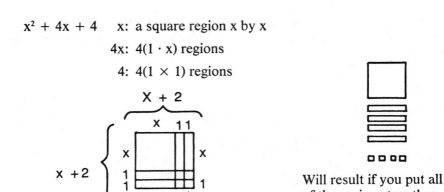

Will result if you put all of the regions together.

The factors of $x^2 + 4x + 4$ are $(x+2)$ and $(x+2)$, $x^2 + 4x + 4 = (x+2)(x+2)$; therefore, to divide $\dfrac{x^2 + 4x + 4}{x + 2}$ we factor $\dfrac{(x + 2)(x + 2)}{(x + 2)}$ and reduce to lowest terms: $x + 2$.

Diagrams are essential elements in the teaching and learning of geometry since geometry has a unique symbolic code. For example:

implies that $\triangle$ ABC is congruent to $\triangle$ DEF by a side-angle-side correspondence. While we can model many geometric relations, the concepts are somewhat complex at the tenth grade level and require a verbal coding understanding. For this reason we are continually moving back and forth from symbols to pictures to objects and vice versa in an attempt to produce an understanding of geometry. This places a limit on the amount of diagnostic, prescriptive teaching we can accomplish in geometry as our domain is extensive at the beginning. The preliminary work of geometry becomes the source for development of proof, a higher level of behavior. Multiple experiences in different modes of operation (teaching and learning) provide a good framework for learning-disabled individuals to find a mode with which they can be successful.

From geometric models, which are somewhat abstract in nature, we often use models of real objects. For example, a small model car provides a truer representation of an automobile than a geometric cone does for an ice cream cone. Learners can name, identify with labels, and draw pictures of real objects or representations (models) of real objects. Counting, sorting, classifying, and describing objects are prerequisite activities for developing number concepts and skills. When we must go to this level of assessment to obtain success, we begin a developmental procedure. Very seldom do we need to go to this extreme, but it is sometimes necessary to use some type of representation for numerical values. With experience a clinician will be able to prescribe the most direct route from problem error to defining difficulty to finding a successful mode of functioning. What is important is to branch from specific systematic errors so as not to lose sight of the beginning.

To illustrate the total individual assessment (diagnostic) process a sample procedural flowchart is presented in Figure 5-1. While the flowchart contains a simple example, it represents an effective general model.

## ASSESSMENT TECHNIQUES IN HIGHER LEVEL MATHEMATICS

In the first section of this chapter we examined assessment procedures in general mathematics from grades 5 through 12, in algebra 1 from grade 7 through grade 9, and in geometry for grades 9 or 10. The focus of this section will be on upper level mathematics: geometry, algebra 2, elementary functions, analysis, or selected semester courses in advanced mathematics. Students involved with these courses have already demonstrated that they can succeed in mathematics. Our task is to provide them with the opportunities to continue to be successful in their study and learning of mathematics.

The *Scholastic Aptitude Test* (SAT) provides the major hurdle that students in grades 10, 11, and 12 will face in regard to evaluation procedures. Since it is given in a paper and pencil format, learners with disabilities in language acquisition may have additional difficulties. Alternative testing modes should be available for learners with disabilities; however, no such provision has thus far been made. We can only prepare students within the restrictions imposed. Other similar situations involve prognostic and standardized achievement tests in the areas of advanced mathematics.

In teacher-made tests we have some opportunities for adjustments if we want to find out what learners can do if certain restrictions are removed. This is the area that will be addressed in this section and much of the discussion will concern alternative strategies for presenting a given concept.

Some students have difficulty establishing and using a general form of the equation for a straight line, $y = mx + b$, where m is the slope and b is the y-intercept even though they can solve an equation in one unknown.

**Figure 5-1** Procedural Flowchart for Individual Assessment

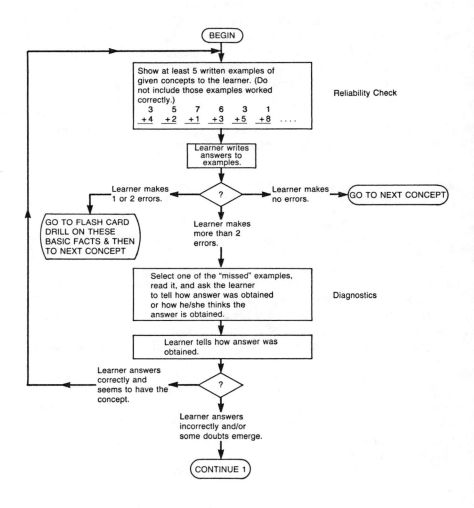

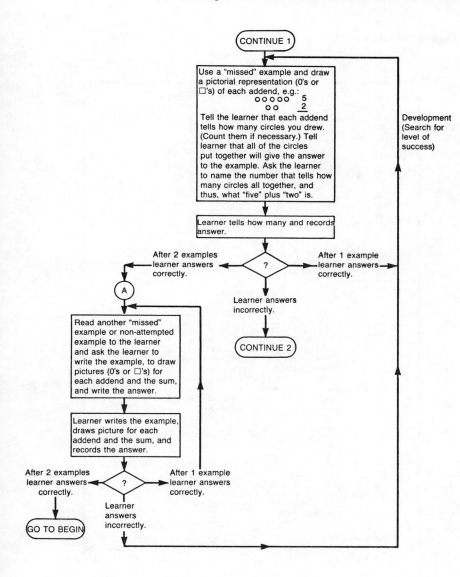

## Figure 5-1 continued

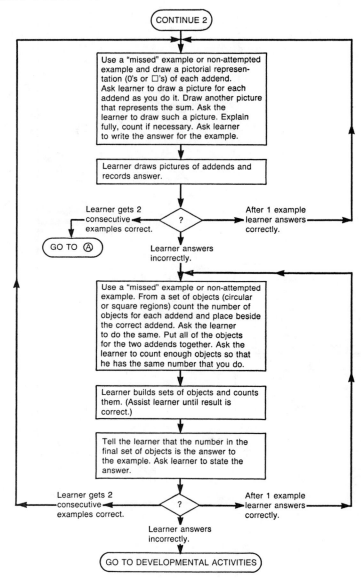

To develop the general form of the equation, the following strategy is suggested.

1. Graph y = x by selecting values for x and plotting the ordered pairs.
2. Graph y = 2x to discover that as the numerical coefficient of x increases the slope of the line of the graph gets steeper.
3. Graph y = $\frac{x}{2}$ to discover that as the numerical coefficient of x decreases the slope of the line of the graph gets flatter.
4. Generalize that y = mx changes as m changes.
5. Graph y = x + 4 to discover that as a number is added or subtracted from x the graph of the line moves away from the origin and passes through (0, b).
6. Generalize that y = mx + b changes as m and b change.
7. Write the equation in other forms:
   y − mx = b or mx = y − b
8. Take general examples and write in standard form and identify slope and y-intercept.

$$\begin{array}{r} y + 7x = 9 \\ - \qquad 7x = 7x \\ \hline y = -7x + 9 \end{array} \qquad m = \frac{-7}{1} \qquad b = 9$$

9. Interpret m as "rise over run" or $\frac{dy}{dx}$ and b as (0,9).
10. Graph equations for straight line by plotting (0,b) and then going up or down the y axis the number of steps in the rise (dy) and to the left or right the number of steps in the run (dx) to plot a second point. Through the two points draw a line that is the graph of the equation.

Assessment involves determining where a learner is in the developmental process, reinforcing this step, and moving toward step 10 for this particular concept. Similar procedures may be used for quadratic equations.

1. Graph $y = x^2$
2. Graph $y = 2x^2$
3. Graph $y = \dfrac{n^2}{2}$
4. Generalize equation $y = ax^2$
5. Graph $y = n^2 + 4$
6. Generalize equation $y = ax^2 + c$
7. Graph $y = (x + 1)^2$
8. Generalize equation $y = a(x + n)^2 + c$

The example serves to define assessment within a given content area. Many topics in higher mathematics are sequential and must be presented in a developmental approach if complete learning is to occur. Any reteaching or assessment procedure involves determining a starting point along the sequence of steps that lead to an understanding of the concept.

## SUMMARY

In this chapter we have described general assessment procedures in grades 5 through 12. Beginning factors and current conditions were presented along with specific examples that served to describe variations among learners. A teacher-made test was given and the results were discussed. A specific example of difficulties exhibited by one learner was outlined. Individual assessment was then presented with specific examples from general mathematics, algebra, and geometry for various diagnostic procedures. An overview of assessment techniques in higher mathematics served to illustrate the limits and different procedures that may be used at this level.

# Chapter 6

# Assessment of Mathematics in the Real World

*Mahesh C. Sharma*

Brought about by the rapid changes within American society and the technological demands of today's living, new concerns are arising regarding the mathematical preparation of our high school and college graduates. Educators, along with business and industrial leaders, are trying to articulate and relate this technological explosion to curriculum outcomes. As a result there is a new emphasis on the set of behaviors and competencies needed to function in today's society and to be successful in the future and with this emphasis the hope that students will be better prepared in the areas of mathematics and science.

## MATHEMATICS EDUCATION

In many countries, including the United States, there has also recently been a growing interest in the problems of mathematics education. This growth of interest is directly related to the steadily increasing importance of mathematics in today's society. Higher competence in mathematics is necessary for progress and effectiveness in all major fields of knowledge. The sciences especially are becoming more mathematical; this applies not only to physics, chemistry, astronomy, and engineering but also to such sciences as modern biology, archeology, medicine, meteorology, economics, planning, linguistics, and to many others. Mathematical methods and the mathematical style of thinking are penetrating all areas of study and all professions. The need for mathematics and mathematically trained persons is increasing every year. As a result, college entrants are required to have more and better preparation in mathematics. Similarly, more and more entry-level jobs require better preparation in mathematics. And this is not just in the case of those jobs where there is an inherent demand for mathematics competence but also in those jobs where the use of mathematics is quite limited.

For most of the past decade, the mathematics education community has been involved in an effort to reshape the school curriculum. Changes in mathematics, societal needs, and especially technology have made mathematics curriculum revision necessary. Much attention has been devoted to elementary and middle school programs, particularly in relation to broadening the emphasis beyond computation.

Mathematics teaching occupies a central position in the school curriculum. A student spends eight years studying mathematics in the elementary school and two to four years in high school. Employers expect definite mathematics competence and knowledge as an outcome of this long experience. They also want to make sure that the student has the ability to apply this knowledge to real-life situations. In the past, graduates of high schools were automatically assumed to possess this competence. Not today. Several factors have contributed to this erosion of credibility on the part of schools. The pool of high school graduates is much larger and more diverse than before. Several studies (Boyer, 1983; Wirtz, 1977) have demonstrated that scores on national examinations and tests have declined steadily during the last two decades. The curricular offerings in high schools are much more varied and some people claim that they are much less rigorous today. As a result it is not possible to assume that each and every graduate is able to demonstrate the mathematical capability needed and required for successful functioning in today's jobs. Moreover, the mathematical knowledge and competence requirements of the business and industrial world are much higher and more complex today than at any other time in history. At the same time many prominent business and industrial leaders believe that the amount and quality of mathematics knowledge required to function optimally in the world are not directly proportional to the amount of knowledge imparted in schools.

Polls (Gallup, 1982; National Commission on Excellence in Education, 1983) have shown that the public considers mathematics to be essential for all students. As the public demands more accountability from educators, the need for better teaching, better curricula, and better indicators for learning outcomes also increases. Students want to know that what they are learning will increase their capabilities for quality performance and satisfaction in the world of work. However, students in most states are required to take no more than one year of mathematics in secondary school. Employers from industry and business believe that the amount of mathematics experience in schools for an average student is inadequate. From their point of view, it is now essential to make sure that prospective employees are tested to evaluate their mathematical preparation. Those who are deficient must be provided with remedial mathematics and more training in the application of mathematics to their jobs.

## ASSESSMENT TECHNIQUES

The importance of assessment techniques in schools and outside has never been greater than today. The scope of mathematics assessment is getting broader as educators seek to demonstrate changes in students' ability in applying mathematics concepts to real-life situations rather than simple computation abilities. They want more than simple recognition and recall of information relating to simple manipulation of formulas and algorithms.

If mathematics skills assessment procedures are to adequately meet the needs of students, teachers, administrators, and, more important, future employers, the examination techniques employed in schools in mathematics courses must be substantively and methodologically related to competence in the postsecondary school world of work. Therefore, many of the leaders in industry have instituted remedial and teaching programs in mathematics in their plants and have drastically upgraded their entrance requirements. Today, industry and business have more training programs than the programs in institutions of postsecondary education. The major part of this inhouse training is the teaching of basic skills and mathematics related to that particular industry, but it also includes higher mathematics. At the same time, several states and businesses are taking the lead in urging schools to require high school students to take more years of mathematics.

It is true that the curricular changes in schools have tried to keep pace with the changing needs of the society. But most curricular changes, particularly the course offerings at the high school level, have affected the able pupil. Because of neglect and poor teaching methodologies, the curriculum for the average student at all levels has gone through drastic changes in a negative direction. As a result, the performance in mathematics of the average high school graduate is not of the same caliber and quality that it once was. This is not a nostalgic statement but one that reflects the concerns of many educators as evidenced by numerous reports by several commissions in recent months (National Commission on Excellence in Education, 1983; Boyer, 1983).

While educators have paid special attention to the special needs students, and their efforts have definitely helped this group, there is an unwanted negative effect on the general curriculum. In order to accommodate the special needs students in regular classes, many authors of mathematics textbooks, hoping to appeal to a larger segment of the student population, have compromised the contents of mathematics textbooks and mathematics teaching.

To ensure that employers are able to get the type of employees they are looking for, many businesses have instituted their own assessment programs. The objective of these assessment programs is twofold: first to ensure the quality of the mathematics preparation of incoming employees and second to ensure their proper placement in order to best use their strengths and help realize their potential.

This thrust has two major implications for learning-disabled adults. First, the tests and examinations used for these purposes are not designed with the learning-disabled person in mind. Second, the learning-disabled individual's poor performance on such examinations results in improper job placement and poor job performance evaluations. Certainly, this does not mean that learning-disabled adults should be excluded from any kind of evaluations and assessments. What is being emphasized here is that the learning-disabled adult's disability puts particular constraints on his or her performance on certain kinds of tests and this must be kept in mind when such a person is being evaluated in mathematics. By and large learning-disabled individuals' test results do not reflect their actual level of ability.

## WHAT CONSTITUTES MATHEMATICS COMPETENCE?

The determination of what constitutes mathematics competence in the real world must be the basis for the construction of appropriate tests. The development process for such tests should logically begin with the identification of specific mathematical knowledge, skills, abilities, and other performance characteristics related to tasks and jobs in the real world. The assessment of performance involving the application of mathematics is a difficult task compared with testing for narrowly defined computations and mathematical formulas. The mastery exhibited in academic situations may not readily be transferable to the real world; it needs to be examined in the context of the real world.

Efforts to find out what constitutes competence in applying mathematics have resulted in the expenditure of millions of dollars on the part of employers and considerable personal anxiety on the part of test takers, all with limited meaningful outcomes. To be able to predict future success in the world of work based on the results of tests is elusive. In order to expedite the assessment process and have control over the subject matter, we tend to conceptually oversimplify the task by taking the simpler route of utilizing standard examinations and tests. This means manipulating test items that may not provide a clear understanding of the nature of human behavior. This is particularly so in the case of a person who is constrained in giving his or her best performance on examinations because of a learning disability. In most cases, it means oversimplification of complex human behavior through tests involving simple tasks and skills. Such a process is questionably suited even to an "average" person, let alone the learning disabled, who have been victimized by this very process all through their academic lives.

Even those individuals who are not going to join the work force right after graduation are also subject to examination in mathematics. About 1.5 million people take the *Scholastic Aptitude Test* (SAT) every year and millions more take similar tests such as the *Graduate Record Examination* (GRE), Civil Service examinations, and IQ tests. Taking these standardized tests is, for most people, an anxiety-laden ordeal that must be undergone at one time or another. If the stakes were not so serious—acceptance to college, to professional schools, to the professions themselves—they would simply be annoying intrusions in one's life. But, as we all know, they do matter, even to the point of determining our future course in life and in some cases, regrettably, our own self-esteem. In the case of those who have been facing difficulty not because of lack of ability but because of the way their ability is tested, the impact is considerable.

The best example is the *Scholastic Aptitude Test* (SAT), which students take for college entrance. It is the most widely taken test, and its structure is fairly typical of all others. This test examines mathematics concepts from arithmetic, algebra, and geometry and the applications of the concepts from these areas (see Exhibit 6-1). Generally, students who have taken at least two years of mathematics do quite well on the SAT. The performance gap between the students who have more than two years of mathematics and those with less or equal to two years is substantial, sometimes as much as 100 and 200 points. The case of the learning-disabled student is even more pronounced. Not only the mathematics material but the time constraints that are present during the examination also contribute to poor performance. The time pressure, the unrelenting barrage of hundreds of questions, the hard-backed chair, the ritual of booklets and answer sheets, and the atmosphere of everyone else's nervous energy is a different and difficult kind of experience for every test taker and it takes its toll, but in the case of the learning-disabled student this effect is magnified.

Even though the College Entrance Examination Board, the administrator of these tests, began allowing the identified learning-disabled students to take an untimed test, this concession has improved the test taking conditions for the student but it has not resulted in a substantial improvement of scores. The nature of the items is still the same: multiple-choice

**Exhibit 6-1** Sample Items from a Scholastic Achievement Test

1. If $x + 4x^2 = 105$, then $x =$
   (a) 2
   (b) 5
   (c) 4
   (d) 6

2. If p, q, and r are integers and q/p and r/q are both integers greater than 1, which of the following is not an integer?
   (a) p/r
   (b) r/p
   (c) rp/q
   (d) rq/p
   (e) qr/rp

3. The sum of ten numbers is what percent of the average of ten numbers?
   (a) 0.001%
   (b) 10%
   (c) 200%
   (d) 2%
   (e) 1,000%

4.      AB
     + AB
     ‾‾‾‾
        CD

   A, B, C, and D are different digits in the correctly worked sum of 2 two-digit numbers above. If A and B are even numbers and if B is equal to twice A, then C is

   (a) 2
   (b) 4
   (c) 6
   (d) 7
   (e) 9

5. If $x + 2$ is an even integer, which one of the following is NOT an even integer?
   (a) $2x + 2$
   (b) $2x + 4$
   (c) $x - 2$
   (d) $x$
   (e) $x + 1$

6. If
$$J = \frac{rK}{M + r}$$

then r =

(a) $\dfrac{JM}{K - J}$

(b) $\dfrac{JM}{J - K}$

(c) $\dfrac{JM}{K - 1}$

(d) $\dfrac{M}{-K}$

(e) $\dfrac{M}{K}$

7. In the currency of the country of Rorwana, 15 saks are equal to 1 peta. If 10 saks are equal to 1 pancham, what is the value in petas of 6 panchams?

(a) 1/15
(b) 2/5
(c) 3/2
(d) 3
(e) 4

8. After John gave 6 marbles to Bill, they each had the same number of marbles. John originally had how many more more marbles than Bill?

(a)  3
(b)  6
(c)  9
(d) 12
(e) 15

Directions: The following questions from 9–14 consist of two quantities, one in column A and in column B. You are to compare the two quantities and select your answer as follows:

(a) If the quantity in column A is greater
(b) If the quantity in column B is greater
(c) If the two quantities are equal
(d) If the relationship cannot be determined from the information given

9. On a certain day, 80 percent of the girls and 75 percent of the boys were present in a mathematics class.

| Column A | Column B |
|---|---|
| The number of girls present | The number of boys present |

**Exhibit 6-1** continued

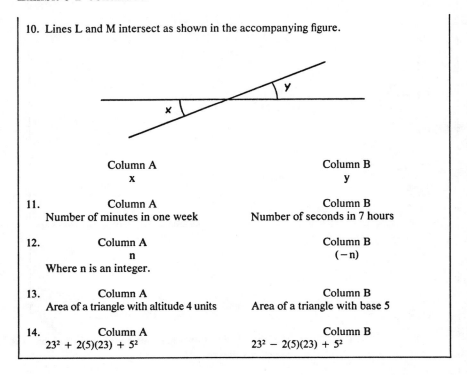

10. Lines L and M intersect as shown in the accompanying figure.

|  Column A | Column B |
| :---: | :---: |
| x | y |

| 11. | Column A | Column B |
| :---: | :---: | :---: |
|  | Number of minutes in one week | Number of seconds in 7 hours |

| 12. | Column A | Column B |
| :---: | :---: | :---: |
|  | n | $(-n)$ |
|  | Where n is an integer. | |

| 13. | Column A | Column B |
| :---: | :---: | :---: |
|  | Area of a triangle with altitude 4 units | Area of a triangle with base 5 |

| 14. | Column A | Column B |
| :---: | :---: | :---: |
|  | $23^2 + 2(5)(23) + 5^2$ | $23^2 - 2(5)(23) + 5^2$ |

answers, spot checking of the skills in several areas of mathematics, poor application examples, and too broad a pool for items.

The Educational Testing Service (ETS), the developer of the test, declares in the SAT brochure that coaching and preparation for the test do    not improve the scores significantly. However, experience has shown that working with both learning-disabled students and others has improved scores substantially (more than the normal gain accounted for by natural growth and maturity). Many commercial test preparation services have shown that it is possible to increase the scores of almost all students on these examinations by employing better test-taking techniques, reviewing the material, and providing practice opportunities. The Association of Supervisors of Mathematics in Schools and the National Association of Secondary School Principals (1980) have also felt that through appropriate study methods and techniques it is possible to increase one's score on the SAT by a substantial amount. This applies to both the average student and the learning-disabled student.

The analysis of the kind of tests that high school graduates are asked to take will be included later in this chapter but first we will discuss the mathematical content that is expected to be mastered by high school graduates, both college bound and noncollege bound.

## MATHEMATICS REQUIREMENT OF THE COLLEGE-BOUND

A good working knowledge in at least two areas of mathematics is required of college-bound students who are going to study any of the major science and social science fields. The two areas of mathematics that provide the most adequate preparation in order to do well in college courses, needing mathematics either directly or indirectly, include the following:

1. a traditional complete pre-calculus sequence
2. a good foundation in statistics and probability, mathematical modeling techniques, and computer science

The College Entrance Examination Board (1983), in its recent report, *Academic Preparation for College: What Students Need To Know and Be Able To Do,* listed objectives for the basic mathematics proficiencies needed by college entrants:

- ability to apply mathematical techniques in the solution of real-life problems and to recognize when to apply those techniques
- familiarity with the language, notation, and deductive nature of mathematics and the ability to express quantitative ideas with precision
- ability to use computers and calculators
- familiarity with the basic concepts of probability and statistics
- knowledge in considerable depth of algebra, geometry, and functions

Another report (National Association of Secondary School Principals, 1980) stated that students in college-preparatory courses need to:

- recognize what basic algebraic forms they have and which they want, in order to select appropriate mathematical models and computer software
- apply algebraic methods to geometric concepts, analytic geometry, and vector algebra

- develop and apply the idea of functions
- develop and analyze algorithms, and then program a computer to perform algebraic operations

If we focus on the analysis of mathematical requirements for the college bound and many more recommendations that are being made by a host of commissions and study groups, we find that there are serious implications for mathematics education at the high school level for every student, but for the learning-disabled there is a significant impact on their educational plans. Throughout their elementary and junior high school years learning-disabled students are placed in the lowest level of mathematics grouping and as a result do not reach the level and the content of the high school algebra and geometry that constitutes the core of the examinations required for college and job entrance. For example, the recommendations of many of the commissions (see references) to introduce the following into the secondary school curriculum are of no value if the student does not have the preparation for these concepts and skills:

- discrete mathematics (e.g., basic combinatorics, graph theory, discrete probability)
- elementary statistics (e.g., data analysis, tables, graphs, survey, sampling)
- computer science (e.g., programming, algorithms, iteration)

Requirement for more mathematics naturally raises three very important points:

1. What special provisions are being made for the teaching of these mathematics courses to the learning-disabled students in mathematics?
2. Have we identified the preparatory special skills that will be needed by learning-disabled students to be able to complete the kind of mathematics sequence that is being suggested and that is already in place at present in the schools today? Because we do know that certain special constraints are placed by the student's learning disability on learning in general and mathematics in particular these questions are of extreme importance to the learning disabled.
3. Does the school mathematics content being suggested and presented to these students have relevance to the real world?

## MATHEMATICS FOR NONCOLLEGE-BOUND STUDENTS

The second largest employer group that uses tests for recruitment and placement purposes is the Civil Service. In addition to other criteria, each job, except the top political jobs, is filled upon successful performance in an examination or sequence of tests administered by Civil Service boards in different municipalities, states, and the federal government including defense services.

The mathematics content of these tests is similar to that of the SAT. In some instances the type of application examples are more demanding than that of the SAT. Here again the student who has completed two or more years of high school mathematics generally fares much better than the student who has completed only one or two years of high school mathematics. The examination conditions and most of the test preparation and item selection techniques are similar. Therefore, the learning-disabled student faces the same difficulties as he or she would in taking the SAT.

The requirement for more mathematics is not limited to just the college bound but to all the students. Mathematical needs can be divided into three categories: mathematical knowledge for daily living, mathematical knowledge to be successful in one's profession, and mathematical insight for one's recreation and leisure. In addition to the basic arithmetical and mathematics concepts noncollege-bound students also need mathematics skills in these areas: (1) mathematics for technical and vocational skills and (2) mathematics for consumer and other citizenship skills.

As technology has become more complex, the technician requires a strong mathematics background. For example, any potential machinist must be able to perform technical applications of mathematics. The apprentice to an electrician, a mason, a carpenter, a cosmetologist, etc., is asked to take mathematics examinations that have large samples of mathematics concepts (a sample test is included in Exhibit 6-2). Even those whose career use of mathematics appears minimal are required to possess mathematics skills related to consumer applications dealing largely with informal statistics—finding, organizing, and using information; drawing inferences from data; and conducting experiments to generate data. Basic arithmetic skills and rudimentary knowledge of algebra and geometry, particularly the applications of this material, are also expected.

## ANALYSIS OF SOME POPULAR TESTS

The understanding of number concepts is an important part of intellectual development, especially in a highly numerical, scientific and techno-

**Exhibit 6-2** Sample Items from an Employment Test*

---

1. Calculate:

   (a) $\begin{array}{r} 453 \\ + 962 \\ \hline \end{array}$   (b) $\begin{array}{r} 548.02 \\ - 199.67 \\ \hline \end{array}$   (c) $2.9\overline{)58116.29}$   (d) $.42\% =$

   (e) $\frac{1}{2} + 3\frac{1}{2} =$   (f) find the average of 24, 54, 78, 93, and 44

2. Is it cheaper to hire an apprentice at $3.95 per hour for 15 hrs. for a certain piece of work or a master carpenter at $12.00 per hour if he can do the same job in 3 and $\frac{1}{2}$ hrs.?

3. If an oil engine requires $\frac{7}{8}$ of a pint of oil per hour, what will be the cost of running an engine for 8 hours with oil at $21.42 per barrel? (Take a barrel as 31 and $\frac{1}{2}$ gallons.)

4. If the outside diameter of a pipe is 2 and $\frac{1}{4}$ inches and the inside diameter 1 and $\frac{7}{8}$ inches, how thick is the pipe? What is the volume of the pipe?

5. The force (pressure) of the wind in pounds per square inch may be determined by using the formula $P = .005 \, V^2$, in which P equals the force and V equals the velocity in miles per hour.

6. The cool air enters a transformer room through a square pipe which is attached to and has the same area as a rectangular pipe 5 feet 4 inches wide and 16 inches high.
   (a) What is the size of the square pipe?
   (b) Which would be cheaper to build, one foot of length of the square pipe or the same length of the rectangular pipe? Assume the same price per square foot.

7. A booth at the fair ground has the shape of a hexagon and covers 375 square feet. An electrician estimates that the cost of installing wiring around the outside of the booth will be 39.44 cents per foot. What will be the total cost of the wiring?

8. An item is put on sale at a discount of 35% of the original price of the item. If the item is selling for $68.55 now, what was the original price of the item?

9. A typing pool can handle the task of the department in 8 hrs. if the whole staff of 5 secretaries is present. How long will it take them if 2 secretaries are absent? (Assume that each secretary works at approximately the same speed.)

10. The meter in a taxicab registers $0.50 for the first $\frac{1}{5}$ of a mile and $0.10 for each additional $\frac{1}{5}$ of a mile. How many miles is a trip for which the meter registers $2.50?
    (a) 5
    (b) 4 and $\frac{4}{5}$
    (c) 4 and $\frac{3}{5}$
    (d) 4 and $\frac{2}{5}$
    (e) 4 and $\frac{1}{5}$

*Employer not identified by request.

---

logically oriented civilization. The language of number, of quantity, measurement, and comparison has become so much a part of everyday life that we are hardly aware of it. When we speak of a "50-50 chance of rain," for example, we do not realize that we assume a knowledge of percentages.

"Two on one" in basketball has to do with ratio as well as defensive strategy. Whether it's cooking, odds in a contest, batting averages, mileage, or buying paint, the things we talk about very often have a quantitative basis. Moreover, in the general public's mind, arithmetic skills and mathematical thinking provide a basic measure of an individual's ability to work with real-world problems in a logical, organized, and intelligent manner. Therefore, performance on arithmetic tests and arithmetic subtests of intelligence tests has important implications for making judgments about a person's likelihood of success in the real world.

## Wechsler Intelligence Scales

One of the most important tests used for many placement purposes is the *Wechsler Intelligence Scale for Children-R* (WISC-R) in schools and the corresponding *Wechsler Adult Intelligence Scale* (WAIS) in postsecondary situations both in college entrance of the learning disabled and the world of work. The underlying assumption of the WISC-R is that by the observation of certain behaviors we can measure the intelligence of a person. For example, in the arithmetic subtest of this test, one assumes that by answering arithmetic problems the person gives evidence of mental alertness. The arithmetic subtests of WAIS and WISC-R require meaningful manipulation of complex thought patterns and the subject must demonstrate the ability to translate word problems into arithmetic operations and vice versa. It is a measure of the individual's ability to utilize abstract concepts of number and numerical operations, which in turn themselves are measures of cognitive development.

The WAIS subtest is based on the conceptual assumption that the ability to manipulate number concepts is one of the criteria of intelligence and, furthermore, that everyday existence in a culture in which manipulation of numbers and measurement are quite common will provide the opportunity for a person to extract number relationships and generalize these relationships. This process of abstraction and generalization is one of the indicators of the presence of intelligence. In ordinary circumstances that abstraction is possible if the person is of average to higher intelligence and is not a victim of any kind of learning disability. Such assumptions are shared by the general public. Therefore, quite often employers insist on giving arithmetic tests to all job applicants in order to ascertain their levels of intelligence.

Many of the problems on arithmetic tests require a direct focusing of concentration, and identification and extraction of basic arithmetical relations involved. To do this, the subject must understand and attend to the pattern of the four basic operations (addition, subtraction, multiplication, and division) as well as the abstract concept of number patterns and their relationships.

Since in essence concentration and attention are noncognitive development functions and the manipulation of number operations is cognitive, this test is of value in that it furnishes a demonstration of how the individual relates cognitive and noncognitive factors in terms of thinking and performance. As for learning-disabled students, because of the general conditions of the examination and the time constraints of the test, many are not able to demonstrate their actual level of cognitive development or show their sophistication in handling that kind of material.

Wechsler (1974) specifically warns examiners not to introduce this test as a test of arithmetic. The words "arithmetic" or "mathematics" often cause subjects to expect severe failure. For those subjects for whom the word "arithmetic" is significant as a negative conditioned response, dealing with the content of this subtest can be perceived as traumatic. Many individuals react quite dramatically, often stating that they are stupid and cannot do such examples, and even refusing to try simple problems. Such a strong emotional reaction in what are otherwise normal individuals lowers scores, often to the lowest possible score on the test. By the end of high school, such a condition does exist with the majority of students who have seen failure in mathematics. Critical analysis of the test has revealed that results are very susceptible to the effects of anxiety. When these types of tests are used as assessment tools at the time of entry to the world of work, the person may bring the same apprehensions and fears that he or she had experienced in school.

Students with higher mental capacities will presumably be able to turn to internalized patterns of numerical functions in order to solve a problem presented to them. Students not defeated by the schooling process and who have not developed any kind of anxiety (particularly mathematics anxiety) are able to produce that material they have learned. However, anyone with any kind of mathematical learning problem is likely to do poorly on WISC, WAIS, and other similar tests and measurements.

In general, arithmetic is more likely than some of the other subtests to reveal important clues to personality and attitudes toward school achievement. For instance, individuals who have had negative experiences involving mathematics in school are bound to do poorly on this subtest even if they actually know more than what they attempt on the test or any other such test. A low score can indicate poor attention and distractibility caused by anxiety invading the thinking processes. It may also demonstrate poor school achievement perhaps because of rebellion against authority or cultural disadvantage. Transient emotional reactions can cause marked variation in scores for this subtest. Any of these factors may not have any relation to the actual working environment or the requirements of the new job. And in such a situation using such a test is of dubious value for getting the results the employer is expecting.

Difficulties in immediate memory, concentration, or conceptual manipulation and tracking can prevent even very mathematically skilled individuals from doing well on orally administered tests. Some individuals typically can perform the first several items quickly and correctly since they involve only one operation, a few elements, and simple, familiar number relationships; but when there is more than one operation, several elements, or less common number relationships requiring "carrying," these individuals lose or confuse the elements or goals of the problems. They may succeed with repeated prompting but only after the time has expired, or they may be unable to do the problem "in their head" at all, regardless of how often the question is repeated.

The total arithmetic score on the WAIS of a bright, nonlearning-disabled person will include both number of correct responses and time credit points. In the case of a slow responder who takes longer than the time limit to formulate the correct answer, the total arithmetic score may not reflect arithmetic ability so much as response rate. Each of these persons may get the same number of responses correct, say 11; but the first subject could earn a raw score of 12 and a scaled score of 11, whereas a learning-disabled individual whose arithmetic skills are comparable might receive a raw score of only 8 or 9 and a scaled score of 7 or 8. To do justice to the slow responder and gain a full measure of data about this person, the examiner should obtain two arithmetic scores: one based on the sum of correct responses given within the time limits plus time bonuses and the other on the sum of correct responses regardless of time limits. The first score can be interpreted in terms of the test norms. The second gives a better indication of the individual's arithmetic skills and may be used for placement and job-related information. The results under comfortable and unstressful conditions might be better indicators of the future employee's mathematical ability.

### Scholastic Aptitude Test (SAT)

The College Entrance Examination Board, the administrator of the SAT, "knows that some people are uncomfortable when they are faced with the prospect of taking any test, but that there is even greater uneasiness before taking national standardized tests such as the Scholastic Achievement Tests (SAT)" (1984). For the learning disabled there are several reasons for uneasiness about the SAT. We have already identified some of the general ones relating to test taking and examination conditions. Others stem from the content and teaching methodology prevalent in teaching learning-disabled students. Most are "tracked" into consumer and life skills types of courses during the high school years. The content of these courses is basically the direct application of formulas and procedures. There is no interaction from different areas of mathematics. As a result students solve only those problems that are direct applications of the formulas. Consequently, they are not able to and prepared to handle the content of the SAT. They find it difficult to solve those problems in which one has to apply original thinking. For example, let us consider the following problem from the SAT:

> If the symbol $\oplus$ between two expressions indicates that the expression on the right exceeds the expression on the left by 1, which of the following is (are) true for all real numbers x?
>
> I. $x(x + 2) \oplus (x + 1)^2$
> II. $x^2 \oplus (x + 1)^2$
> III. $\dfrac{x}{y} \oplus \dfrac{x + 1}{y + 1}$
>
> (a) None (b) I only (c) II only (d) III only (e) I and III.

This kind of problem involves working with a newly defined symbol. The learning-disabled person who has no experience in dealing with new concepts will have difficulty dealing with such a problem.

Some questions in the mathematical sections of the SAT are like the questions in usual junior and senior high school textbooks. Those questions that ask the student to do original thinking may not be as familiar. The questions are designed for students who have had a year of algebra and geometry. Many of the geometric ideas involved are usually taught in the junior and high school years, but a few of the questions involve topics that are taught in high school geometry. A student is asked to actually apply the concepts.

## CORE CONTENT OF MATHEMATICS TESTS FOR HIGH SCHOOL GRADUATES

An analysis of many of the tests given by industry, businesses, the College Entrance Examination Board, and Civil Service boards at different levels—municipal, state, and federal—indicates that planners and users of the test results believe there is a core of mathematical knowledge that the test takers must possess and that the schools should teach to equip high school graduates to be successful in their future ventures. Such a core content list includes:

- performing basic arithmetic operations (addition, subtraction, multiplication, and division) with whole numbers, rational numbers (fractions), decimal numbers, irrational numbers; even and odd numbers; prime numbers; signed numbers; divisibility tests; quantitative comparisons; and simple applications of arithmetic operations

- applying the concepts of averages, percents, ratio and proportion, along with arithmetic operations to real-life situations

- understanding simple algebraic concepts: variables, expressions involving variables; simplification of and operations with algebraic expressions; setting up simple equations; solving equations; roots and exponents; rates and slopes; relations; functions and graphs; factoring; linear equations; inequalities; simple quadratic equations; and applying algebraic concepts to real-life situations

- understanding geometrical concepts: important postulates, theorems, and results relating to points, lines (parallel and perpendicular lines), planes, geometrical shapes (quadrilaterals, polyhedra, etc.); concept of proportion and similarity in geometrical shapes; areas and perimeters of simple closed geometrical figures (square, rectangle, triangle, and circle); perimeter of a polygon; circumference of a circle; surface areas and volumes of simple solid shapes; special properties of isosceles, equilateral, and right triangles; 30-60-90 and 45-45-90 triangles; locating points on a coordinate grid; finding the midpoint between two points; finding distance between two points; and applying these concepts to real-world problems

- understanding elementary probability and statistics and its applications

- applying mathematical reasoning and approach to problems in everyday situations

- estimating, approximating, measuring, and testing the accuracy of mathematical applications

- general skills: maintaining personal bank records, planning personal and family budgets and maintaining them, understanding different kinds of interest rates and their comparisons, calculating interests on given amounts for specific periods, estimating real costs and values of items, computing taxes and investment returns, and appraising insurance and retirement benefits

## SUMMARY

Better methods of assessment and evaluating a student's preparation for the world of work are needed. Participation by school mathematics teachers in the evaluation process will play a useful role: first, in order to bring the difficulties of learning-disabled students to the attention of the people from the world outside academia and second to bring to teachers' attention what mathematics is needed in the real world so that they can adjust programs accordingly.

**REFERENCES**

College Entrance Examination Board (1983). *Academic preparation for college: What students need to know and be able to do.* New York.

College Entrance Examination Board (1984). *Ten scholastic aptitude tests.* New York.

Boyer, E.L. (1983). *High school: A report on secondary education in America.* The Carnegie Foundation for the Advancement of Teaching. New York: Harper & Row.

Gallup, G.H. (1982). Gallup poll of the public's attitude toward the public schools. *Phi Delta Kappan,* September.

National Association of Secondary School Principals. (1980). *State-mandated graduation requirements, 1980.* Reston, VA.

National Commission on Excellence in Education. (1983). *A nation at risk.* Washington, DC: Government Printing Office.

Wechsler, D. (1974). *Wechsler intelligence scale for children—Revised.* New York: The Psychological Corporation.

Wirtz, W.W. (1977). *Report of the advisory panel on the scholastic aptitude test score decline.* New York: College Entrance Examination Board.

# Chapter 7

# Nonmathematics Appraisal

*John F. Cawley*

This chapter focuses on the process of appraisal in areas that may or may not be directly related to mathematics but that are part of a typical appraisal battery. It is designed to provide an overview of selected appraisal techniques and needs and their implications for the development of a greater understanding of the concept of learning disability.

The nonmathematics appraisal will

- assist in establishing a foundation for a rule-based interpretation of learning disability
- identify patterns of strengths and weaknesses in areas other than mathematics through attribute-based instruments
- enable one to partial out the effects of one disability upon another
- identify areas of development that can be enhanced by experiences in mathematics
- assist in the selection of the most appropriate service delivery model

As was described in Chapter 1, the term *appraisal* refers to a three-stage process that includes measurement, assessment, and diagnosis. For the most part, appraisal is conducted with standardized tests or batteries, although this chapter will also stress the potential of informal approaches. Table 7-1 lists a number of instruments, some combination of which might be found in a typical appraisal.

## SOME IMPORTANT DISTINCTIONS

Appraisal instruments are composed of sets of items that appraise combinations of knowledge and behavior. It is important to differentiate knowl-

**Table 7-1** Appraisal Instruments by Category

|  | Ability | Achievement |
|---|---|---|
| Measurement | Peabody Picture Vocabulary Test-R | Gray Oral Reading Test |
|  | Raven's Progressive Matrices | Roswell-Chall Auditory Blending Test |
|  | Columbia Test of Mental Maturity | Slosson Oral Reading Test |
|  | Developmental Test of Visual Motor Integration | Test of Early Mathematics Ability |
| Assessment | Woodcock-Johnson Psycho-educational Battery | Woodcock-Johnson Psycho-educational Battery |
|  | K-ABC | K-ABC |
|  | WISC-R | Wide Range Achievement Test |
|  | WPPSI | Peabody Individualized Achievement Test |
|  | WAIS |  |
|  | Illinois Test of Psycho-linguistic Abilities |  |
|  | McCarthy Scales of Children's Abilities |  |
| Diagnostic | Bender-Gestalt Visual Motor Gestalt | Diagnostic Protocol for Reading |
|  | Minnesota Test for Differential Diagnosis of Aphasia | Gates-McKillop Reading Diagnostic Test |

edge from behavior so as to obtain a clearer picture of the differences between discrepancy and disorder and between those factors that comprise the patterns of individual strengths and weaknesses.

## Discrepancies and Disorders

A *discrepancy* exists when an individual is performing below a set standard of expectancy. This expectancy may be based on chronological age or on combinations of chronological age and ability. These combinations tend to be confusing when one uses them across the spectrum of handicapped children. For example, the child who is defined as mildly retarded may manifest a discrepancy between present level of functioning and chronological age. This is a natural expectancy in that the handicap of mild retardation results in slower rates of development, which lead to the subsequent discrepancy. This individual is not considered learning disabled because the level of functioning might be consistent with mental age.

In the case of an individual with average to near-average ability, the level of expectancy approximates chronological age. Thus, a significant discrepancy between present level of functioning and chronological age could be indicative of a learning disability.

It is possible for the mildly retarded individual to meet the rule-based standard of discrepancy for learning disability. Such a case would exist when the discrepancy between level of functioning and level of expectancy is based on mental age, not chronological age.

A *disorder* exists when the performance of the individual is characterized by aberrations or distortions. Whereas the individual with a discrepancy is performing below expectancy, that performance may be satisfactory for the lower level. A seventh-grade child who is discrepant and reading at the third-grade level should be reading third-grade material in a reasonable manner. The child who is disordered is unlikely to perform any items in a reasonable manner. Thus, on any test, the disordered individual's raw score should be extremely low and unreliable (e.g., in a two-choice task, the response pattern is erratic). Children who are discrepant tend to get certain items correct (i.e., they establish a basal level) and then fall into a failure pattern (i.e., they reach a ceiling when the items become difficult for them). Children who are disordered generally fail to establish any meaningful basal level.

The processes of measurement and assessment are more appropriate for the child who is discrepant. Children who are disordered comprise the more severely learning disabled and the process of diagnosis should be used with them.

**Behavior or Knowledge?**

All approaches to appraisal combine behavior and knowledge. Some rely more upon one than upon the other. For example, the *Peabody Picture Vocabulary Test-R* is constructed upon a single behavior. That behavior has the examiner stating a word and the individual pointing to one of four pictures that represent the word. It is the increase in difficulty of the words (i.e., knowledge) which gives the PPVT its discriminatory capability across ages.

Most instruments vary both knowledge and behavior on every subtest. For this reason, it is often difficult to stipulate whether the individual's discrepancy is attributable to a lack of knowledge or a lack of task or behavioral capability. An examination of the raw scores will shed some light on the differentiation. The individual who can respond to a subtest with some reliable set of raw scores is likely to be an individual whose discrepancy is knowledge based.

In mathematics, the child who can do some of the multiplication items is not a child in need of task or behavior-based instruction (i.e., he or she does not need to be taught to multiply, per se). This would be a child in need of knowledge-based instruction (i.e., he or she needs to be taught the correct responses to the items).

## TYPES OF APPRAISAL INSTRUMENTS

Tables 7-2 to 7-4 show three sets of instruments. Table 7-2 lists ability only instruments. Table 7-3 lists instruments that contain both ability and behavioral sections and Table 7-4 lists instruments related to achievement only.

### Ability-Only Instruments

In a general sense, ability-only instruments have been developed to classify students or to make predictions as to present status or future levels of performance. The professional community has generally accepted the correlations between tests of ability and achievement as being of sufficient magnitude to warrant confidence in making predictions about a typical population. However, the learning disabled do not represent a typical population. In fact, they represent a direct contradiction to the ability-achievement prediction. This is evidenced by the rule-based stipulation that a learning disability exists only when there is the prediction that performance will be high but the level of functioning must be low.

The set of ability measures used in special education can be divided into two groups. One of these is rooted in intelligence. The others are rooted in various combinations of cognitive, perceptual, or information processing.

Intelligence has historically dominated the ability component of appraisal and the tendency has been to use the intelligence test as the basis for establishing the level of expectancy. Intelligence has generally been viewed as something that should not be tampered with or subjected to direct stimulation or remediation. This hands-off policy has tended to mask out the fact that there is considerable real growth by an individual whose ability score (i.e., IQ) remains constant over time. Table 7-5 lists the raw scores of four different subtests of the *WISC-R* across four different age levels. The numerator represents the score for an individual whose IQ would permutate to about 70 if all scores fell at a comparable level. The

**Table 7-2** Ability-Only Instruments

| SRA: *SRA Primary Mental Abilities* | STANFORD-BINET: *Stanford-Binet Intelligence Test L-M* | WISC-R: *Wechsler Intelligence Scale for Children-R* |
|---|---|---|
| Ages: 7–11 | Picture Vocabulary | Information |
| 1. Verbal-Picture-Meaning | Naming Objects from Memory | Comprehension |
| 2. Space | Opposites Analogies | Arithmetic |
| 3. Reasoning: Word Grouping | Pictorial Identification | Similarities |
| 4. Reasoning: Figure Grouping | Discrimination of Forms | Vocabulary |
| 5. Visual Discrimination | Comprehension | Digit Span |
| 6. Number | Memory for Sentences | Picture Completion |
| | Pictorial Similarities & Differences | Picture Arrangement |
| | Three Commissions | Block Design |
| | Picture Completion | Object Assembly |
| | Definitions | Coding |
| | Copying a Square | Mazes |
| | Patience: Rectangles | |
| | Vocabulary | |
| | Differences | |
| | Mutilated Pictures | |
| | Maze Tracing | |
| | Picture Absurdities | |
| | Similarities | |
| | Repeating Digits Forward | |
| | Repeating Digits Reversed | |
| | Memory for Stories | |
| | Verbal Absurdities | |
| | Similarities and Differences | |
| | Naming Days of the Week | |
| | Memory for Designs | |
| | Rhymes | |
| | Abstract Words | |
| | Finding Reasons | |
| | Problem Situation | |

denominator represents the score for an individual whose IQ would permutate to almost 100 if all scores fell at a comparable level. In each instance, the ability indicator, IQ, remains constant over time. However, each is expected to make reasonable and near equivalent increments (e.g., 20 points each from 6-6 to 15-6 in Picture Arrangement) in actual performance. Although direct instruction to improve scores is generally frowned upon, there is clearly the expectancy that the natural experience of the individual will result in real growth.

**Table 7-3** Ability and Achievement Tests

| Woodcock-Johnson Psychoeducational Battery | K-ABC | Mann-Suiter Developmental Screening Tests |
|---|---|---|
| Ability | Ability | Ability |
| Picture Vocabulary | Magic Window | Visual Motor |
| Spatial Relations | Face Recognition | Visual Figure Ground |
| Memory for Sentences | Hand Movements | Visual Discrimination |
| Visual-Auditory Learning | Gestalt Closure | Visual Memory |
| Blending | Number Recall | Visual Closure |
| Quantitative Concepts | Triangles | Auditory Discrimination |
| Visual Matching | Word Order | Auditory Closure |
| Antonyms/Synonyms | Matrix Analogies | Auditory Memory |
| Numbers Reversed | Spatial Memory | Alphabet Speech Screen |
| Concept Formation | Photo Series | Visual Language Classificaton |
| Analogies | | Visual Language Association |
| | | Auditory Language Classification |
| | | Auditory Language Association |
| Achievement | Achievement | Achievement |
| Letter-Word Identification | Expressive Vocabulary | Letter Names |
| Word Attack | Faces and Places | Letter Sounds |
| Passage Comprehension | Riddles | Blends and Digraphs |
| Calculations | Reading Decoding | Spelling Inventory |
| Applied Problems | Reading Understanding | Reading Inventory |
| Dictation | Arithmetic | Word Reading |
| Proofing | | Paragraph Reading |
| Science | | Listening Comprehension |
| Social Studies | | |
| Humanities | | |

The *WISC-R* and the *Stanford-Binet* have been the most popular measures of ability within special education. As can be seen, they are quite different and produce markedly different sets of attribute-based descriptors.

There are many other types of ability-only instruments. These are used to appraise psycholinguistic abilities (e.g., *The Illinois Test of Psycholinguistic Abilities*), perceptual development (e.g., *The Developmental Test of Visual Perception*), or perceptual-motor development (e.g., *The Developmental Test of Visual-Motor Integration*). This latter group differs from the intelligence tests in that they often express direct linkages to instruction and remediation.

**Table 7-4** Achievement-Only Tests

| Durrell-Listening-Reading | Gates McKillop: Gates-McKillop Reading Diagnostic Test | Test of Written Language |
|---|---|---|
| Listening<br>  Vocabulary Listening<br>  Paragraph Listening<br><br>Reading<br>  Vocabulary Reading<br>  Paragraph Reading | Oral Reading<br>Words: Flash<br>Words: Untimed<br>Phrases<br>Recognizing and Blend-<br>  ing Word Parts<br>Giving Letter Sounds<br>Naming Capital Letters<br>Naming Lower Case<br>  Letters<br>Nonsense Words<br>Initial Letters<br>Final Letters<br>Vowels<br>Auditory Blending<br>Spelling<br>Oral Vocabulary<br>Syllabication<br>Auditory Discrimination | Vocabulary<br>Thematic Maturity<br>Spelling<br>Word Usage<br>Style<br>Thought Units<br><br>Handwriting |

**Table 7-5** Growth Patterns on Selected *WISC-R* Subtests

|  | Vocabulary | Arithmetic | Similarities | Picture Arrangement |
|---|---|---|---|---|
| *Age* | | | | |
| 6-6 | 11/16 | 4/6 | 3/7 | 5/13 |
| 9-6 | 21/27 | 8/11 | 8/11 | 16/24 |
| 12-6 | 29/38 | 11/14 | 11/17 | 21/30 |
| 15-6 | 36/46 | 12/15 | 15/20 | 25/33 |
| Total Growth | 25/29 | 8/9 | 12/13 | 20/20 |

## Ability and Achievement Instruments

Another set of ability tests are those that combine ability and achievement items. Those listed in Table 7-3 emerge from distinctively different theoretical orientations. The *Woodcock-Johnson Psychoeducational Battery* takes a general cognitive approach. The *K-ABC* is rooted in the specific theoretical orientation of Das (Das, Kirby, & Jarman, 1979) and his work on simultaneous-successive information processing. The *Mann-Suiter* reflects perceptual-language orientation.

A major difference among these exists with regard to instructional planning. For the most part, the *Woodcock-Johnson* does not make extensive instructional projections relative to techniques or to learning styles. The *K-ABC* manual does contain explicit recommendations for instruction and supports these by citing research that has validated these claims. The *Mann-Suiter* has extensive instructional implications and many materials have been developed to support it.

Throughout its brief history, the field of learning disabilities has been peppered with instruments purporting to provide a basis for remediation or treatment. In the main, the instruments and the programs designed to accompany them have yielded only limited success.

### Achievement-Only Instruments

Instruments designed to appraise achievement are numerous. These include group and individual tests and batteries for just about every basic skill and subject matter topic. Reading dominates. It seems that reading is the area of predominant interest, both in terms of appraisal and instruction. Special education has given little attention to mathematics. The three instruments shown in Table 7-4 are quite different. The *Durrell* combines both reading and listening. The *Gates-McKillop* breaks reading down into a number of subcomponents and skills. The *TOWL* is a test of written language, an area that has been sadly neglected.

The variability across the hundreds of ability and achievement tests exacerbates the problem of developing any attribute-based description of the learner.

Assume, for purposes of illustration, that two children have been referred for appraisal because of difficulty in mathematics. Each has been administered the *Mathematics Concept Inventory*. One child was then administered the *WISC-R*, the *Woodcock-Johnson* and the *TOWL*. The other child was administered the *WISC-R*, the *K-ABC* and the *Gates-McKillop*. Given that each has an element of commonality in the *Mathematics Concept Inventory* and the *WISC-R*, how does one integrate the remainder of the battery and develop descriptions of need and instructional or curriculum recommendations when they are so markedly different? One alternative is to focus interpretations on task or behavioral commonalities and differences.

**Behavior-Only Interpretations**

There are numerous instances when the nomenclature used to name or describe a test suggests that one test item is different from another. Such a situation is illustrated in Table 7-6. Four different sets of nomenclature are used to describe the same task. The primary difference in the four instruments is that the sentences are composed of different content. The requirements imposed upon the child are essentially the same for all tests.

Rather than getting confused with the mixture of content and task, it is best to differentiate the two and to examine the attributes of the learner according to task specificity rather than test title or content.

Consider the following objective:

Given a written sentence describing Christopher Columbus, the child will rewrite the sentence to express a similar meaning.

Examine the objective as rewritten:

Given a written sentence, the child will rewrite the sentence to express a similar meaning.

And, again, as :

Rewrite sentence to express similar meaning.

The first illustration specified both task and content. The behavioral component was contaminated by the need to know about Columbus. In the second illustration, the reference to Columbus was eliminated and the task

**Table 7-6** Behavior-Only Instruments

| Test | Task | Subtest |
|---|---|---|
| *Detroit Tests of Learning Aptitude* | Examiner states sentence and child repeats sentence | Auditory Attention Span for Related Syllables |
| *McCarthy Scales of Children's Abilities* | Examiner states sentence and child repeats sentence | Verbal Memory 11 |
| *Meeting Street School Screening Test* | Examiner states sentence and child repeats sentence | Repeat Sentences |
| *Menyuk Memory for Sentences* | Examiner states sentence and child repeats sentence | Memory for Sentences |

could be conducted with any set of content. Thus, the task could be performed on a topic about Jedi, a building on fire, or any other content.

The third example is in the form of a shorthand referred to as *Desired Learner Outcomes* (DLOs). The act specifies the behavior of the examiner or teacher (i.e., the input) and the learner or child (i.e., the output). The cognitive qualifier is designated (i.e., similar meaning). The DLO is illustrated below.

| *Input* | *Output* |
|---|---|
| Examiner says word. | Child points to picture representing word. |
| Examiner says word. | Child says definition for word. |
| Examiner shows written word. | Child performs action indicated by word. |

The first illustration is that of the *Peabody Picture Vocabulary Test-R*. The second is that of the vocabulary subtest of the *WISC-R*. The third is that of the reading understanding subtest of the *K-ABC*. Note that each is described only in terms of the task required of the examiner and the child. It is possible to take any instrument that contains a set of tasks and different sets of content across these tasks and convert it so that only one or the other varies at any given time. As an illustration, Schenck and Levy (1977) developed a curriculum-based or informal simulation of the *WISC-R*, as seen in Exhibit 7-1. They followed the administrative directions of the *WISC-R* and substituted content from the field of mathematics, selecting their content from grade level texts in mathematics for grades 5 through 8. In administering the instrument they found the expected trend. That is, fifth grade children responded best to items at the fifth grade level. Eighth grade students got high percentages of items correct on content taken from grades 5 through 7 and their performance decreased for items from the eighth grade texts.

In contrast to the approach where one uses the same content across a number of different behaviors or tasks, one can use different content across the same behaviors. Table 7-7 shows two subtests of the *WISC-R*, Vocabulary and Similarities, with a number of different content areas. Thus, one can take a set of tasks with which the learner is capable and construct items from different topics and levels to appraise knowledge. Or, one can use a set of known and familiar knowledge across different tasks to measure skill or behavioral capability. This type of control is important at the assessment stage and essential at the diagnostic stage. In a situation in which a youngster is given a question to answer and difficulty is encountered, is the problem in knowledge of the content, understanding the question, or the ability to provide an answer? Does, for example, the individual truly understand the intent and requirements of the question?

**Exhibit 7-1** Sample Items from Mathematics Version of *WISC-R*

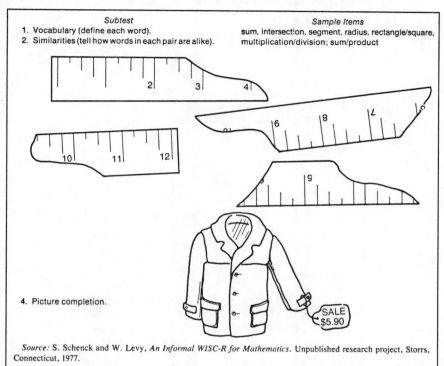

| Subtest | Sample Items |
|---|---|
| 1. Vocabulary (define each word). | sum, intersection, segment, radius, rectangle/square, |
| 2. Similarities (tell how words in each pair are alike). | multiplication/division; sum/product |

4. Picture completion.

*Source:* S. Schenck and W. Levy, *An Informal WISC-R for Mathematics.* Unpublished research project, Storrs, Connecticut, 1977.

If not, the answer may not be appropriate, but the difficulty may not be due to the fact that the child cannot express an answer or that the answer is not known.

The difficulty may be that the question is not understood. Systems that seek attribute-based information need to distinguish among the components of performance, especially with the more severely handicapped.

## THE INTERACTIVE UNIT AND TEST CODING

As described in Chapter 1, the interactive unit (IU) is a mechanism for defining the interaction among child and teacher and materials during instruction or among examiner, child, and materials during appraisal. It is possible to take nearly all items contained in appraisal instruments and code them to one, or, at the most, two, combinations of interaction during

**Table 7-7** Use of Common Behaviors Across Multiple Content

| | Math | Science | Social Studies | English |
|---|---|---|---|---|
| *Vocabulary Subtest* | | | | |
| Input: Says Word | | | | |
| Output: Says Definition | "sum" | "telescope" | "president" | "comma" |
| | "product" | "microscope" | "governor" | "period" |
| *Similarities* | | | | |
| Input: Says two words | | | | |
| Output: Says how words are similar | "product"/"sum" | "telescope"/"microscope" | "president"/"governor" | "comma"/"period" |

appraisal. This enables the examiner or the district to review the character and pattern of the appraisal instruments and to determine the distribution of items. Table 7-8 lists items compiled from selected items from the *WISC-R,* the *Detroit Tests of Learning Aptitude,* and the *K-ABC.* Each is coded by test name, examiner, and child behavior and by interactive unit combination.

Figure 7-1 shows how these would look if placed into the interactive unit. Note the emphasis on aural input and oral outputs. In an examination of over 1,000 subtests of commonly used appraisal instruments, the Reading Understanding test of the *K-ABC* is the only instance found where the individual reads and then performs the act stipulated. Yet this is one of the most popular social behaviors and an integral component of any mathematics because it is the one in which the child would examine an item (e.g., 5 or 3 + 2 =) and be requested to represent either of these with blocks, toothpicks, or some other objects.

An examination of patterns of appraisal within the interactive unit would help to shed some light on the characteristics of the individual with regard to learning style. For example, many individuals examine performance to determine the extent to which the individual is an "auditory learner" or a "visual learner." For the most part, they fail to organize the information in such a way as to provide for such an examination. What if the total

**Table 7-8** Coding Subtests to Interactive Units

| Test | Examiner | Child | Interactive Combination |
|---|---|---|---|
| *WISC-R* | | | |
| Vocabulary | Says word | Says definition | Say/Say |
| Similarities | Says two words | Says how similar | Say/Say |
| Information | Says question | Says answer | Say/Say |
| Picture Completion | Shows picture | Says what is missing | Say/Say |
| *Detroit* | | | |
| Verbal Opposites | Says word | Says word with opposite meaning | Say/Say |
| Pictorial Absurdities | Shows picture of absurd situation | Says what is absurd | Display/Say |
| *K-ABC* | | | |
| Reading Decoding | Shows written word | Says name of word | Write/Say |
| Reading Understanding | Shows written word(s) | Perform action stipulated by word | Write/ Manipulate |

**Figure 7-1** Subtest Placement in Interactive Unit

| | | Examiner | | |
|---|---|---|---|---|
| | | Manipulate | Display | Say | Write |
| **Learner** | Manipulate | | | | Reading Under- standing |
| | Identify | | | | |
| | Say | | Picture Comple- tion<br><br>Pictorial Absurdi- ties | Vocabulary Similarities Information Verbal Opposites | Reading Decoding |
| | Write | | | | |

appraisal includes 12 subtests in the cell marked say/say and half of these showed high performance and half showed low performance? How would one make any statement as to "auditory learning?" Perhaps the search would be more wisely directed toward the use of alternative instructional combinations rather than the search for preferred combinations.

**READING AND MATHEMATICS**

The most popular area of appraisal is reading. The relationships between reading and mathematics have been examined from a number of perspectives. Vocabulary and comprehension have been studied most extensively. The general finding is that there is a positive correlation between reading and mathematics and that improvement in reading often results in improvement in mathematics. Literature indicating that improvement in mathematics will improve performance in reading is less common.

Nolan (1984) describes math materials as being written in a terse, unimaginative style, with few cues to help in decoding meaning. The process of reading mathematics materials requires slow, deliberate reading. Math materials are presented in five different contexts, pictorial or graphic, computational or symbolic, verbal, textual, and testing. Included in these five contexts are four types of vocabulary: words having same meanings as in general use, technical words, symbolic vocabulary, and words with multiple meanings.

To deal with the complexity of the math materials, Nolan recommends a number of strategies to assist the pupil. He suggests that word problems can be rewritten to make them easier. However, it often happens that when one rewrites a problem to make it easier, one takes out the components of the problem that made it a problem. In other words, a problem becomes a nonproblem.

Teaching vocabulary is important. Youngsters can build their own dictionaries. Teachers could create informal reading inventories for mathematics and match students with specific texts.

It is common to find reading performance described in stages. Although different authorities may use different combinations and criteria to establish these stages, the two stages most relevant to mathematics are the independent reading level and the instructional reading level. The independent reading level is the level at which an individual knows about 95 to 99 percent of words and understands about 90 percent of the material when entering the reading task. The instructional level is the level at which the individual knows about 90 to 95 percent of the words and understands about 75 percent or more of the material when entering the reading activity. Note that the criteria for these are used to stipulate entering level standards.

The mathematics teacher who is going to have the children do an assignment they read to themselves must realize that the independent reading level requires almost perfect reading performance. The independent reading level is the level at which the child can read without assistance. At this level, the child should be able to interpret directions, understand task requirements, and comprehend the vocabulary and the meanings of the context. In mathematics, this includes the messages of symbols, formulae, and other specialized codes. The youngster must be able to relate the message to specific operations and to the sequence of steps within the operation.

Because the independent reading level has such stringent criteria, the mathematics teacher will have to be certain that the child has all the prerequisites. Homework cannot be done if the requirement is that the child read at the independent reading level and it is beyond the level at which the child reads. Classroom assignments will not be done quickly or efficiently if the child cannot read the material.

The independent reading level is the level at which the teacher should be able to say, "Locate page 12 in your book and complete the assignment. You will have 30 minutes to complete this task," or "Tonight's assignment is to complete the problems on page 16." The expectancy is that the assignment is within the independent reading level of the student. Anything short of this makes the assignment inappropriate.

The instructional level is the level at which the teacher and the student are directly involved in the interaction with the reading material. The teacher is providing instruction and the learner is responding to this instruction. While there are established criteria by which we can specify the instructional level, the fact remains that one clear measure of the appropriateness of the instructional level is given in the standard that states that "the instructional level for the child is the level at which the teacher teaches such that the child does not make any more mistakes that the teacher can properly correct." In effect, when the performance of the learner is characterized by excessive errors, the instructional level is inappropriate, no matter how much help the teacher gives the child. Should the learner require excessive correction, assistance with new words and terminology and with the interpretation of material, the instructional level is too high and some adjustment is necessary. This is easier said than done when the topic is mathematics, for it is difficult to find material with different reading levels and equivalent mathematics. Just how does the teacher provide the child with a sixth grade math assignment when the child is a first grade equivalent reader? Unfortunately, the teacher does not have any choice because to give the learner an inappropriate combination is to acknowledge a planned effort at inappropriate instruction.

Some children may be able to operate within the classroom instructional setting because they capitalize on verbal cues and explanations and on the illustrations and physical representations presented by the teacher. These same youngsters may be totally unable to manage material when asked to work alone. The teacher mistakes the ability of the youngster to function in the instructional setting for the ability to function independently and fails to understand when the child says "I didn't understand the stuff." Some learning-disabled children are able to function in a setting in which multiple instructional interactions are taking place. These same youngsters do not function independently.

The matter of independent and instructional levels in reading has an extensive history. Little or no attention has been given to the concepts and skills in mathematics. Certainly, they are just as meaningful and, although there are no specific data to support the following standards, they may serve as a beginning:

- Independent Mathematics Level: the level at which the individual can complete all problems or computational items without assistance.
- Instructional Mathematics Level: a rate at which the child can respond to items when they are first taught. Rate is comparable to that of other learners at the same level. Number correct should be four to five times greater than number incorrect at any time.

Several aspects of reading are important for mathematics and other subject areas. These are:

1. Word recognition and the understanding of the meanings of individual words in specific contexts
2. Interpreting the meanings within and among sentences
3. Interpreting and generalizing the meanings of paragraphs or page-length materials that vary from one contextual setting or demand to another
4. Interpreting, graphs, charts, and formulae and the interrelationships among these

The importance of vocabulary and reading of mathematics materials is gradually attaining greater attention among those interested in appraisal. The *Test of Reading Comprehension* (Brown et al., 1978) includes a measure of math vocabulary, as seen in Exhibit 7-2.

The *Test of Mathematics Abilities* (Brown & McEntire, 1983) also contains a vocabulary test. In this instance, the learner is given a set of terms (e.g., *dozen*) and requested to write a definition for each term.

Cox and Wiebe (1984) describe an inventory for estimating first through third grade children's ability to read mathematics vocabulary and to understand concepts. This inventory, seen in Exhibit 7-3, contains four parts. In Part 1, the teacher says a word and the child marks the word. In Part 2, the child reads a word and marks an instance of the concept for the word. In Part 3, the child reads a word and marks a word that represents a similar meaning. Part 4 consists of a cloze task in which the child inserts a word to given meaning to an expression.

Prior or concurrent knowledge is an important element of reading. Word meanings are important because they signal degrees of available knowledge. Over the years, vocabulary training has been considered an impor-

**Exhibit 7-2** Mathematics Vocabulary Test of TORC

---

### TORC SUBTEST #4: MATHEMATICS VOCABULARY

DIRECTIONS for each item:
1. Read the 3 words in the box. Think about why they might go together, or how they are alike.
2. Read all the words under the box. Choose the 2 you believe are most like the two words in the box.
3. Put X's over the letters that stand for the 2 words you chose.

EXAMPLES :

▲  2  5  6
A. 8
B. Z
C. 3
D. T

●  more than  longer  bigger
A. blue
B. larger
C. food
D. greater

---

▼ 1.  20  30  10
A. 40
B. 50
C. 15
D. 05

6.  10  15  5
A. 01
B. 20
C. 51
D. 25

11.  above  right  inside
A. pair
B. beside
C. long
D. near

2.  one  five  three
A. ten
B. fine
C. eight
D. ate

7.  $2+1=3$  $2+2=4$
   $5+1=6$
A. $6-1=5$
B. $6 \div 3=2$
C. $3+1=4$
D. $2+3=5$

12.  IX  X  III
A. ten
B. 5
C. XIV
D. V

3.  twenty  thirty  ten
A. fifty
B. forty
C. fifteen
D. zero five

8.  high  middle  over
A. hundred
B. far
C. above
D. light

13.  $+$  $=$  $>$
A. ?
B. $<$
C. ¢
D. x

4.  morning  noon  evening
A. afternoon
B. breakfast
C. midnight
D. pound

9.  $\div$  $-$  $+$
A. %
B. $
C. $=$
D. x

14  pay  save  buy
A. spend
B. wait
C. sell
D. penny

5.  take away  $(-)$  minus
A. $2-1=1$
B. add
C. difference
D. $5 \times 1=5$

10.  ten  fifteen  five
A. fifty-one
B. twenty
C. zero one
D. twenty-five

15.  2  8  6
A. 9
B. 4
C. 10
D. 3

Go on to the next page. ➡

16. two   eight   six
   A. three
   B. ten
   C. four
   D. nine

17. cupful   pint   gallon
   A. tallest
   B. ruler
   C. liter
   D. spoonful

18. triangle   square   rectangle
   A. sides
   B. altitude
   C. area
   D. zero

19. decimal   .01   ten
   A. 4/10
   B. 0.1
   C. divide
   D. 4.25

20. big   large   short
   A. high
   B. few
   C. man
   D. tree

21. dm.   km.   cm.
   A. hm.
   B. mm.
   C. oz.
   D. p.

22. three   seven   one
   A. nine
   B. two
   C. five
   D. six

23. eighth   sixth   third
   A. twelve
   B. half
   C. fourth
   D. nine

24. yard   pint   mile
   A. meter
   B. foot
   C. quart
   D. gram

25. angle   vertex   line
   A. arc
   B. triangle
   C. circle
   D. axis

— STOP —

*Source:* V. Brown, D. Hammill, and J.L. Wiederholt. *Test of Reading Comprehension.* Austin, Texas: Pro-Ed. 1978.

tant facilitator of improved mathematics performance. This training enables the individual to perform better in mathematics. However, there are instances where this type of training has long-term negative effects on the learning-disabled child. For example, Reutzel (1983) describes a six-component model to teach arithmetic story problem solving. The first stage, concept clarifying, involves extensive use of manipulatives to develop the appropriate mathematics concepts. In the second stage, the use of context clues is rehearsed using the cloze technique, where specific words are deleted. Composing is a third component. Here the child is exposed to real experiences involving quantity and number. In the next stage, chaining and classifying, the integration of the elements of a problem takes place. Children identify relevant information and devise plans or routines, part of which is the development of a semantic map. To this point, the model seems most appropriate. It is at the next stage, clues and calculations, that the problem solving is turned to rote activity. Here Reutzel identifies a list of key words associated with each operation (e.g., left = subtraction), and suggests that they be taught. Given this approach, how does one explain the following:

The girl has 3 apples left after she gave 2 apples to the boy. How many did she start with?

**Exhibit 7-3** Wiebe/Cox Mathematical Vocabulary Reading Inventory

Part I

| 1. once | ones | won | no | none |
|---|---|---|---|---|
| 2. hoot | flute | foot | foil | fate |

Part 2

| 1. Ten | ○ | ⬤ (dots) | 🛖 | (dots) | **346** |
| 2. Cent | 5¢ | 1¢ | 1 One 1 | ☆ | 👞 |

Part 3

| 1. missing |
|---|
| gone        more        mission        found        middle |
| 2. shape |
| short        square        sharp        formless        size |

Part 4

| 1. Five is _____ ten. |
|---|
| more than        less than        equal to        one third of        four times |
| 2. The _____ for addition is a plus. |
| second        score        sign        rename        division |

*Source:* J. Cox and J. Wiebe. (1984). Measuring Reading Vocabulary and Concepts in Mathematics in the Primary Grades. *The Reading Teacher, 37* (47), 405–409. Reprinted with permission of the authors and the International Reading Associations.

or

The girl has 5 apples after having added 2 apples to her pile. How many did she start with?

Rather than adding cue words to the existing list as suggested by Reutzel, it might be best to drop this component altogether with the learning disabled. The sixth step involves checking.

Some have felt that vocabulary training helps the individual to "think." A more realistic interpretation would suggest that the added vocabulary experiences extend the knowledge of the person and the person is then able to relate specific meanings to the situations.

Sentence meaning is probably more important to mathematics than to reading per se or to other subject areas. For this reason, appraisal needs to be directed toward the specific interpretations individuals make of single sentences and of sequences of sentences that are brief and direct. The reason for this is that mathematics is a system of communication that is highly sentence specific. Word problems typically consist of 3 or 4 sentences. Each sentence provides detailed and specific information and each needs to be interpreted.

The written sentence of mathematics contains special symbols or arrangements that are often accompanied by their own system of punctuation. The items $3(2 + 3)$ and $2(4 + 2)$ might also be written in an applied manner as:

The 3 children in one group each had 2 pears and 3 apples. The 2 children in another group each had 4 oranges and 2 grapes. How many pieces of fruit in all?

Paragraph or page-length sets of reading material constitute the makeup of financial reports, columns on the sports page, newspaper articles discussing the new budget, and many other types of quantitatively specific information. These types of experiences should be more fully integrated into the mathematics program for the learning disabled.

In *Project MATH* (Cawley et al., 1976) paragraph or story activities are an integral component of the problem-solving activities. Exhibit 7-4 is an illustration.

The inclusion of the paragraphs enables one to approach the needs of the learning-disabled child in an integrated manner (Cawley, 1984). A number of purposes are served:

1. In-depth analysis and search of reading material for relevant quantitative information is encouraged.
2. The stimulus properties of mathematics are incorporated into the reading program and the relationship between them is strengthened.
3. Attention is directed to a common set of information from which multiple mathematics activities can be generated.

As one develops the appraisal process, there is a need to incorporate the appraisal of many types of reading. This can be accomplished at the measurement and assessment stages. Any youngster whose reading prob-

**Exhibit 7-4** Problems in Story Format

---

**APPLE PICKING**

Austin and five of his classmates picked apples one fall for a week. The workers were paid by the basket, so they wanted to work as quickly as they could. On Monday, Austin filled only 8 baskets. On Tuesday, he filled 12 baskets. On Wednesday, he filled 16 baskets, and he filled the same number of baskets on Thursday. On Friday, Austin was tired and managed to fill only 14 baskets. Austin's friend Jack picked 9 baskets on Monday and picked the same number of baskets as Austin did on Tuesday and Wednesday. On Thursday, Jack picked 15 baskets, and he also picked 15 baskets on Friday.

1. How many baskets of apples had Austin picked by Wednesday night?
2. How many baskets of apples in all did the two boys pick on Monday and Tuesday?
3. What was the total number of baskets of apples that Austin picked?
4. How many baskets in all did Jack pick?
5. Which boy picked the greater number of baskets of apples?
6. By Wednesday night, which boy had picked the greater number of baskets of apples?
7. How many baskets of apples did Jack pick on his three best days?
8. How many baskets of apples did Austin pick on the three days that he picked the fewest number of baskets?
9. What was the total number of baskets of apples picked by both boys?

*Source:* J.F. Cawley, A.M. Fitzmaurice, H.A. Goodstein, A. Lepore, V. Althaus, and R. Sedlak. *Project MATH* (Tulsa, Okla.: Educational Progress, Inc.), 1976.

---

lems are so severe as to warrant appraisal at the diagnostic stage would clearly be an individual whose reading is inoperative for use in mathematics. Placement should be considered accordingly.

## LANGUAGE AND MATHEMATICS

For purposes of discussion in this section, language will be defined as those exchanges between senders and receivers that involve oral, gestural, or written messages. Reading, per se, will not be included.

In the mathematics classroom or during the mathematics lesson, combinations of language activities are used to organize and direct the lesson and to receive information, to request clarification, to store and retrieve information, and to organize and use symbols and terms to demonstrate proficiency. Some specific facets of language functioning are:

1. Listening for short and long periods of time
2. Interpreting directions
3. Mapping spoken, written, and gestural language simultaneously as the teacher says something, scribbles on the board, and gestures to

represent a concept. The learner needs to translate the common language meanings of each of these systems

4. Comprehending and expressing meaning of words, symbols, and sentences
5. Producing written language responses

Language is an unusual phenomenon when it comes to mathematics. It is often said that mathematics is "done in the head." This does not mean that it is done in a vacuum or that it is done subconsciously. The doing of mathematics "in the head" is a conscious undertaking that is mediated, at least according to some perspectives, by language. The doing of mathematics in the head may involve subvocalization and employ a kind of talking to oneself.

We recognize that many young children perform math tasks without the conscious or metacognitive use of language. We also recognize that by the time children are five or six years of age, they have extensive linguistic capability. Given the fact that many learning-disabled children have severe cognitive-language impairments, it is incumbent upon the appraisal specialist to uncover what they are and to provide a description of strengths and weaknesses.

Millgam (1973) notes that a person's cognitive competence attains biological maturity in late adolescence, whereas basic linguistic competence is probably attained by age six, or thereabouts. What seems to take place is that the language embellishments (e.g., enriched and specific vocabulary) continue to build upon linguistic competence and interact with cognitive growth over time as the individual moves toward cognitive maturity. If this maturity is viewed in a Piagetian perspective, it would be characterized by those behaviors associated with formal operations. This would involve the acquisition of a combinatorial or interpropositional logic that deals with the construction of possible rather than necessary realities. In effect, the individual constructs abstractions of abstractions. Millgam (1973) goes on to say that we are often so impressed with the oral-aural communication system of the child that we lose sight of the difficulties children encounter in using the verbal medium for cognitive purposes.

Children whose educational experiences in math are limited to concrete, rote learnings can be expected ultimately to manifest less than efficient systems of cognitive-language use. Thus, it is important to consider a variety of cognitive-language dimensions in the appraisal process. Some of these might include the vocabulary and similarities tests of the *WISC-R*, the verbal opposites test of the *Detroit*, the analogies test of the *Woodcock-Johnson*, the mathematics vocabulary test of *TOMA*, and others as desired.

The cognitive-language appraisal needs to differentiate the impact of language and cognition across discrepancies or disorders. Informal or curriculum-based assessment represents a means for developing instruments that will provide the necessary differentiation. In the informal assessment, the examiner can systematically vary content (e.g., level of words) by task (e.g., analogies) through interactive combination (e.g., written stimulus: written response). These could be backed up by the use of standardized measures to provide group comparisons. The analogies test of the *Beginning Educational Assessment* uses a pictorial format to assess analogical reasoning, whereas the analogies test of the *Woodcock-Johnson Psychoeducational Battery* employs a combination of oral and written inputs and an oral response. The *Miller Analogies Test* employs written input and written responses. Combinations could be constructed as desired.

### LISTENING AND MATHEMATICS

There is an element of both the independent level and the instructional level in listening. At the independent level the individual can listen to a lecture, lesson, or discussion for whatever period of time the activity is conducted. During this period, the individual would be able to mediate his or her behavior by taking notes, reflecting upon the material being presented, thinking ahead, making analogies, and raising questions. The individual would understand the terms, concepts, and principles and would be able to generalize these to other areas as they are being presented. Essential to effective listening is the ability to recognize when one is not comprehending or when one has lost track. This could be a serious problem with the learning disabled in that they do not recognize that they are not listening effectively.

The instructional level for listening would be characterized by a situation in which the teacher monitors his or her presentation knowing that the child has only a modicum of prequisite capability for the presentation. At the instructional level, it is the teacher who must anticipate the need to explain just one more time, to illustrate in another way, or to query the child regarding the material as it is presented. For instructional purposes, the teacher needs to be aware that the child is expected to leave the setting with the proper understanding of the new knowledge or procedure. To accomplish this, the teacher might conduct an informal inquiry before the start of the lesson by engaging the class in dialogue or by checking the level of knowledge of the class on that topic. Vague expressions or unanswered questions would certainly indicate a need for more background.

The use of oral exchanges in the listening setting is an efficient means by which to judge this readiness.

## WRITING AND MATHEMATICS

Written language is used extensively in social, vocational, or academic settings. Unlike spoken language, which people use in a perfunctory and general manner, written language activities are ordinarily undertaken for a purpose. Whereas spoken language is a group-oriented activity, written language is individually oriented. Five persons may sit about a table discussing something, but it is unlikely that five persons will sit about a table writing something as a group.

Whereas spoken language is a sequential activity (i.e., one waits for another to finish before speaking), written language is a simultaneous activity (i.e., everyone can be working on the same material at the same time). The teacher uses written language in a group context (e.g., writing illustrations on the chalkboard, preparing dittos, assigning pages in a book), whereas for the learner written language is more an individual activity (e.g., given a ditto, doing one's own work, not looking at anyone else's paper).

There are marked differences in the written and spoken uses of language in mathematics and other subjects. In spoken language, the effects of punctuation can be noted by inflection, intonations, and pauses. These same effects require written symbols in written language. In some areas, there are no direct transformations. For example, the spoken sentence "Mary said John has 3 apples" can be intonated and inflected to give the proper meaning. If written, this sentence needs to be formally punctuated, "Mary said, 'John has 3 apples.' "

Given the mathematical sentence $3(32 + 34)$, there is no oral language equivalent without the interjection of terminology "three times thirty-two plus thirty-four, where the term "times" is substituted for the parentheses.

Whereas written English has a specific format, that same format does not hold true for written mathematics. English is written from left to right and it is interpreted from left to right. Mathematics may be written left to right and then interpreted right to left. Such a case exists in:

$$\begin{array}{r} 362 \\ \times\ \ 14 \\ \hline \end{array}$$

where we have the added condition of writing top to bottom or in the case of subtraction where we read bottom to top.

While these may not seem to be major obstacles to most children, they can be serious problems for the learning disabled. Again, the appraisal specialist must be able to determine the effects across the different areas of academic functioning and to transmit this information to the teacher.

Copying from the board or taking dictation are important skills for mathematics. Whereas the individual may be able to summarize or make anecdotal notes from history, science, or other subjects, note taking in mathematics often requires an exact copy. Any single variation can destroy the concept or skill presentation. Many learning-disabled children are slow in this area. Often, the amount of time they have to take notes or copy examples is too short and they fail to get the material. The result is they cannot practice it or complete assignments, not because they cannot do the work but because they did not get the proper material in the first place.

Individuals working with the learning disabled would do well to provide ditto copies and avoid the difficulty of copying from the board. The teacher could place the same material on a transparency and explain each item. Should the teacher have to go on, the item will not be erased but will be available for the student to refer to in asking questions. Many teachers are frustrated when approached for help with a problem they put on the board and erased. The student says "I didn't understand what you were doing" but has no record or recall of the exact nature of the problem or the difficulty encountered.

## INTERPRETING APPRAISALS

The diversity in approaches to appraisal in ability and achievement provides a basis for understanding the difficulties encountered in reaching an understanding of the attributes subsumed under the concept of learning disability. Given the fact that we have literally hundreds of alternatives and combinations of alternatives to draw from, it is no wonder that the term *learning disability* means something different to everybody. We can understand this. What is less understandable and, to an extent, bewildering, is the fact that many individuals who review the same material come to different conclusions as to what it means about a given learner. This lack of reliability among interpreters is a serious problem because it invalidates the actual appraisal process. Two factors contribute to the situation. One is that not all persons attending the meeting of the appraisal team have a common understanding of the instruments or approaches used in the appraisal. One person might understand the *WISC-R,* another might not. A second factor is related to the manner of presentation. Typically, each member of the appraisal team presents his or her results individually during the meeting. This often includes a statement as to the present level of functioning, an interpretation of this statement, and a set of suggestions or recommendations. When one person has finished, the next person reports. This procedure requires that all participants be able to integrate the results and comments of all other persons into some wholistic depiction of the child. In reality, many attend to their own reports and often the information presented by others is less than fully utilized.

A conscientious school district will implement a policy requiring that all members of the appraisal team have a complete set of information about the child before or at least during the meeting. This information needs to be presented in a manner that allows for independent determination of strengths and weaknesses and the opportunity to ask questions about all the available information. Further, as is the case with the Massachusetts standard, all information should be presented in a common language, that is, so as to be understandable to the least sophisticated or novice member of the group.

## CHOOSING AN APPROACH TO ASSESSMENT

*Subject-matter* or *curriculum-based assessment* are terms used to describe an approach to appraisal that focuses on the subjects or curriculum that are integral to the school or classroom in which the student is enrolled. There are many advantages to such an approach. In the main, they provide direct comparisons of the student with the material that is being presented, a comparison with other learners experiencing the same material under relatively similar conditions, and the opportunity to observe how the student will respond when specific recommendations are made. It is one thing to describe a student in a seventh grade classroom as a third grade equivalent reader and another to take the material the student is required to read and demonstrate specific performance levels reached with that material. The same essentially holds true for mathematics. It is one thing to describe the child as being four years behind and quite another to show the teacher that the child simply cannot deal with the material at either the instructional or independent levels of functioning. The evidence obtained in subject-matter appraisal has direct bearing on the designated level of instruction. Any child making more errors in mathematics than the teacher can correct is a child who has not been assigned to a proper instructional level.

Successful intervention in mathematics rests in the purview of the mathematics specialist, not the special educator. Ideally, in a team approach to mathematics members of the appraisal team, the special education staff, and the mathematics staff work together, with the mathematics specialist having as much opportunity as possible to work with one or two children at a time instead of being assigned to lunch or study hall supervision.

## SERVICE DELIVERY MODELS

Appraisal is integral to the selection of an appropriate service delivery model for the individual. The student whose needs are met at the measurement stage of appraisal should be able to function quite well in the regular class. This means that, with some adjustments, this individual can participate effectively with his or her peers. For example, if the learning disability is in reading, the instructional adjustment during mathematics would be to minimize the role of reading. If the learning disability is math related, the student could remain in the regular math class during math and receive assistance from a resource teacher at another time.

For the student whose appraisal needs have been met at the assessment stage, participation in the regular class would also seem a viable option. It is likely that this student will show a pattern of strengths and weaknesses across different areas in math and each could be adjusted as desired.

The student who is referred for diagnosis would have considerable difficulty functioning in the regular class. There are two exceptions. The first is the student who demonstrates reasonable capability with alternative representations. The second is the student whose rate of learning approximates that of other members of the class even though he or she may be working with material that is of a lower grade level. If a student has neither an alternative capability nor a learning rate approximating others, he or she would be best assigned to some unit other than the regular class.

## SUMMARY

The general nature of human development is such that it is impossible to separate appraisal in an area such as mathematics from areas such as reading and listening. Further, in recognition of the diversity that exists in the instruments used to conduct an appraisal, it is necessary to find simple and common language terms to interpret the results of the appraisal.

All appraisal must have implications for curriculum and instruction. Combinations of norm-referenced and curriculum-based approaches seem the best way to specify these implications. This chapter has described the aforementioned, identified selected issues, and suggested a range of alternatives and considerations.

**REFERENCES**

Brown V., Hammill, D., & Wiederholt, L.J. (1978). *Test of reading comprehensions*. Austin, TX: Pro-Ed.

Brown, V., & McEntire, M.E. (1983). *Test of mathematics abilities*. Austin, TX: Pro-Ed.

Cawley, J. (1984). Selection adoption and development of curriculum and instructional materials. Chapter 10 in *Developmental teachings of mathematics to the learning disabled*, Rockville, MD: Aspen Systems.

Cawley, J., Goodstein, H.A., Fitzmaurice, A.M., Lepore, A.V., Sedlak, R., & Althaus, V. (1976). *Project MATH*. Tulsa, OK: Educational Progress Corporation.

Cawley, J., Fitzmaurice, A.M., Shaw, R.A., Kahn, H., and Bates, H. (1979). Math word problems and suggestions for LD students. *Learning Disability Quarterly, 2,* 25–41.

Cox, J., & Wiebe, J. (1984). Measuring reading vocabulary and concepts in mathematics in the primary grades. *The Reading Teacher, 37,* 402–411.

Das, J., Kirby, J., & Jarman R. (1979). *Simultaneous and successive cognitive processing*. New York: Academic Press.

Millgam, N. (1973). Cognition and language in mental retardation: Distinctions and implications. Chapter 6 in D.K. Roults (Ed.), *The experimental psychology of mental retardation*. Chicago: Aldine.

Nolan, J. (1984). Reading in the content area of mathematics. In M.M. Dupius (Ed.), *Reading in the Content Areas*. Newark, DE: International Reading Association.

Reutzel, R. (1983). C[6]: A reading model for teaching arithmetic problem-solving. *The Reading Teacher, 37,* 28–34.

Schenck, S., & Levy, W. (1977). An informal WISC-R for mathematics. Storrs, CT: Unpublished research project.

# Chapter 8

# Interdisciplinary Assessment of Mathematical Learning Disability: Diagnosis in a Clinical Setting

*Mahesh C. Sharma*

Today, more students than ever before are being referred to mathematics diagnostic and remedial clinics. There are several reasons for this. One is the general public's realization that the mathematical preparation needed to function optimally and realize one's potential in one's chosen field is much more extensive today than at any other time in history. What is required by the mathematical needs of a technological society is far more than the development of computation skills. Another reason is the concern on the part of special educators for the all-around remediation of students' learning problems including their mathematics learning difficulties.

The availability of diverse methods of remediation for reading problems, which has been made possible by interdisciplinary professional interaction, has inspired special educators to involve other professionals in the diagnosis and remediation of mathematics learning problems. Another impetus for the increased emphasis on the identification of mathematics problems is parental awareness. More and more parents are realizing the importance of mathematics in day-to-day living. It has become generally accepted that the aquisition of skills of a higher level of competence in mathematics will make students more employable. Mathematical thinking is a set of skills that cannot be duplicated by machines. Indeed, one needs these skills not only to run machines but also to develop them.

The diagnosis and assessment of mathematics problems reflect these concerns through educators' emphasis on problem solving and application as well as concept development and computation. More and more outside specialists are being involved in the diagnosis of students' learning problems in mathematics.

A caring classroom teacher has ample opportunity to know a learner's deficiencies in mathematics. Through informal observations of behavior in the classroom, seeing his or her performance on formal and informal tests, watching his or her participation in classroom discussions, assessing the quality of his or her interaction with other students, and from interviews with parents, the teacher gains valuable, in-depth information. Such a teacher knows the nature of a student's deficiencies in every subject area including mathematics. But this information has to do with symptoms, and it is not enough. What the teacher needs is the answer to the following questions:

1. What are the causes of the learning difficulties in mathematics?
2. What are the specific kinds of difficulties encountered?
3. What kind of teaching approach will be the most effective remedial strategy?

The teacher is looking for causes, not just symptoms, for ways that can help him or her design better educational programs for students.

Many questions can be answered by specialists participating in the diagnostic process. The clinical diagnostic process defines a role for both the specialists and the classroom teacher. Most medical-facilities-based clinics do not provide teaching and therefore the role of the classroom teacher is still crucial. Even those mathematics clinics that do provide remedial services need the classroom teacher's cooperation in order to get maximum results. The diagnosis at most clinics focuses primarily on the assessment of difficulties and their possible causes. But the objective of mathematics clinics (as an adjunct to a medical clinic) should also be to provide some corrective teaching that builds upon the strengths that have been identified and assessed through the clinical diagnosis. Only through such prescriptive, corrective, and model teaching can interdisciplinary research in mathematics education be transferred to classroom situations.

More and more clinicians—psychologists, neurologists, and physicians—are taking an active interest in the etiology and diagnosis of mathematics learning problems. Only a few years ago the assessment of learning disabilities involved the identification of the factors that contributed to the learning disability as manifested in reading, language, social, and emotional malfunctioning. Now a comprehensive evaluation routinely includes the difficulties experienced by a learning-disabled individual in the handling of quantitative and mathematical information and concepts.

Many learning disabilities and neurological disorders units in hospital settings and psychological and family counseling practices now include mathematics specialists among their staff. This interdisciplinary approach to the diagnosis of mathematics learning problems is beginning to throw light on the interrelationships between mathematical learning difficulties and learning disabilities. The involvement of specialists from many fields has brought a diversity of fresh perspectives to the problem of reading and language. Similar approaches and interdisciplinary perspectives on mathematical learning disabilities are beginning to provide answers to questions such as:

- What constraints are imposed by an individual's learning disabilities on mathematics learning in general and what effects does this have on an individual's performance in mathematics and on other related activities?
- Is there an etiology of mathematics learning disability?
- What aspects of mathematics learning are especially affected by the particular nature of an individual's learning disability?
- What type of compensatory mechanisms are employed by a learning-disabled individual in mathematics learning?

## CHARACTERISTICS OF LEARNING DISABILITY IN MATHEMATICS

Many deficits have been found among groups of learning-disabled students, such as right-left confusion, impairment of form perception, difficulties in spatial orientation. Descriptions of learning-disabled students that have appeared in the literature include diverse characteristics, depending on the describer's perspective about mathematics disability. The following gives some of the important indications:

- Problems in symbolizing concrete and visual experiences into abstract forms, particularly experiences involving quantitative relationships.
- Disturbances in visual-spatial perception and difficulties in visual-motor integration and accompanying disorientation.
- Disturbance in understanding nonverbal experiences and relating them to verbal and abstract experiences.
- Difficulty in comprehending relationships of quantity, order, size, space, and distance.
- Inability to make generalizations or draw the proper conclusions from experiences that ordinarily would lead to the understanding of number and quantity.
- Difficulty with geometric figures, particularly shape and form.
- Lack of integration of the information from the visual, auditory, and kinesthetic modalities. Inability to associate between symbol and meaning and quantity. Inability to associate auditory and visual sym-

bols. For example, being able to count auditorially but not being able to identify the numerals visually.

- Disturbances in body image.
- Inability to establish one-to-one correspondence between collections.
- Lack of estimation skills.
- Inability to count meaningfully. Inability to relate the meaning of cardinality and ordinality. Inability to visualize clusters of objects within a large group: each object in a group satisfies the characteristics of the whole group.
- Inability to grasp the principles of conservation. For example, some learning-disabled individuals are not able to comprehend that ten cents is the same whether it consists of two nickels, one dime, or ten pennies; or that a one pound block of butter is the same as four one-quarter pound sticks.
- Inability to understand process signs. In certain instances that deficiency is related to a perceptual disturbance (inability to distinguish the difference in the plus and multiplication signs). More frequent is the failure to grasp the meaning conveyed by the signs.
- Inability to understand the arrangement of the numerals in a number (place value). Inability to understand the sequence of letters in a word.
- Inability to follow and remember the sequence of steps to be used in various mathematical operations and algorithms. Inability to follow directions.
- Inability to understand the concepts of measurement and inability to read maps and graphs.
- Inability to choose the principles for solving problems in arithmetic reasoning. The learning-disabled student can read the words and do the problems if he or she is given the principle and formula but without assistance cannot determine which process to apply.
- Inability to determine primary concepts and skills in a secondary concept.

## PARAMETERS OF DIAGNOSTIC MODELS

The important progress made in the diagnosis of reading can provide us some direction in developing viable models for the diagnosis of mathematical learning difficulties. The specialists and the disciplines involved in the diagnostic process of reading difficulties range from classroom teacher to neurologists. Similarly, the literature in the field of mathematics learning disabilities has contributions from many specialists. Classroom teachers, certainly, are helping to identify the characteristics and behaviors of learning-disabled students. Special education teachers are observing and studying the effects of the constraints imposed by a student's learning disability on his or her mathematics learning. Diagnosticians are developing diagnostic and screening procedures for learning disability in mathematics. Mathematics educators are studying the appropriateness of a particular content and of teaching methodologies for the learning disabled in mathematics. Psychologists are collecting information regarding the affective aspects of learning disability and the effects of psychological and emotional factors on learning mathematics and are studying the effects of math anxiety. Neurologists are trying to discern the effects and relationships of lesions and insults to the brain with disabilities in general and mathematics disabilities in particular.

All these professional contributions from different fields suggest an interdisciplinary approach to a diagnostic model. On the following pages we first describe what is happening in clinics at the present time and then discuss the development of a diagnostic model. To design a diagnostic model, one has to look at the parameters of the diagnostic process first. In the context of mathematics learning one has to consider the following:

- What is the nature of mathematics—concepts, skills, processes?
- How does one learn mathematics?
- Are there different ways of conceptualizing a mathematical idea?
- What mathematical concepts are in the reach of a child at a particular age?
- Is it easier to learn certain mathematics concepts in a particular sequence?
- What are some of the optimal pedagogies for certain concepts and skills?

Many etiologies have been cited explaining why people have difficulty understanding and manipulating mathematical concepts. These etiologies can be placed into two major categories. One perspective attributes mathematical difficulties to the manner and sequence in which the concepts are presented while the other attributes the difficulties to psychoneurological deficits within the child.

Diagnostic assessment is dependent on the identified goals of mathematics learning for the child to be diagnosed. And the mathematics curricular goals themselves are dependent on the child's cognitive level of functioning, learning style, linguistic development, preparation for mathematics learning, and previous mathematics learning experience and achievement. But all this information is ideally the outcome of the diagnostic process. Therefore, it is not entirely possible to have an *a priori* defined objective for the mathematics diagnostic process. Only the wider parameters and processes can be predetermined and contemplated. For that reason a diagnostic model for mathematics assessment has to be interactive and multidisciplinary—interactive with teaching and interdisciplinary as far as other aspects of a child's learning.

The diagnostic model has to be interactive so that not only the student's deficiencies and strengths in learning mathematics are assessed but his or her limits to learning mathematics are also ascertained. This will provide clues to the student's rate of learning, motivation, and information about the affective component of his or her learning. The model has to be interdisciplinary so that the information gathered by one specialist will be useful to another specialist on the diagnostic team in assessing the student's level of mathematics learning. Learning deficiencies found in one discipline sometimes can explain the difficulty a student might be having in mathematics. For example, if the neurologist finds that there is a definite lesion in the individual's left hemisphere, it will be useful for the teacher to know the effects this lesion might have on the mathematical learning ability of the student. Such information could imply that sequencing might be difficult for the student and that the teacher must use visual/spatial and intuitive means of presenting a mathematical algorithm rather than the usual teaching procedures.

This interactive, interdisciplinary and dynamic process is guided by the goals of the mathematics curricula. The relevant educational objectives and the selection of the diagnostic model in turn guide us in setting goals for the diagnostic process.

Some of the elements to be considered in the diagnostic process are:

- How does the child relate to abstract concepts?
- Is the child ready for the mathematics concepts, skills, and processes being taught?
- What is the student's intellectual level (intelligence)?
- What is the student's cognitive level?
- Does the student need manipulatives and/or concrete models for conceptualization?
- What is the student's rate of learning new concepts?
- What is student's rate and accuracy in recalling arithmetic facts?
- What is the student's learning style?

- What is the student's self-concept, motivation, and affective reaction to mathematics?

- What is the student's neurological, psychological, and emotional profile? For example, are there any neurological impairments, insults, or injuries to the student's brain?

- What is the student's home environment and the attitude of other members of the family towards mathematics now and when they were learning mathematics?

Gathering the answers to these questions involves several specialists: a physician, a neurologist, a neuropsychologist, a behavioral psychologist, a learning disability specialist, the classroom teacher, a mathematics educator, and an educational psychologist. The training and the environment of the specialists involved bring unique viewpoints to the models of diagnosis and to approaches to the remediation. Clinical models involve one or a combination of the following approaches:

- *Medical Approach.* To medical personnel, there are three levels of interest: etiology, dysfunction, and the symptoms. *Etiology* relates to causes. *Dysfunction* refers to malady, disease, difficulty, or a problem. *Symptoms* are observable changes in performances and states that indicate a disorder or dysfunction.

- *Educational Approach.* Educators on clinical teams put their emphasis on individual abilities and disabilities. For example, they are interested in identifying the learner's strengths and weaknesses in such areas as visual and auditory discrimination, sequencing, and memory. They focus on hierarchies of concepts, cognitive processes, and skills that are inherently involved in mathematics learning and a student's preparation in these areas is assessed to provide information for remediation.

The procedures involved and used by these professionals for gathering information useful for diagnostic assessment are diverse, beginning from informal observations by classroom teachers to formal and informal neurological examinations by a neurologist. The diagram shown in Figure 8-1 is an example of a diagnostic model representing cooperative practices between schools and learning disability clinics at hospitals and medical centers in the Boston area.

**Figure 8-1** Diagnostic Model for Mathematical Learning Disability

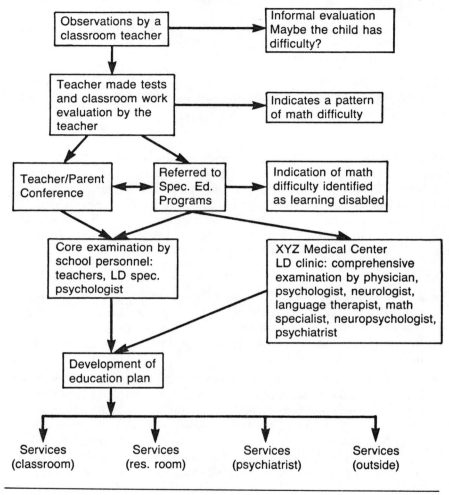

## WHAT IS TO BE DIAGNOSED?

A mathematical diagnosis seeks to determine

1. The student's mathematics skills: computation, problem solving, mathematical modeling, and application of mathematical concepts
2. The student's attitude toward mathematics and its applications
3. The student's rate of learning and retention of mathematics

4. Neurological, psychological, linguistic, cognitive, and pedagogical factors that might be contributing to the student's mathematical learning problems

There is a clear distinction between (1) mathematics learning problems related to the specific functions that constitute mathematics (including mathematics learning problems due to a student's developmental lag) and (2) those specific learning disabilities that diminish the student's level of performance in mathematics because of other than mathematical deficiencies. In other words, some of the mathematical problems for the learning disabled arise because of the complex nature of mathematics and the way it is being taught and others are the result of the constraints their learning disability imposes on learning mathematics. Specialists involved in the diagnostic process must be able to give some idea of this to the teacher so that the teacher can plan remedial instruction accordingly. This kind of diagnosis focuses on the problems within the pupil as explanations of the mathematical disability.

In a clinical setting several areas are explored in order to find contributory factors to the problem. For example, at the Learning Disabilities Clinics at the Children's Hospital Medical Center and Massachusetts General Hospital, both in Boston, and at the Center for the Teaching/Learning of Mathematics in Wellesley and Framingham, Massachusetts, the following areas are emphasized during or prior to the diagnostic evaluation and assessment process (these variables are representative of the emphasis at other such clinics):

- General information about the child and family background
- Physical health and development
- Neuropsychological status
- Psychiatric (mental and emotional development)
- Neurological development and milestones
- Psychological development
- Speech development
- Audiology (status of hearing and audio input)
- Language development
- Reading ability
- Mathematics ability and achievement

Exhibit 8-1 provides a list of variables related to the mathematics learning problem that the different members of the diagnostic team are interested in.

After all the examinations have been made an extensive case conference takes place. All the professionals involved participate whenever possible.

**Exhibit 8-1** Learning Disability Variables

Neurological/Neuropsychological
- Hearing and visual difficulties
- Developmental milestones (motor, speech, dressing skills, peer interaction)
- Family history of medical/neurological disorders
- Oral work
- Handedness
- Visual tracking
- Fine motor skills
- Gross motor skills
- Cerebellar
- Sensory
- Digit span
- Hemispheric specialization
- Lesion location
- Nature of insults to the brain
- Integration of the two sides of the body
- Balance ability
- Motor planning ability
- Eye motor activity
- Difference in performance between right and left side of the body
- Visual perception abilities
- Sensory integration

Developmental (Cognitive)
- Classification, seriation, class inclusion, estimation, conservation tasks (number, length, area, volume, weight)
- One-to-one correspondence
- Relationships (reflexive, symmetric, transitive)
- Primary and secondary concept learning
- Parts-to-whole versus whole-to-parts strategy to puzzle and picture making
- Spatial orientation and space organization
- Reversibility
- Concepts of equality and inequality
- Identification and relationships of variables

Mathematical

- Number concepts and their relationships (counting—forward, backward, skipping by 2's, 5's, 10's, etc.)
- A number bigger than a given number, smaller than a given number, between two given numbers, representation of a given number by concrete materials
- Representation and identification of money—different kinds of coins
- Recognition, copying, and extension of a given pattern
- Identifying and reproducing geometric figures
- Writing and identifying numbers
- Translating mathematical expressions into English statements and vice versa
- Oral mathematics
- Number operations
- Arithmetic operations (according to the age of the child)
- Logical deductions
- Similarities and dissimilarities
- Sequencing
- Analogies
- Attitudes toward mathematics

The discussions consider all the information collected about the child by different professionals on the team. They result in diagnostic data that help in formulating remedial instructional strategies. This diagnostic information and the remedial suggestions are then shared with the parents and the school system through an extensive written report. (Examples are included in Appendixes 8-A, 8-B, and 8-C.) Procedures for follow-up are also outlined.

## DIAGNOSTIC PROCEDURES: WHO DOES WHAT?

The classroom teacher is the first person to detect any problems that a student might be having. The teacher has the maximum information about the nature of the difficulties, i.e., what the student can and cannot do and what he or she needs to do. But what the teacher does not know is the reason for the problems and the student's potential in mathematics. A classroom teacher may not have time or the training to diagnose the difficulties and thus generally refers the student to the special education department or informs the parents either formally or informally during parent-teacher conferences. In the case of reading difficulties, a school system might be able to provide elaborate diagnostic and remedial procedures. But in the case of mathematics difficulties, the procedures that are employed in most school systems are limited.

As we have seen in other chapters, several diagnostic tests have been developed and published for classroom use, and some for individual administration. The most popular is the *KeyMATH Diagnostic Test*. These are very valuable and helpful, but there are several limitations to their usefulness as diagnostic tools. For example, most of them tell us what the student can and cannot do but none tells us why a student is not able to solve certain mathematical problems. They provide us with a profile but not with the suggestions for remediation. Nor do they take into account the possibility that a student may give the right answer for the wrong reasons or an almost right answer and leave out a minor item and therefore receive a substantially lower score.

Written work and probing are necessary ingredients of any diagnostic process. Without this the question of how much the student understands remains unanswered. It is impossible to find out why a student thinks as he or she does without asking the student. Frequently the answers don't fall into the preconceived patterns that are assumed in standardized and formal tests. Wrong answers and mistakes provide us with information about a learner's thinking processes. The only way to find out how well concepts and written work are understood is to analyze error patterns. The diagnostician should ask questions and listen to the answers, and then use these answers to find out information that is not immediately available from ordinary standardized tests. But all this requires time and techniques that elementary teachers may not possess and referral to a specialist becomes necessary.

It is a common assumption on the part of many educators that if teachers know mathematics they will be able to work with children having problems in mathematics. Or if they know how to deal with reading problems they can also deal with mathematics problems. These assumptions are accurate only in a limited number of cases. A person might be an expert in mathematics or in reading but still may not be able to diagnose a student's mathematical problems and design educational plans to correct those problems. To be able to work with children having problems in mathematics, one needs to know the way children learn and acquire mathematical concepts, the nature of mathematical problems, and the type of difficulty that children especially encounter in mathematics.

Only a very small number of schools have trained personnel to do meaningful diagnostic evaluation of learning problems in mathematics. Most special education tutors and resource room teachers are trained essentially in the procedures for reading and language disabilities and therefore they have difficulty with students who are having problems in mathematics. The most they do is administer the *KeyMATH Diagnostic Test* or something parallel to it and then design an educational plan based on that limited information. Once they have developed an educational plan, the methods they employ for remediation are not much different from those in the regular classroom.

The person who can fulfill the requirements of a good diagnostician and a remedial tutor for the learning-disabled student in mathematics must possess:

1. A good grasp of mathematics and its development
2. A positive attitude towards mathematics and mathematics learning
3. A good understanding of how children learn mathematics and the reasons one might experience learning difficulties in mathematics
4. An understanding of the constraints imposed by the learning disability on a child's ability to learn mathematics

Many children have problems in learning mathematics—many exhibit problems only in the area of mathematics. The nature of their problems varies. The causes also are many, as are the solutions, from simple educational to neuropsychological adjustments. Referral to professionals outside the school system is important if we are to fulfill our responsibilities to all learners.

## THE DIAGNOSTIC/REMEDIATION CASE FOLDER

The diagnostic/remediation folder contains medical and developmental histories, test results, recommendations, letters and forms to schools and parents, progress reports, lesson plans, progress charts, samples of work, and ongoing work reports. All information concerning the student is considered highly confidential and discussed only in a conference class or only with the parties concerned.

## ASSUMPTIONS ABOUT THE NATURE OF MATHEMATICS LEARNING

The processes involved in the learning of mathematics are of critical importance to the description, screening, diagnosis, and remediation of learning problems in mathematics. The problems associated with learning disabilities in mathematics have concerned researchers for a long time. As early as 1919, neuropsychologists were investigating the causes of dyscalculia. The results of these studies have provided a body of knowledge concerning the behavioral and cognitive characteristics of children with specific learning disabilities in mathematics. As more information about dyscalculia has become available, educators have become concerned with the application of this knowledge to diagnosis and remediation.

## COGNITIVE DEVELOPMENT AND MATHEMATICS LEARNING

Any mathematics diagnosis is guided by the diagnostician's understanding about the mathematics learning processes and his or her perspective on these processes. Theoretical orientations range from behavioral management to Piagetian theory of cognitive development. For example, we see two positions regarding mathematics readiness: behavioral and cognitive. Behaviorists believe that learning is the outcome of response to a given stimulus, whereas the cognitivist posits that learning is more the formation of cognitive structures that are the result of a learner's experiences from different modes and time periods.

While it is true that the acquisition of lower-level mathematical skills and the mastering of basic facts involve  associations akin to the behavioral approach, in conceptualizing higher-order mathematical concepts and processes it is the restructuring of preexistent cognitive schemata and the development of new ones that are operative. The major part of mathematics learning is the result of cognitive activity. Mathematics learning is meaningful when the student can demonstrate it not just as responses to certain associations and stimuli under specific conditions but as the presence of and the ability to apply concepts, algorithms, skills, and processes. At the same time the child has the flexibility to change and develop these schemata according to the need, context, and the experiences that result in that learning. Demonstrations of these skills are not functions of the stimuli but they represent the student's understanding and mastery of concepts at that time. This understanding helps the student in restructuring his or her reality. Psychologists, therefore, during the diagnostic process are interested both in the behavioral responses of the child to a particular stimulus and the presence or absence of cognitive structures.

Earlier mathematical concepts, particularly primary concepts (whether by a child or an adult), are learned through the senses (Skemp, 1963). Mathematical information is first received by the learner's senses, then perceived by the senses and sent to the appropriate processing mechanism in the learner's neuropsychological systems. Piaget (1965) and Piaget and Inhelder (1965) also consider the interplay of perceptions or sensations as the ingredients for the formation of intelligence. Piaget adds that sensory motor activities prepare the child for logical operations. Thus, logic, particularly in the earlier stages of a child's development, is based on the general coordination of actions, and later it is the product of interactions between language and concrete actions. Basic, then, to the learning of mathematics, at the earliest level, is perception, the process of organizing the raw data obtained through the senses and interpreting its meaning through the perceptual and logical operations in the brain. The basic sensory modalities through which mathematical information passes are visual, auditory, tactile, and kinesthetic. During the diagnosis, the neurologist and the neuropsychologist are interested in the sensory integration and perceptual integration processes.

Formation and conceptualization of every new mathematical concept is dependent on one's earlier knowledge and skills. For example, multiplication is dependent on addition; solving quadratic equations is dependent on algebraic manipulations such as factoring and the collecting of like terms. These in turn are dependent on the commutative and distributive laws and other foundations of algebra.

For the mastery of any mathematical content, we need both kinds of information: rote and schematic. When there is a schematic dependence between concepts and processes, the presence of prerequisite schemata is a must. Where the appropriate schema for the learning of a specific content is absent, some kind of learning is possible. But without the knowledge that is necessary to give meaning to the new material it will be learning without understanding. This latter kind is isolated learning, whereas in schematic learning new knowledge builds upon the previous knowledge and existing schemata. In schematic learning new schemata are formed and old ones are restructured and refined into new schemata and learning. Retention in rote learning is short lived and selective, whereas in schematic learning the learned material can be used after a long time. The intact and efficient memory system, therefore, is an essential requirement for optimal functioning in mathematics. Psychologists, therefore, are interested in assessing a learning-disabled student's performance on tasks involving short- and long-term memory.

## MATHEMATICS LEARNING PERSONALITY AND MATHEMATICS LEARNING

Some neurological research (Denckla & Marolda, 1979; Wheatley, 1978) is emerging which throws light on mathematics learning from a psychological and neurological perspective. This research addresses, to some degree, the question whether children's mathematical learning is associated with their mathematical learning style, and in turn, whether learning style is dependent on neurological development and in particular specialization of one's brain. Neurological research is beginning to associate specific components of mathematics learning and achievement to the hemispheric specialization of an individual's brain functioning (Wheatley, 1978). Based on these observations, it seems that there are two types of mathematical learning personalities: quantitative and qualitative.

A child with a quantitative mathematical learning personality (Quant-P) is one who has left hemispheric orientation. This child is good in language and verbal expression, in solving problems bit by bit (in components), in quantifying and in quantitative operations, and especially good in operations that build up sequentially, such as counting, addition, and multiplication. Such a child has specific solutions to specific problems rather than general rules. He or she uses a "one step at a time" approach to problem solving. When given a word problem, this child looks for a familiar algorithm to solve the problem.

A child with a qualitative mathematical learning personality (Qualt-P) is one who has a right hemispheric orientation. This child looks at the problem wholistically and explores general approaches to solutions; he or she is good in identifying patterns—both spatial and symbolic—is more creative, intuitive in approaching new problems, shows good performance on counting by patterns, estimation, and applications of mathematical concepts. When given a word problem this child seems to play with the problem in a nondirected metaphoric way before beginning to solve it.

The matching of a child's mathematical learning personality with the instructional materials being used and the teaching style that a teacher employs—the way the teacher asks questions and presents new information and organizes the classroom—is crucial for optimal learning. For example, if the teacher's teaching style is more qualitative, intuitive, and divergent, then the student with a qualitative learning style will feel more comfortable, and therefore will learn better and produce more. On the other hand, if the teacher is more sequentially oriented and convergent in his or her questioning approach, then the student with a quantitative learning style will learn better because of the needed structure.

The same principle applies regarding the choice of instructional materials; children are more comfortable when the match between the instructional material and their learning style is optimal. Qualitatively oriented children learn better by using visual/spatial materials such as Cuisenaire rods, graph papers, etc. Quantitatively oriented children learn better by using sequential materials such as the number line, fingers, numerical blocks, unifix cubes, etc. Clearly, diagnostic information about a child's learning style has important implications for the planning and implementation of remedial programs for the learning-disabled student in mathematics.

## MATHEMATICS AS LANGUAGE

Mathematics, at one level, is a form of language involving the communication of concepts through symbols. Among the concepts embodied in this unique language are, at the primary level, classification and ordering of objects, quantity, size, order relationships, space, form, distance, and time. On another level, mathematics as a language is used to convey the results of logical thinking and reasoning, collection and classification of data, analysis and interpretation of information, and finally to solve problems and convey the results in a useful form for meaningful purposes. Thus mathematics may be regarded as a symbolic language whose practical function is to express quantitative and qualitative relationships and communicate concepts through symbols, and whose theoretical function is to facilitate thinking.

Appropriate language facility—vocabulary, syntax, translation from mathematics to a child's language and from his or her language to mathematics, use and understanding of symbols—must be intact for smooth learning of mathematical concepts and their competent use. The principal functions of a symbol and language in mathematics are to designate with precision, clarity, and brevity. The reward is, as Alfred North Whitehead put it, "by relieving the brain of all unnecessary work, a good notation sets it free to concentrate on more advanced problems, and, in effect, increases the mental powers of the race." In point of fact, without the process of abbreviation, mathematical conceptualization is hardly possible. The demands of precision require that the meaning of each symbol or each symbol string be unambiguous.

We act on mathematical symbols in two very different ways: we calculate with them and we interpret and use them to conceptualize ideas, and many times these symbols help us to represent and recreate the effect of the concrete experience. In a calculation, a string of mathematical symbols is processed according to a standardized set of agreements and converted into another string of symbols. To interpret a symbol is to associate it with some concept or mental image; to assimilate the two results in learning. Symbols involve images; many times those images are quite vivid and are good replacements for concrete objects. Symbols can be looked upon as the mechanism by which the brain makes meaning out of discrete pieces of information.

The symbol, then, is a mechanism for understanding. The symbol transcends the limits of the physical sense. Goethe has said, "In the symbol, the particular represents the general." Symbols by their nature can resolve paradoxes and create order from disorder. A symbol stands by itself, as a whole. In its wholeness it produces an understanding beyond verbal explanations. The mastery of mathematical concepts to a great extent depends on the child's facility to understand and acquire mastery in the use of mathematical language and symbols.

Problems in dealing with these symbols (numbers and operational symbols) may result from language disorders, inability to deal with spatial/temporal relationships, and/or other specific processing deficits. Learning disabilities that affect reading, writing, and spelling tend also to affect arithmetic skills acquisition. No one basic task area can be considered in isolation in attempting to diagnose the problems of the learning-disabled student in mathematics.

## LEVELS OF KNOWING MATHEMATICS

To master a mathematics concept, whether simple or complex, one has to pass through several levels of understanding. The levels range from an intuitive understanding of the concept to the ability to communicate it to others, to apply it to real-life situations, or connect it to another mathematical and cognitive task. The levels are:

1. Intuitive
2. Concrete
3. Representational
4. Abstract
5. Application
6. Communication

Many times a teacher has the wrong impression about a child's level of knowing a particular mathematics concept. As a result his or her teaching may be mistargeted as far as the level of teaching that particular concept is concerned. Furthermore, most mathematics teaching, even in earlier grades, takes place at the abstract and semiabstract level. That is not appropriate for the child who is functioning at a lower cognitive level and the child who has limited concrete experiences. The diagnostic information about the child's level of mastery in mathematics concepts, therefore, is important for remedial teaching.

## PREREQUISITE AND SUPPORT SKILLS

Another factor that contributes to a child's learning difficulties in mathematics is the absence of prerequisite and support skills. Before a child can meaningfully understand and use a mathematical concept he or she needs to have these prerequisite skills. Anyone who has worked with a child with reading problems has realized that readiness skills are necessary before a child can make meaningful progress in actual reading. A similar situation holds true for mathematics. The major difference is that the prerequisite and support skills in the case of mathematics are closely related to cognitive skills and a skill that is a prerequisite skill for subtraction becomes a support skill for division and other related topics. Therefore, it is important to find out if the child has all the necessary prerequisite skills before we begin to teach a particular concept. As a rule, a certain portion of a child's time should be devoted to the development of prerequisite skills such as

- classification/class inclusion
- matching/one-to-one correspondence
- ordering and sequencing
- following sequential directions
- spatial orientation and space organization
- estimation
- visual clustering
- pattern recognition and extension
- logical deduction and induction

This list is not exhaustive but indicates how nonmathematical skills such as these effect mathematical conceptualization. These skills are best acquired in a nonmathematical context. Nevertheless, their presence is definitely needed in a child's repertoire, as can be illustrated by the following example. Let us assume that a child has to find the product of

$$\begin{array}{r} 49 \\ \times 58 \\ \hline \end{array}$$

To find this product, one has to follow more than 10 sequential directions. If the student is not able to follow sequential directions, he or she may have difficulty in any of the many algorithms at the elementary level and beyond. The same thing can be demonstrated about all of the prerequisite skills.

## APPROACHES TO LEARNER DESCRIPTIONS: REPORTS FROM CLINICS

Various approaches are taken to describe the findings about mathematically learning-disabled students. In the latter part of this section, we will give examples of a few reports. But first it is important to discuss what information is of value to the users of this information: the student, parents, the classroom teacher, the remedial teacher, the resource room teacher/tutor, and others who are going to provide services to this student.

Bateman (1967) identified and discussed three approaches to learner descriptions: etiological, diagnostic-remedial, and task-analytical from a more general point of view of the Specific Learning Disabled (SLD) child. Using the same approach, we can describe the mathematics learning problems of and the related findings about the SLD child.

The etiological approach, which focuses on the causes of the disability, is generally involved with descriptions of the types of deficiencies and the damages to the child's psychological, neurological, and cognitive system that may cause a specific type of mathematics disability. Though this type of description and information is meant for everyone concerned, classroom teachers and remedial tutors find it inadequate. They are not able to or not trained to transform this information into practical use for the users, particularly the school personnel. The amount of technical data and the approach to the description of the child are not in the reach of many. This type of information has to be supplemented by information that can directly tell the teacher to do what is needed. Neurological reports and other reports from medical centers fall in this category.

The diagnostic-remedial approach to description, which was developed to bridge the gap between etiologically oriented diagnosis and educational programming, focuses on the outcome of the assessment procedures that provide information about basic disabilities in the perceptual-motor processes, expressive, receptive-integrative language functions, cognitive development, neurological functioning, quantitative behavior, and appropriate prerequisite mathematical skills. In this approach information about perceptual-motor deficits, language difficulties, and quantitative learning deficits is correlated and implications are spelled out in order to make this information meaningful to remedial teachers, tutors, and classroom teachers.

The task-analysis approach to the description of learners is very much an educational deficits approach and is most popular with educators involved with children who have learning problems in mathematics. This approach deemphasizes processes within the child and emphasizes the specific educational tasks the child needs to accomplish and be taught. Tasks are designed to assess the pupil's status within the task hierarchy (i.e., what he or she knows, does not know, needs to know, etc.). In the determination of the learning/skill hierarchies in content, guidance is provided by established scope and sequences lists and curriculum guides by such researchers as Gagné (1977) and Brownell (1929).

Appendixes 8-A, 8-B, and 8-C include reports that incorporate the elements discussed above. They include diagnostic information, a description of mathematical deficiencies, possible etiologies of problems, and remedial suggestions.

The reports give an example of the information that is being provided by many of the mathematics clinics to the parents and teachers of children who are having difficulty in learning mathematics. These mathematics clinics are serving three most important functions:

1. They provide an important service—diagnosis, remedial suggestions, placement in appropriate learning environment—to the children with learning problems in mathematics.
2. They involve professionals from different fields in order to bring a wider perspective to the problem, which thus far had been limited to the explorations by educators and isolated specialists.
3. They bring the research from different fields and specialists to the classroom teacher and other school personnel's attention through the diagnostic reports and interactions that these clinical settings provide.

## SUMMARY

This chapter has shown that clinical diagnosis in mathematics is a growing and developing field. Work in mathematics clinics is going to have important effects on the teaching of mathematics and dealings with children and adults who have disabilities in mathematics. Secondly, it will have a major impact on mathematics curricula, training of mathematics specialists—diagnosticians and tutors—and research on mathematical conceptualization. Mathematics clinics will provide the platform for interaction among professionals working on the problems of mathematics learning and children with mathematics disability.

**REFERENCES**

Bateman, B. (1967). Three approaches to diagnosis and educational planning for children with learning disabilities. *Academic Therapy Quarterly.*

Brownell, W.A. (1929, September). Remedial cases in arithmetic. *Peabody Journal of Education.*

Connelly, A.J., Nachtman, W., & Pritchett, M. (1976). *KeyMATH diagnostic arithmetic text.* Circle Pines, MN: American Guidance Service, Inc.

Denckla, M., & Marolda, M. (1979). Private communications and conversations relating to their work with children with learning disabilities and mathematics learning problems.

Gagné, R.M. (1977). *The conditions for learning*. New York: Holt, Rinehart and Winston.

Piaget, J. (1965). *The child's conception of number*. New York: Norton Library.

Piaget, J., & Inhelder, B. (1965). *The psychology of child*. New York: Norton Library.

Skemp, R.R. (1963). A three-part theory of learning mathematics. In F.W. Land (Ed.), *New approaches to mathematics learning*. London: Macmillan & Co. Ltd.

Wheatley, G.H. (1978, January). Hemispheric specialization and cognitive development: Implications for mathematics education. *Journal for Research in Mathematics Education*.

# Appendix 8-A

# Diagnostic Evaluation of Mathematics Learning and Achievement

This is a report from the Center for Teaching/Learning of Mathematics.

Mark was referred to the Center by Dr. Margaret B., Massachusetts General Hospital, Boston. Her report indicated that Mark showed marked deficiencies in the area of mathematics. During the formal and informal testing procedures Mark was very cooperative. Although Mark's mother reported that Mark was reluctant to attempt mathematics tasks, Mark was very polite and attentive during all the evaluation activities. Mark did make some comments about his not doing so well on mathematics tests and examinations. He also made it clear that he is always anxious about mathematics. Even before the testing he said that he expected to do poorly on the testing because he thought he did not remember many things in mathematics. This attitude, we feel, may have affected some of his performance.

On the *Concrete Operational Reasoning Test* and *Formal Operational Test,* his performance on many of the activities indicated that he is operating in the beginning to middle part (approximately 14 years of age) of the formal operational stage of cognitive development (this stage extends from 12 years to 16 years of age in most children). He missed items on the *Concrete Operational Reasoning Test* and several items on the *Formal Reasoning Test,* showing that there is a carryover from the concrete operational stage. This means that intellectually (cognitively) on mathematics ideas he is operating at a slightly lower level than his chronological age. The implication of this finding is that many of the mathematical concepts (particularly the abstract form of the concepts), if not presented to him through concrete models and experimental activities, may be difficult for him to concep-

Reprinted with permission of the Center for Teaching/Learning of Mathematics.

199

tualize. Therefore, he still needs some concrete and visual models to understand and conceptualize abstract mathematical ideas. Mathematical instruction using concrete models and activities will definitely help him to make up for this developmental lag. For example, even in quantitative concepts he needs to see a concrete model to understand an abstract concept. Repeated abstract work without concrete examples will continue to compound the problem.

Apart from this cognitive developmental lag, another reason for Mark's problems in mathematics seems to be contributed by his difficulty with prerequisite and support skills such as classification, class inclusion, sequential logic, transitivity, estimating, pattern recognition (and its extension to generalize concepts), visualization and visual clustering. Work with mathematical operations (addition, subtraction, multiplication, and division) will be meaningless, particularly with fractions, signed numbers, decimals, percentages, etc., until Mark has a good understanding and grasp of the concrete models of these concepts and these pre-skills. For example, because of the lack of estimation, Mark does not question his answers to see whether he is in the range of right answers or not and as a result either he does not check his answers or when he checks them he repeats the same procedure with the same mistakes. Difficulty with transitivity results in difficulty with proofs and multistep operations. His spatial orientation/space organization ability is better but because of limited training in using this ability he has great difficulty in visualizing math problems, particularly problem solving and the applications of mathematical ideas.

Mark shows a high level of anxiety in doing mathematical problems. This anxiety seems to be the result of continuous failures in mathematics and is now beginning to affect his self-concept. Failure in mathematics in the earlier grades results in the lowering of the student's self-concept, which in turn results in mathematics anxiety. Thus mathematics anxiety in the earlier grades is the symptom of mathematics learning problems. In the later grades this mathematics anxiety becomes the cause of mathematics learning problems.

During the evaluation, Mark's approach to reproduction tasks is global in nature; when it comes to analyzing and focusing on the components of the task he was not able to do so. On the successive administration (copying a drawing first when it is in front of him and later from memory at different intervals of time—

immediately after, 20 minutes after, and a week later) we observed that he left out successively more items (more than usual) on the details aspects of the picture but not on the global aspects of the diagram, showing that his approach to learning concepts and to processing of information about problems is more global in quality. This indicates that his approach to learning mathematics is to look for the whole-to-part information first and then for specific idea and pattern. Mark processes mathematical information visually/spatially, wholistically, and intuitively, indicating that he has a qualitative mathematical personality. This means that to conceptualize mathematical ideas he needs visual/spatial and continuous (Cuisenaire rods, Dienes' blocks, etc.) materials. He is good in the qualitative aspects of mathematical concepts (geometry, applications of mathematics). His approach to problem solving is inductive, qualitative, and therefore many times Mark misses the specific idea and is not able to connect ideas and concepts.

This lack of generalization results in Mark having no or very little understanding of interrelationships between different mathematics concepts and facts. In other words, when he learns the mathematics concepts he does not see the interconnections between those concepts. Also if he is not asked to point out the specifics of the problem he misses the details of the problem resulting in his feeling that he knows the concepts but actually he does not. Most arithmetic concepts and many of the algebraic concepts are sequential in nature and they are presented in a sequential manner and a student like Mark who needs to see the connections between different concepts from a global point of view misses out. The "whys" of these students must be answered in order to give them the security needed in the learning process. In a classroom situation (or other tutoring situations) Mark will benefit tremendously if most of the mathematics material is presented to him in a visual/ spatial manner.

Mark's understanding of mathematical concepts is superficial—having no concrete or visual models behind the concept; therefore he is not able to apply and connect ideas together. He relies heavily on his memory rather than understanding. More specifically, his mastery of arithmetic facts is not automatic. His estimates of computations are very far from the range of acceptable answers. His understanding of fractions is very superficial; conversions from fractions to decimals and vice versa are very difficult for him. He has very little understanding of percents, ratio, and proportion concepts. He can manipulate simple algebraic concepts if the arithmetic involved is simple and the concept is a primary one. Word problems involving even the simple arithmetic concepts are difficult for him and he refuses to attempt them. He has a fairly good understanding of geometrical shapes and their relationships. In summary, his mathematical performance is several years lower than his grade level.

**Suggestions for Remediation**

1. Mark's mathematics program should not only include mathematical content but should also include working with mathematical support skills: estimation, transitivity, pattern recognition, sequential logic, and spatial orientation/space organization tasks. Lack of mastery in prerequisite skills is contributing to his difficulty with the basic arithmetical operations.
2. All of the planned activities should begin with giving him a concrete model of the mathematical idea first and then the abstract representation of that concept. There should be a conscious effort to connect arithmetic concepts to algebraic concepts, i.e., begin with an arithmetic idea and then extend it to show its generalization into the algebraic concepts. Mark needs to be helped in seeing the connections between different mathematical concepts, relations, and facts.
3. Before Mark performs any arithmetic operations he should be asked to give an estimate first. He should be asked to verbalize the procedures he is going to adopt in solving the problem and when he has completed the problem he needs to compare his estimate of the answer. If there is any discrepancy between the two he should be encouraged to discuss the reasons. He should also articulate the steps he has taken in completing the problem and should be asked whether he knows any other problems that are similar to the one he just completed.
4. Since Mark is hasty and careless when doing mathematics work it might be useful to devise structural procedures such as developing lists of steps to be checked off during problem solving.
5. Mark needs one-to-one individual mathematics tutoring together with continued small group instruction. He has the potential to do simple algebra work if the appropriate preskills are inculcated and if the proper connections between arithmetic and algebraic concepts are made.

6. Every remedial session with Mark should have the following components:

   - developing of preskills (¼ of the total session time)
   - arithmetic work (¼ of the total session time)
   - visualization of problems and ideas (¹⁄₁₀ of the tutorial time)
   - verbalization of the procedures (¹⁄₁₀ of the tutorial time)
   - helping Mark to form problems relating to the concept (¹⁄₁₀ of the tutorial time)
   - working with related algebraic concepts (⅕ of the total tutorial time)
   - Each remedial session with Mark for the next few months should have the following components:
     —counting forward beginning with a given number, e.g., begin with 53 and count forward by 2's, 3's, 5's, 10's, .1, ⅕, etc.
     —counting backwards beginning with a given number, e.g., begin with 97 and count backward by 1's, 2's, 5's, 10's, ⅙, .2, etc.
     —showing patterns of number facts, e.g., $4+4=8$ then $4+5=$  ; $0+8=8$, $8+10=18$, then $18+10=$  ; $a$, $a+x$, $a+2x$, $a+3x$, what will be the next entry, etc.
     —visualization of number operations, e.g., think of the number 16 in your mind. What is two before, what is two after it, etc.

7. Since Mark is conscious of his failures in mathematics he needs to see some success. It is, therefore, important to begin with a topic where he has not seen any failure and where it is relatively certain that he will experience some definite success.

8. Mark will have a better time with geometry if he is first helped by providing structures for proof and then a complete proof. He needs to be asked to give several examples for a given definition. He should be asked to make hypotheses, conjectures, and generalizations from a given set of information. Mark should be asked pointed questions about the written math material to check his reading comprehension about the given reading material in mathematics. Many of the problems stem from the lack of reading with meaning.

# Appendix 8-B

# Mathematics Diagnostic Evaluation and Assessment

This report is an example of a diagnostic evaluation from the learning disabilities clinic attached to a major hospital in the Boston area.

10 February 1982
RE: SCOTT H.
D.O.B.
D.O.E.
C.A.
GRADE 8

SCOTT H. was interviewed to assess his achievement, ability, and learning style in mathematics. He is reported to have had persistent difficulty in finding success in mathematics. This difficulty was noted early and pursued in a learning disabilities evaluation at the Massachusetts General Hospital. Mrs. H reports the finding of the evaluation noted dyscalculia and dysgraphia. Scott describes math as his worst subject and notably different from his good skills in reading and English. The purpose of this evaluation is to closely scrutinize Scott's achievement and learning style in mathematics so they may be considered in his future education plans.

TEST ADMINISTERED: *Mathematics Diagnostic/Prescriptive Inventory*

DISCUSSION:

Oral Counting: Appropriate Responses

Reprinted with permission of Diagnostician Maria Marolda, author of *Mathematics Diagnostic and Prescriptive Inventory*, Learning Disabilities Clinic, Dept. of Neurology, Children's Medical Center, Boston, Massachusetts.

Scott could count forward, count on, and count backwards satisfactorily. He could skip count by 10's, 5's, and 2's. When asked to generate an unfamiliar skip counting sequence (count by 10's starting at 7), he effectively used additive strategies, building up to an appreciation of the governing pattern.

## Basic Quantitative Concepts: Appropriate Responses

All basic quantitative concepts, including place value, seemed established, as would be expected. Basic fraction concepts seemed established, but more subtle interpretations and applications seemed elusive. Scott could interpret numbers with both discrete (set) continuous (rod) models, but was notably more facile with set models.

In the numerical problem-solving activities, Scott used direct, inductive strategies.

## Numerical Symbolism: Appropriate Responses

Scott could read and write numerals for whole numbers, fractions, and decimals.

In the dictated arithmetic activities, he relied on reauditorizing to recall the elements. He demonstrated appropriate use of operations signs and organizational skills in producing the problems.

## Arithmetic of Whole Numbers

Scott can find solutions to one-digit arithmetic facts, but is somewhat slow in actually producing them. In longer calculations, calling up the necessary facts was quite deliberate.

Scott can implement all four arithmetic operations accurately. However, once again he is somewhat slow in actually working through each step to reach a final solution.

Qualitatively, Scott seemed to benefit from "talking" himself through the various calculation procedures. This strategy seemed helpful in organizing and sequencing the necessary steps and, indeed, in slowing him down from his tendency to impulsively rush to a solution.

## Arithmetic of Fractions and Decimals: Some deficits

Although Scott is familiar with fraction notation, the rules for computing with fractions were not reliably available. He knew some, was unsure of some, and confused yet others. In contrast, decimal operations seemed well established. Scott seemed to have appropriate skills with percents and in translating from fractions to decimals to percents.

## Pre-Algebra Skills: Some Deficits

Although Scott reports he is familiar with integers, few reliable skills were present. He could evaluate sample algebraic expressions when substituting whole number values. He demonstrated few skills in solving simple algebraic equations.

## Informal Geometry

These informal geometric activities are particularly useful in providing clues about the predisposition of a child's particular cognitive style, postures brought to bear on learning experiences. The activities are informal, unpracticed, and unlearned. Thus, an individual's natural instincts are elicited and can be observed. Any difficulties or interferences with effective responses that are noted could then be considered to be potential compromises to formal mathematical activities.

Scott was familiar with the names of basic shapes. In the activities on the geoboard he seemed more comfortable. He relied on and effectively used the inherent structure of the geoboard to organize his approaches. Organizational difficulties, previously noted, seemed thus circumvented.

In three-dimensional geometric activities, Scott responded adequately. In the geometric problem-solving activities, he initially had difficulty formulating an approach. However, once the approach was clear he diligently pursued the presented problems, generating correct solutions.

In these activities and in others where highly perceptual cues were involved, Scott seemed to find the perceptual requirements and judgments difficult. He often used verbalization to interpret perceptual situations.

## Intuitive Problem Solving

Scott nicely applied arithmetic to real-life situations. His strategy was to interpret the situation with arithmetic sentences and then to do the appropriate calculation.

When asked to discern patterns governing analogues, sequences, and sets of objects, Scott responded quite nicely, with elegant solutions in the activities with sequences. This would indeed document good thinking strategies, typical of a bright boy.

## Behavioral Aspects

Scott was cooperative and hard-working throughout all tasks. Nevertheless, his lack of confidence in his mathematical ability and his subsequent chagrin at not seeming "smart" were always visible. He talked conversationally through all the activities. It seemed by doing so he (a) bought time to organize a strategy, (b) prepared an excuse for what he anticipated to be a failure, and (c) diverted the examiner from judging him not to be "smart" when indeed he thought he was/would like to seem "smart."

## Impression

Scott's skills in arithmetic are totally established and well-implemented with a familiar (for his age) exception in fraction operations. Pre-algebra skills are quite primitive, with few reliable skills with integers and solutions to simple equations present. Qualitatively, he was notably deliberate and at times downright slow in producing arithmetic facts and multistep calculations. Unfortunately, he seems to associate quality of performance with speed and then he rushes, often producing incorrect solutions. In longer calculations, his control of arithmetic facts deteriorates and imprecision intrudes.

Scott is most effective when he writes down all calculations and implements them in a "recipe" or "flowchart" manner, carefully verbalizing each step. These strategies seem to effectively address the idiosyncrasies of his learning style.

Scott demonstrates subtle recall deficits within mathematical contexts, specifically, recall of arithmetic facts and visual memory of overall designs.

Stylistically, he clearly prefers discrete stimuli and verbal interpretations. He approaches situations with step-by-step inductive strategies, gradually building to more general perspectives.

Under the stress of complexity, Scott's efforts are undermined by organizational, integration, and recall deficits. The issues seem to be primarily in producing fast, exact results. His efforts are further complicated in familiar activities with the presumption that he will not be successful and his self-deprecation further interferes with efficient production of solutions.

Scott seems considerably less effective when perceptual cues are present or perceptual judgments required. It should be noted that all of his deficits are of a subtle, high-level variety and emerge most dramatically with new or complex activities.

Scott's overall "math sense" is a source of real encouragement with good, sometimes elegant, thinking strategies available. Nevertheless, his efforts in familiar contexts are sometimes compromised by his prejudgment that he will not be successful and then he gives up. In unfamiliar activities for which he can make no prejudgment, he clearly likes to be challenged and is quite tenacious.

## Recommendations

With a mathematical profile like Scott's, where organizational and production issues predominate, the setting and atmosphere of the instructional situation are of paramount concern. Scott would seem to function well in small, structured, not particularly highly competitive (and thus highly production-oriented) situations. His and his parents' search for such a placement is highly endorsed.

Once in such a setting, the mathematical approaches should be carefully presented, with each step clearly identified, particularly organized, and sequenced for Scott, and then rehearsed often. The production requirements for speed and number of problems will have to be carefully monitored, since "overload" indeed affects his performance. Initially, for purposes of self-esteem, no particular modifications need be required. The instructor might merely be apprised of Scott's possible difficulty. However, in time, special considerations might be put in place when warranted. An important factor in Scott's success will be the nurturing of self-esteem with respect to his mathematical skills. To this end, circumstances to enhance his chances of success might be carefully orchestrated. Although more work with fractions, integers, and pre-algebra skills may be a part of his eighth grade year, some gentle review and refreshing of skills might be offered during the summer months to make him confident as he enters his new setting. Further, provisions for regular tutorial opportunities at home to review and mediate algebraic learning ongoing in the classroom might be helpful.

Scott should not be placed in the most competitive algebra grouping, but he also would not seem to benefit from a basic skills/pre-algebra course.

With mathematical profiles like Scott's, where learning idiosyncrasies are focused on issues of organization, production, and complexity, a continuing supportive effort should be anticipated. "Compensation" rather than cure might seem the concern.

With Scott's learning style instructional strategies should develop segmented strategies with meaningful, smaller components that are then carefully organized, sequenced, and rehearsed. A flowchart format is often a useful scheme to implement these strategies. The spiraling of such procedures to keep them current is essential.

Estimation skills and application of procedures may not be easy for Scott. Special strategies to approach situations, to evaluate their thrust, and then to estimate the solution should be developed. These strategies might themselves be verbal, step-by-step processes that can be easily assimilated and implemented.

A particular emphasis of the instructional program should be a conscientious presentation of "overview," whence the concept comes and where it goes, for Scott does not spontaneously appreciate these considerations. Indeed, he is likely to become "lost in the trees and overlook the forest."

Problem-solving activities should be an essential part of Scott's mathematical program. The mathematical thinking strategies they develop will help him in life. Further, they will build confidence in him by rewarding him for good thinking.

Furthermore, with students like Scott, formal standardized group tests are likely to reveal a minimal rather than a maximal level of skills. The requirements for precision and intricate organizational strategies are common to such tests and yet they are counter to Scott's learning postures. Interestingly, the multiple-choice format might be an advantage to him, since it provides some focus and approach strategy.

Scott is a nice young man and I wish him success in his future pursuits. If I can be of any further help, feel free to contact me at . . . . . . . .

# Diagnostic Evaluation of Mathematics Learning and Achievement

This is a report from the Center for Teaching/Learning of Mathematics.

Richard was referred to the Center by his mother. His mother indicated that Richard showed marked deficiencies in the area of mathematics and during this academic year had not performed well on class tests and examinations.

Our evaluation procedures were conducted to determine Richard's potential in learning mathematics, his mathematics learning style, his preparation for learning mathematics (prerequisite and basic skills needed to learn mathematics), his level of mathematics achievement and mastery, and his approach and attitude toward mathematics learning and its application to problem solving.

During the formal and informal testing procedures, Richard was very cooperative, polite, and attentive. Richard was very deliberate in performing the tasks to the point of perseverance.

On the *Concrete Operational Reasoning Test* and the *Formal Operational Test,* his performance indicates that he is operating in the later part (approximately 15 years of age) of the formal operational stage of cognitive development (this stage extends from 12 years to 16 years of age in most children). He missed only a few items on the *Concrete Operational Reasoning Test* and some items on the *Formal Reasoning Test,* showing that there is some carryover from the concrete operational stage. This means that intellectually (cognitively), he is operating at an appropriate level for his chronological age. But on the test of mathematical concepts we found that his performance indicates that he is operating at a much lower level than his grade level and his chronological age. It was also apparent that he has definite gaps

Reprinted with permission of the Center for Teaching/Learning of Mathematics.

in mathematical concepts. His mathematical knowledge is spotty to the point that many of the current concepts are difficult for him to conceptualize. On many of the algebraic concepts he made mistakes or gave partial answers because either he had limited information about the related arithmetic concepts or the mastery of the prerequisite skills from the earlier grades was quite limited. The implication of this finding is that many of the mathematical concepts (particularly the abstract form of the concepts) may be difficult for him to conceptualize if the related arithmetic concepts and the prerequisite skills are not mastered beforehand. Therefore, he has a good deal of making up to do. Mathematical instruction that incorporates work from earlier grades along with the corresponding prerequisite skills will definitely help him to make up for this performance lag.

Richard's problems in mathematics seem to be accentuated by his difficulty with prerequisite and support skills such as deductive and inductive logic, estimating, pattern recognition (and its extension to generalize concepts), and visualization. Work with algebraic operations will be meaningless, because he has not mastered many of the prerequisite skills such as fractions, signed numbers, decimals, percentages, and ratio and proportion, and translating mathematical expressions into English and vice versa. It seems that his work during the previous academic years was quite deficient. He needs to make up the work from the previous academic years to do well in current algebraic work and future mathematics learning. Although it will take much disciplined and regular work on Richard's part, he has the intellectual capability to be able to make up for this deficiency. He needs to develop organizational skills and better study habits. To develop a positive attitude towards mathematics he has to experience some success in mathematics.

Richard exhibits anxiety in doing mathematical problems. This anxiety seems to be the result of earlier failures in mathematics and is now beginning to affect his self-concept.

During the evaluation, Richard's approach to reproduction tasks was sequential in nature. He can analyze and focus on the components of the task but he was not able to generalize the global concepts. On successive administration (copying a drawing first when it is in front of him and later from memory at different intervals of time—immediately after, 20 minutes after, and a week later), we observed that he was good in short- and long-term memory and this fact can be a plus factor in his remedial program. His approach to learning concepts and to processing information about problems is more sequential in nature. This indicates that his approach to learning mathematics is to look for the part-to-whole information, that is, focusing on specific information first and then looking for the general idea and pattern. Richard processes mathematical information from component to component, logically indicating that he has a quantitative mathematical personality. This means that to conceptualize mathematical ideas he needs a sequential approach. He could do quite well in algebra once the deficiencies are made up.

His approach to problem solving is deductive, quantitative, and therefore many times Richard misses the general idea and is not able to see connecting links. This lack of generalization of ideas from particular to abstract results in mathematics facts that for him have no or very little relationship with each other. In other words, when he learns mathematics concepts he does not see the interconnections between those concepts. Also if he is not asked to point out the general relations he himself may not be able to form those connections. He misses the details of the problem resulting in his feeling that he knows the concepts but actually he does not. Since most arithmetic concepts and many of the algebraic concepts are sequential in nature and are presented in a sequential manner, a student like Richard who has that ability can do quite well, but at present he has developed an attitude that is getting in the way of learning. He needs structure and training in organizing incoming information. These students do not ask pertinent questions and therefore the teacher has to provide all the necessary information that is needed but not asked for. In a classroom situation (or other tutoring situations), Richard will benefit tremendously if before he begins to solve the problem he is asked to articulate the procedure he is going to follow and after he is finished with the problem he is asked again to repeat the steps he had taken in solving the problem. He should also be encouraged to make visual and oral models of mathematical problems.

Richard's understanding of many of the mathematical concepts is superficial—having few concrete or visual models behind the concepts—therefore, he does not apply the ideas and generally does not connect ideas. He relies heavily on his memory rather than understanding. He should be guided to make connections between different mathematical concepts by discerning emerging patterns between them.

**Suggestions for Remediation**

1. Richard's mathematics program should not only include mathematical content but should also include working with mathematical support and arithmetic skills: estimation, pattern recognition, sequential logic, basic facts, fraction word problems, and spatial orientation/space organization tasks. Lack of mastery in prerequisite skills is contributing to some of his difficulty with basic arithmetical operations.

2. All of the planned activities should begin with giving him a concrete model of the mathematical idea first and then the abstract representation of that concept. There should be a conscious effort to connect arithmetic concepts to algebraic concepts, i.e., begin with an arithmetic idea and then extend it to show its generalization into the algebraic concepts. Richard needs to be helped in seeing the connections between different mathematical concepts, relations, and facts.

3. Before Richard performs any algebraic operations he should be asked to give the procedure for solving the problem. For example, in the case of a problem that involves numerical values, he should be asked to verbalize the procedures he is going to adopt and give an estimate of the answer. When he has completed the problem he needs to compare his estimate of the answer with the actual answer. If there is any discrepancy between the two, he needs to be encouraged to discuss the reasons for that discrepancy. He should also articulate the steps he has taken in completing the problem and should be asked whether he knows other problems that are similar to the one he just completed.

4. Richard needs a good deal of extra special individual mathematics tutoring and an organized plan of action. His work has to be closely monitored and regular mathematical activity has to be included in the study time. For example, he needs to do a certain amount of mathematics every day in a structured environment. He has the potential of making up the missing work and even doing well in mathematics including algebra. His success in mathematics is conditioned on his making up the missing preskills and basic arithmetic concepts: fractions, percents, averages, ratio and proportion, etc. He should also develop efficient methods of solving arithmetic problems. At present his methods are very inefficient. This is one area where he might benefit from some tutoring in order to develop effec-

tive methods to improve his performance on examinations and tests.

In summary, Richard is an intelligent and capable student who does have some difficulty in learning mathematics and with some effort, discipline, and structure can realize his potential. Once he makes up the deficiencies in arithmetic skills he will do well in algebra and geometry. If you have any questions about this report and if we can provide any help please feel free to call me at . . . . . . . .

# Chapter 9

# Assessment Techniques and Practices for Classroom Behaviors, Social/Emotional Factors, and Attitudes

*Mary E. Cronin*

Although learning-disabled students receive special education services for an academic problem such as math, many are considered to be classroom behavior problems as well. Some learning-disabled students are unable to interact with peers or teachers appropriately. Many exhibit inappropriate behaviors such as fighting, swearing, roaming about the room, not working, or destroying property. Still others are withdrawn, negative toward school, or have poor work habits. McLoughlin and Lewis (1981) identified five categories of behavior that interfere with a student's capacity to deal with nonacademic demands of the instructional environment. Those categories include (1) classroom behavior, (2) study skills and work habits, (3) social interactions and relationships, (4) a student's attitude, and (5) the influence of environment on a student's behavior.

Some teachers are not properly trained to pinpoint a student's actual problem, be it academic or behavioral. Many times teachers are unable to separate the two problems. Nevertheless, teachers are considered to be the best source in evaluating classroom problems (L. Brown, 1983). The focus of this chapter is to help the teacher identify those nonacademic problem behaviors in a school situation. Three general areas will be addressed (1) general classroom behaviors, (2) social/emotional factors, and (3) attitudes. A brief overview of each category will be given. In addition, assessment procedures appropriate for each category will be presented. Those procedures include a summary of the ecological approach, informal assessment methods, and available norm-referenced/published instruments.

## GENERAL CLASSROOM BEHAVIORS

Every teacher at one time or another experiences students who are behavior problems in the classroom. Classroom behavior, according to

McLoughlin and Lewis (1981), refers to the student's capacity to deal with the nonacademic demands of the instructional environment. It is those students who fail to deal with the nonacademic demands that present the major behavioral problems in the classroom. Failure to hand in homework, complete work, follow rules, bring materials, cope with stress, or control anger often produces such inappropriate behaviors as withdrawal, swearing, fighting, refusal to cooperate, yelling, kicking, and the like.

It goes without saying that learning-disabled students are not immune to such behaviors. Quite the contrary. Many learning-disabled students exhibit these behaviors and more. Many times students with learning problems will demonstrate a sampling of such behaviors out of frustration, anger, fear, or the inability to perform tasks. The teacher's ability to identify when, where, and why these behaviors are happening is essential in programming a student's success in the classroom.

## SOCIAL/EMOTIONAL FACTORS

Social/emotional factors play a primary role in the learning-disabled student's achievement in the classroom. If a learning-disabled student has difficulty following rules and interacting with peers, teachers, and other adults, more than likely the student will experience negative feelings, rejection, and a general dislike for school.

Consequently, when a student is not functioning adequately both socially and academically in school, emotional factors tend to pervade. The student then shows signs of frustration, anger, anxiety, fear, sadness, mood swings, and becoming overly upset under normal circumstances. Lack of attention to social/emotional development clearly presents a barrier to learning.

Many students, especially those with learning problems, tend to display social/emotional problems in relation to a specific academic area such as mathematics. Parents and teachers alike often give their children the impression that learning mathematics is difficult, not pleasant, and an almost impossible task at times. Admittedly, this is the consequence of poor learning experiences in mathematics on the part of the parent and/or teachers. Many students suffer "emotional" or stress attacks (e.g., stomach ache, sore throat, crying, headache, panic, etc.) prior to math class. A student's emotional well-being and favorable attitude toward school-related tasks are essential prerequisites to effective learning.

## ATTITUDES

The attitudes of a learning-disabled student will affect his or her feelings toward peers, teachers, school, academic subjects, and the learning process in general. In addition, the classroom behavior of the learning-disabled student may be influenced by the feelings and attitudes of others.

Attitude is defined as a general emotional disposition towards any person, place, or thing. Many believe that people's attitudes or feelings toward themselves, others, and tasks given will affect their success or failure in a particular situation (Estes, Estes, Richards, & Roettger, 1981; Haladyna, Shaughnessy, & Shaughnessy, 1983; McLoughlin & Lewis, 1981; Michaels & Forsyth, 1978; Shaughnessy, Haladyna, & Shaughnessy, 1983). Teachers believe this is particularly true of students' attitudes toward subjects studied in school (Michaels & Forsyth, 1978). Consequently, of all the academic areas taught, the negative feelings of students toward mathematics appear to be the area of most concern to teachers.

It is most important that teachers are aware of students' feelings toward academic subjects. Frustration with rules, poor academic performance, and social problems give the students negative attitudes. Many times these attitudes contribute to such negative behaviors as tardiness, absenteeism, and inappropriate classroom behaviors (McLoughlin & Lewis, 1981).

The ability of a teacher to identify and understand a student's classroom behavior, social/emotional development, and attitudes will assist in programming for that student's success. The following section will outline assessment techniques available to the teacher in order to obtain this type of information.

## ASSESSMENT OF CLASSROOM BEHAVIORS, SOCIAL/EMOTIONAL FACTORS, AND ATTITUDES

The assessment of classroom behavior, social/emotional factors, and attitudes is necessary if a teacher is going to plan a comprehensive program geared to the needs of a student. Such assessment is often more difficult than assessment of academic performance. Ingram (1980) offers the following reasons:

1. It is not always possible to establish absolute criteria to differentiate between normal and abnormal behavior.
2. Teacher training in the social/emotional area is more highly varied than in the academic areas.
3. Emotional problems are often manifested as inappropriate classroom behavior. The teacher is forced to deal with a symptom instead of a cause. Referral for further assessment on the basis of the symptom is occasionally interpreted as a lack of ability on the part of the teacher to maintain effective disci-

pline. Therefore, teachers may be hesitant to make a referral for further assessment. (p. 242)

Traditionally, classroom behaviors have been assessed by asking teachers and parents to identify students' problem behaviors. The same is true when assessing factors affecting a student's social/emotional development and attitudes. This section will address three major aspects related to the assessment of classroom behavior, social/emotional factors, and attitudes of students. Those trends are the ecological approach to assessment, informal methods, and norm-referenced/published instruments.

### Ecological Approach to the Assessment of Behaviors

The assessment of classroom behaviors traditionally focuses on the negative attributes of specific students such as peer problems, attitudes, inappropriate behaviors, etc. In recent years many educators have promoted investigating not only individual student behaviors but also the environments in which the student functions (L. Brown, 1983; Feagans, 1972; Laten & Katz, 1975; Wallace & Larsen, 1978; Wiederholt, Hammill, & V. Brown, 1983; Wright, 1967). This particular approach to assessing student behavior is referred to as the *ecological approach*.

The ecological approach is a comprehensive system of data collection on various behaviors (classroom, academic, social/emotional, attitude, etc.) of students in the many environments in which they operate. The three major environments studied in most ecological assessments are school, home, and community. Each of these major environments can be studied in terms of the smaller ecologies existing within them. Wiederholt, Hammill, and V. Brown (1983) suggest that teachers limit their investigations to the environments subsisting within the school. Examples of such ecologies include the classroom, gym, math class, music room, art room, resource room, cafeteria, social studies class, playground, etc. Wiederholt et al. (1983) recommend that a comprehensive ecological assessment outside the school environment is too time-consuming and should be done by other professionals (e.g., the social worker or school psychologist).

L. Brown (1983) cites two problems that are avoided when employing ecological assessment procedures. First, this approach provides a broader and more natural picture of the student than more traditional methods. The second problem avoided is misjudging where the problem lies. Ecological assessment assumes that many factors may cause or aggravate behavioral problems, whereas customary assessment techniques assume the student is or has the problem.

The versatility of the ecological approach is endless. Not only can negative aspects of a student or environment be studied but also the positive elements can be highlighted (Wallace & Larsen, 1978). This alerts the teacher to the methods, techniques, or aspects of a particular ecology that are different from the ones employed in their classroom. The awareness, and hopefully, if appropriate, even the incorporation of those discrepancies may make a difference in the student's level of success (both academic and behavioral) in a particular classroom situation.

Laten and Katz (1975) suggest a five-phase approach when undertaking an ecological assessment. Those phases are:

1. Referral
   a. Engaging the environment for data collection on perceptions of the problem.
   b. Gathering information from the system which triggered the referral.
   c. Gathering information from the systems which support the referral.
   d. Gathering information about the systems which do not support the referral.
   e. Mapping the information.
2. Expectations
   a. Gathering information about expectations from the problematic situations.
   b. Gathering information about expectations in successful situations.
   c. Mapping the expectations.
3. Behavioral Descriptions
   a. Data collection on the interactions and skills of the people involved in the problematic situations.
   b. Data collection on the interactions and skills of the people involved in successful situations.
4. Summary of Data
5. Setting Reasonable Expectations (pp. 40–41)

One way of visually representing an ecological study of a student is an ecological map (see Figure 9-1). This illustration indicates the various school environments that Sandy frequents during a school day. Sandy's math teacher, Ms. Hall, has become very concerned with Sandy's off-task behavior (e.g., out of seat, talking, daydreaming, sharpening pencils, etc.) during math class, especially during individual work periods. After consulting with Sandy's other teachers and collecting data on Sandy in her

**Figure 9-1** Ecological Map of Sandy—Off-Task Behavior

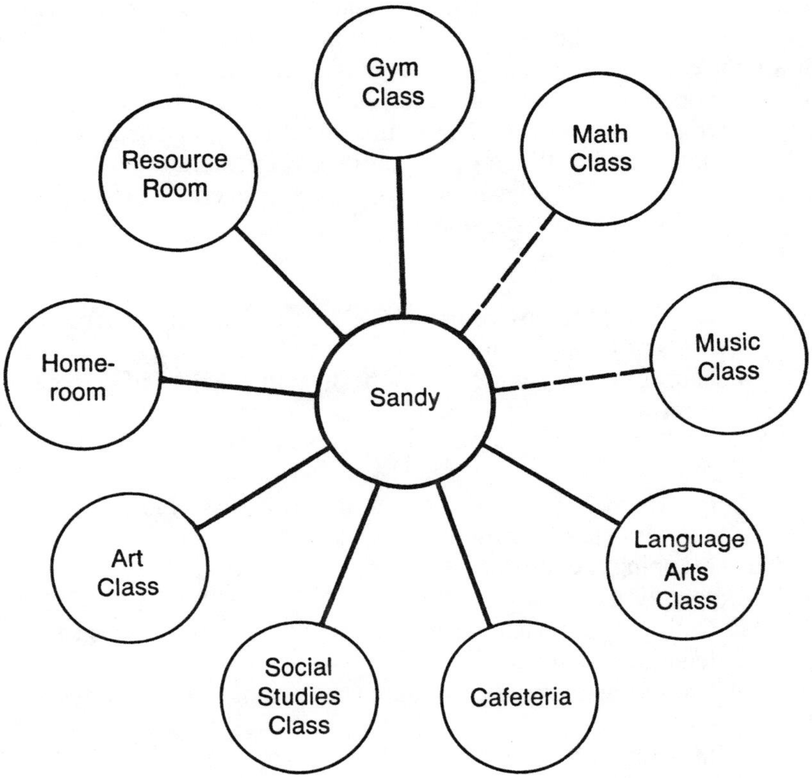

classes, Ms. Hall realized that Sandy was consistently off-task during math and music classes. The two problem classes are indicated by a broken line on the ecological map. Upon further investigation, Ms. Hall noticed that the teachers in social studies, art, language arts and the resource room all gave Sandy shorter assignments more frequently during a class period. In addition, Sandy's other teachers sometimes let her work in a study carrel, which cut down on the stimulus in the environment that usually distracted Sandy from her work. This information led Ms. Hall to a similar plan of action in dealing with Sandy's off-task behavior in math class.

The informal methods and norm-referenced/published instruments discussed throughout the next sections will provide techniques by which teachers can collect data on students when utilizing the ecological approach. Further information on conducting an ecological assessment can be obtained from the following sources: L. Brown (1983); Feagans (1972); Laten and Katz (1975); Wiederholt, Hammill, and V. Brown (1983); Wright (1967); Wallace and Larsen (1978); and Thurman (1977).

**Informal Methods of Assessment**

Teachers use informal methods of assessment on a daily basis. One of the major advantages of informal assessment procedures is their relevance to instruction (McLoughlin & Lewis, 1981). Informal assessment techniques are a means by which teachers are able to collect, evaluate, and use information about the students they teach. These data, either academic, classroom behavior, social/emotional, or attitudinal, are then used to establish goals, select strategies, and measure outcomes (Guerin & Maier, 1983). Selection of a particular method usually depends on (1) time involved, (2) type of data needed, (3) questions to be answered, and (4) type of behavior assessed.

A teacher's ability to systematically utilize informal assessment techniques is critical to the success of students in his or her class. The information obtained from informal procedures is valuable in programming to the demands of the student's environment instead of a norm group (McLoughlin & Lewis, 1981).

This section outlines six popularly used informal assessment procedures commonly employed by teachers. This sample is by no means inclusive of the methods available. It can serve as a catalyst by which teachers may incorporate ideas of their own. Table 9-1 provides a handy reference to guide teachers in selecting the techniques thought to be most useful when assessing classroom behavior, social/emotional factors, and/or attitudes.

**Table 9-1** Informal Methods of Assessment

| Method | Classroom Behavior | Social/ Emotional Factors | Attitudes |
|---|---|---|---|
| Checklists | * | * | * |
| Interviews | * | * | * |
| Q-Sorts | * | * | * |
| Sociograms | | * | |
| Time-on-Task | * | | * |
| Self-Assessment | * | * | * |

## Teacher-Made Checklists

Teachers will find that in a number of instances an informal checklist based on a particular set of classroom and/or academic behaviors is the most helpful assessment device. Only after careful study of student behavior, environments, and management techniques can a useful and efficient instrument be developed.

Wiederholt, Hammill, and V. Brown (1983) recommend that generally a checklist should cover three categories of behaviors: (1) student behaviors, (2) teacher-student interactions, and (3) student-student interactions. The number of specific behaviors that can be itemized under each of the categories is endless but should be limited to as few questions as possible. Another suggestion offered by Wiederholt et al. is that after determining the problem in a specific category one should probe the problem in depth.

A sample behavior checklist adapted by V. Brown (undated) from a checklist by Dawson, McLeod, and Mathews (1976) is presented in Appendix 9-A. The *Behavioral Checklist for Determining Match of Student: Class/School* addresses general school behaviors rather than subject specific or academic behaviors.

## Interviews

Conducting an interview is a helpful informal technique to obtain information regarding a student. Interviews can be conducted with the student, teachers, and/or parents. Specific goals as to the purpose of an interview should be established beforehand.

Several types of information can be gathered during an interview session with a student. Basic demographic data on the student (e.g., age, grade, health, family information, etc.), perceived academic strengths and weaknesses, social contacts, relationships, and perceptions of teachers and/or the school environment are but a few of the topics that could be covered. Similar information gained from parents and/or teachers of the student would be appropriate in many instances.

The interview technique has been found to be quite useful in specific academic areas. Lankford (1974) offers an oral interview specifically designed for computation. Wiederholt, Hammill, and V. Brown (1983) suggest that Lankford's ten questions will help a teacher get started with mathematics interviewing in almost any situation. Wiederholt et al. point out that a "question" in a math interview is not necessarily asked in an interrogative format but provides a means of probing a student's thoughts or ideas:

1. Tell me about how you. . . .
2. Why did you. . . ?

3. How else could you. . . ?
4. As I do this problem, you tell me what you think I'm doing for each step.
5. You work this problem. As you do it, tell me out loud what you are doing.
6. How did you happen to. . . ?
7. How can you be sure that. . . ?
8. How can you find out if. . . ?
9. Show me how. . . .
10. If . . . then. . . ?

*Q-Sorts*

Q-Sorting is a technique used by teachers to compare interpretations of a single set of behaviors. The behaviors compared might be associated with classroom or home behaviors (Kroth, 1975) or with a specific set of skills such as independent study behaviors (V. Brown, undated). Some combination of teacher, parent, or student responses on a specified set of questions might be studied to determine differences of perceived knowledge.

A set of Q-Sort questions may be developed to evaluate a student's and/ or teacher's perceptions about the student's attitude in a specific academic area. The following Q-Sort statements were developed to evaluate the students' perceptions of themselves in math. After reading the math descriptors, the student is asked to arrange the descriptors twice on a chart such as the one illustrated in Exhibit 9-1. The student is first asked to sort the cards or statements according to the students real perceptions of his or her behaviors. The second sort represents the student's ideal view of himself or herself relative to those specified behaviors.

The Q-Sort format forces a relative evaluation of a student on a specific set of behaviors. The sort may be lengthened or shortened by expanding or reducing the number of items and the number of squares in the pyramid.

## *Math Q-Sort Descriptors*

1. don't like going to math class.
2. want to be a math teacher.
3. like to add.
4. like to subtract.
5. like to multiply.
6. like to divide.
7. like to use metrics.
8. understand math.

**Exhibit 9-1** Q-Sort Board

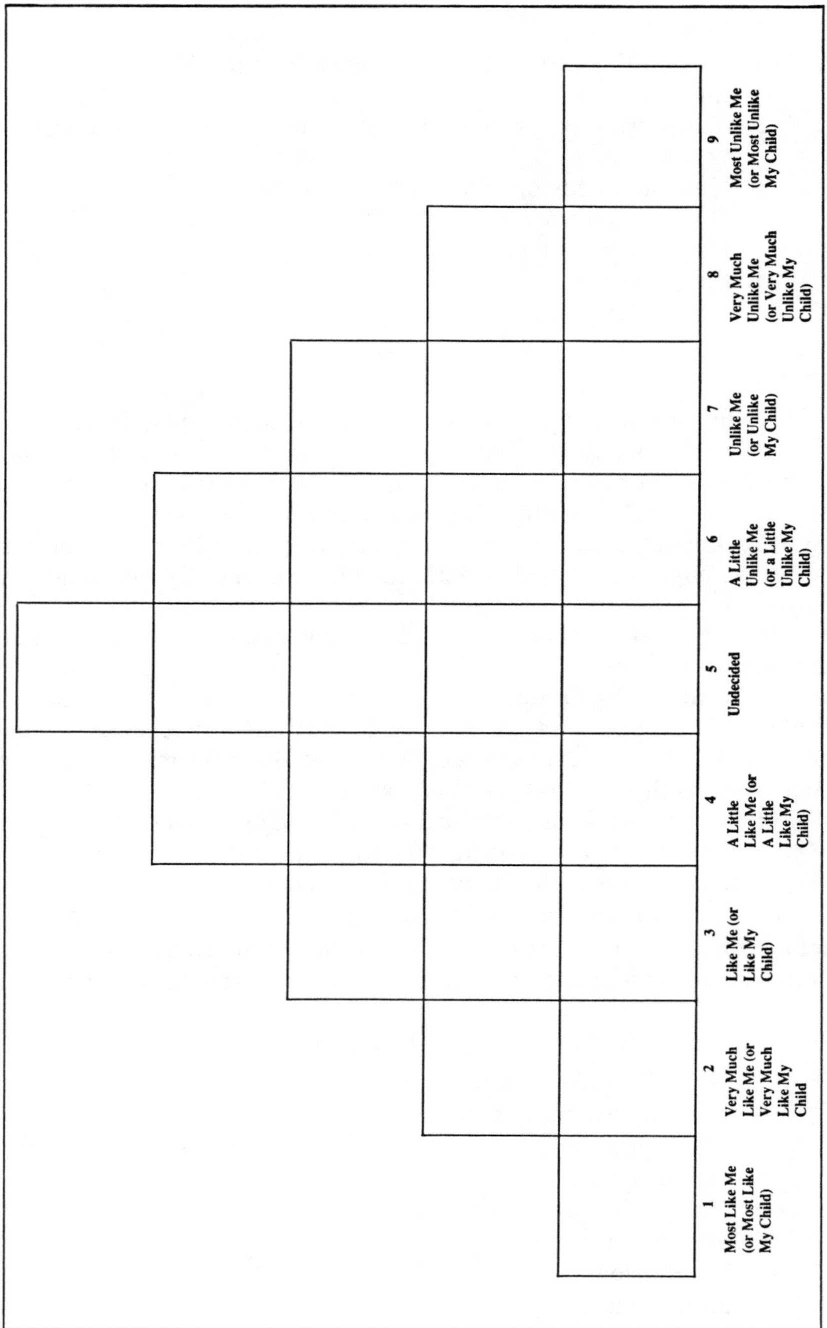

1
Most Like Me (or Most Like My Child)

2
Very Much Like Me (or Very Much Like My Child)

3
Like Me (or Like My Child)

4
A Little Like Me (or A Little Like My Child)

5
Undecided

6
A Little Unlike Me (or a Little Unlike My Child)

7
Unlike Me (or Unlike My Child)

8
Very Much Unlike Me (or Very Much Unlike My Child)

9
Most Unlike Me (or Most Unlike My Child)

9. would rather use a calculator.
10. enjoy math.
11. do as well in math as my friends.
12. ask for help in math.
13. would rather study math than anything else.
14. don't understand most math assignments.
15. finish all math assignments on time.
16. do as well as I can in math.
17. usually understand most math assignments.
18. like my math teacher.
19. score high on math tests.
20. like word problems.
21. like fractions.
22. like geometry.
23. enjoy using a ruler and compass.
24. would rather have math for homework than anything else.
25. like to solve problems.

## Sociograms

One technique of assessing a student's standing in a class is through a sociogram (Moreno, 1953). A sociogram is a measure of attractions and repulsions among members of a group, such as a class, based on an activity specified in stimulus questions. Students are asked to nominate the student(s) with whom they would like to play, eat, work, or perform any other type of classroom or social activity. The number of choices the student is permitted is limited to two or three classmates. This type of information will help the teacher in discerning the social structure within the group.

Figure 9-2 illustrates a sociometric analysis. In this example, the students were asked "Who would you like to tutor you in math?" As you can see, Brian was chosen by five of the twelve students as a good potential math tutor. Lee, Mary, Beth, and Linda were perceived as possible tutors by one other person. Ginger, Fred, Becky, Jim, Pat, and Gaye were not chosen.

L. Brown and Hammill (1978) offer two recommendations when using sociograms. First, at least twenty students should participate and, second, students taking part should have been in the class at least six weeks in order to permit the formation of relationships measured by sociograms.

### Time-on-Task

Time-on-task (TOT) is an open system of descriptive observation that is easy to learn and provides a way to restate behavior that would otherwise be possible through the use of video equipment (Wiederholt, Hammill, & V. Brown, 1983). The TOT format discussed here was adapted by V. Brown (undated) from Balla (1967).

The Brown-Balla system supplies traditional information (first three items below) such as that provided by Hall (1974) as well as additional information helpful to planning instructional activities (Wiederholt, Hammill, & V. Brown, 1983):

1. Percentage of time on task.
2. Percentage of time off task.
3. Ratio of on-task to off-task behaviors.
4. Patterns of work (e.g., rarely on task, work evenly paced over time allocation, sporadically paced over time allocation, etc.).

---

**Figure 9-2** Sociogram

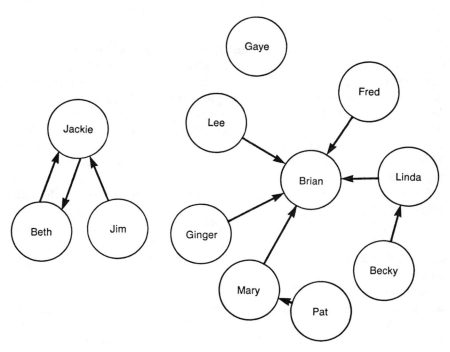

5. Behaviors that are incompatible with working (e.g., going to the wastebasket, daydreaming, or talking).
6. The percentages of time spent in each off-task activity.
7. What specifically seems to be distracting to the student—peers, self, objects, or atmosphere.

The system involves continuous recording of what the student does during a particular work or class period by an observation in 15-second intervals. A coding system is used in order that the behavior sequence can be read back. A sample of the recording procedure as suggested by V. Brown (undated) is shown in Exhibit 9-2. This four-minute sample of a math class shows Peggy to be on task approximately 25 percent of the time. Peggy spent the other 75 percent of her time talking to Bill, Mary, and Fred; playing with her ruler; and walking around the room.

---

**Exhibit 9-2** Time-on-Task for Peggy
Teacher Expectation: Complete assignment on fractions, alone, in 15 minutes at work station.

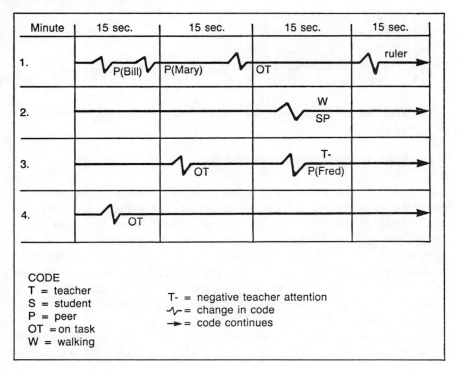

| Minute | 15 sec. | 15 sec. | 15 sec. | 15 sec. |
|---|---|---|---|---|
| 1. | P(Bill) | P(Mary) | OT | ruler |
| 2. | | | W / SP | |
| 3. | | OT | T- / P(Fred) | |
| 4. | OT | | | |

CODE
T = teacher
S = student
P = peer
OT = on task
W = walking

T- = negative teacher attention
ᐯ = change in code
→ = code continues

Wiederholt, Hammill, and V. Brown (1983) suggest that TOT can be used to generate hypotheses about a student; confirm or disconfirm comments made about the student's behavior in the classroom; and find out what does capture his or her attention. Although this method is subjective and observer judgment is difficult to verify, it is helpful to record all student behavior during specific time periods.

*Self-Assessment*

Glynn, Thomas, and Shee (1973) identified three basic components of behavioral self-control: (1) self-assessment; (2) self-monitoring; and (3) self-reinforcement. One of the components, self-assessment (SA), has been used effectively to gather data on various student behaviors (Blackwood, 1970; Bornstein & Quevillon, 1976; Kaufman & O'Leary, 1972).

SA is a procedure by which students systematically examine their own behavior and determine whether or not they have performed a specific behavior. Workman (1982) devised a step-by-step method for implementing SA procedures with students. The steps in setting up a SA program are:

1. Select a target behavior.
2. Devise a rating system.
3. Determine the rating system interval.
4. Design the mechanics of the system.
5. Implement the system. (p. 31)

A sample of the rating form for on-task behaviors during a math class is provided in Exhibit 9-3.

**Norm-Referenced/Published Instruments**

Recently several norm-referenced/published instruments for assessing classroom behavior, social/emotional factors, and attitudes have become available to teachers. Unfortunately, few of these instruments are norm-referenced and yield standardized results (L. Brown, 1983). L. Brown suggests limiting the use of such instruments to general observation and assessment because they provide only rough criteria for interpretation and have not demonstrated adequate reliability and validity data (Spivak & Swift, 1973). Despite their shortcomings, L. Brown does indicate that use is appropriate where they can be of some value.

Norm-referenced tests are difficult to use when assessing classroom behavior, social/emotional factors, or attitudes as it is difficult to establish

**Exhibit 9-3** Sample Rating Form

|        | M | T | W | Th | F |
|--------|---|---|---|----|---|
| 1:10   |   |   |   |    |   |
| 1:20   |   |   |   |    |   |
| 1:30   |   |   |   |    |   |
| 1:40   |   |   |   |    |   |

Each time I instruct you to do so, I want you to rate yourself on how well you have stayed on-task during math class. "On-task" means working on math problems, reading instructions from the math book, or looking at and listening to me while I demonstrate a problem on the board. Give yourself a "0" if you haven't been on-task at all, a "1" if you've been on-task part of the time, and a "2" if you've been on-task the whole time.

**Table 9-2** Norm-Referenced/Published Instruments

| Instrument | Classroom Behavior | Social/ Emotional Factors | Attitudes |
|------------|:------------------:|:-------------------------:|:---------:|
| BRP | * | * | |
| WPBIC | * | | |
| Perceived Competence Scale | | * | |
| Estes Attitude Scales | | | * |
| MAI | | | * |
| Inventory of Teacher Concern | * | * | * |

"norms" for these domains. Therefore it should not be surprising to discover the lack of appropriate instrumentation.

Six instruments were selected for discussion in this section. Table 9-2 lists the tests and the general area assessed (classroom behavior, social/ emotional factors, and/or attitudes) by the instrument.

*Behavior Rating Profile*

The *Behavior Rating Profile* (BRP) (L. Brown & Hammill, 1978) is an ecological assessment battery designed to identify students with behavior problems. It includes five norm-referenced scales and a sociogram that is appropriate for students ages 6 to 18 years and their parents and teachers. The six components of the BRP are independent and the individually normed measures can be used separately or in conjunction with other components. This measure includes not only teacher and parent perceptions but also includes student and peer ratings.

Three of the six components involve student input. The student is asked to classify each item given on the three Student Scales (Home, School, and Peers) as True or False. An example of a home item is "I often break rules set by my parents." "My teachers give me work I cannot do" is a sample school item and "I seem to get into a lot of fights" is one of the peer items. The fourth and fifth components of the BRP, the Parent and Teacher Rating Scales, require the informants to read a description of student behavior and respond to a four-point Likert scale: "Very much like my child," "Like my child," "Not like my child," "Not at all like my child." The BRP also allows sampling of the perceptions of the student's peers with a sociogram.

The norms of the BRP are available by the age or grade of the student and results are reported in scaled scores with a mean of 10 and a standard deviation of 3. According to the manual, scaled scores above 13 indicate positive perceptions of the student's behavior and scaled scores below 7 indicate negative perceptions.

The BRP has high internal consistency reliability with both normal and identified special education populations. Reliability coefficients consistently exceed .80. Two of the methods used to test the validity of the BRP include comparing it with several other behavior checklists and comparing results of varying populations (normal, learning-disabled, and emotionally disturbed students).

Results of the various scales of the BRP may be compared. It is possible to study the student's behavior in three settings (home, school, and with peers) and the student's perceptions of those settings. In summary, the BRP combines the strengths of the ecological format, the efficiency of checklists, and the critical information derived from a sociogram in a reliable, valid, and norm-referenced manner (Wiederholt, Hammill, & V. Brown, 1983).

### Walker Problem Behavior Identification Checklist

The *Walker Problem Behavior Identification Checklist* (WPBIC) (Walker, 1976) is a norm-referenced screening device for classroom teachers intended to help identify students with possible behavior problems. The WPBIC is designed for use with students in grades 4, 5, and 6. It is composed of 50 statements to be rated by the teacher. The five general behavior factors the WPBIC measures and a few sample items include: (1) acting out, "Complains about others' unfairness and/or discrimination towards him." (disruptive, aggressive behaviors); (2) withdrawal, "Tries to avoid calling attention to himself." (passive and avoidance behaviors); (3) distractibility, "Does not conform to limits on his own without control from others." (inattentivenes, restlessness); (4) disturbed peer relations, "Has no friends"; and (5) immaturity, "Argues and must have the last word in verbal exchanges."

Ratings by the teacher are converted to an overall total score. The manual states that total scores of 22 for males and 12 for females indicate disturbed performance.

Reliability for the WPBIC was studied by the split half method and a coefficient of .98 was obtained. Validity was investigated by comparing results of normal and disturbed students on the WPBIC. The teacher ratings of these two groups differ significantly. McLoughlin and Lewis (1981) suggested further validity study of the relationship between the WPBIC and other measures of student behavior.

## Perceived Competence Scale for Children

The *Perceived Competence Scale for Children* (Harter, 1979) measures a child's feelings of competence in three skill domains: (1) cognitive or intellectual skills (focus on school performance); (2) social skills (peer popularity); and (3) physical skills (sports and outdoor activities). A fourth component assesses the feelings of worth or self-esteem. The scale is designed for children in grades 3 through 6.

Each of the four subscales contains seven items. Half of the items are worded so that the first part of the statement reflects high perceived competence and the second part reflects low perceived competence.

A teacher's rating form is provided to check the child's perception with that of the teacher. The form contains the same items as the child's. The scoring procedure on both the child's and teacher's forms is the same.

Reliability coefficients range from .73 to .83. Special emphasis is placed on the scale's factor analysis. Validity of the scale was measured by subjecting each subscale to factor analysis across normed age groups.

## Estes Attitude Scales

The *Estes Attitude Scales* (Estes, Estes, Richards, & Roettger, 1981) were devised to measure a student's attitudes toward basic school subjects. The results of the scales provide a quantitative measure of the attitudes of individuals or of groups.

The *Estes Attitude Scales* are published in two forms, Elementary and Secondary. The Elementary Form measures the attitudes of elementary school children toward three school subjects (reading, mathematics, and science). The three 14-item Likert-type scales are intended for use with children from the end of second grade through sixth grade. Since no reading is required of the elementary children, the item content is easily understood by most. Each scale may be administered separately, or the entire battery may be given at one sitting.

The Secondary Form assesses the attitude of students in grades 7 through 12 toward one of the content areas: English, mathematics, reading, science, and social studies. The five 15-item Likert-type scales have readability levels of sixth grade. As with the Elementary Form, each of the scales may be administered separately or at one sitting.

Both the Elementary and Secondary Forms of the scales were examined for four types of validity: content, factorial, convergent, and discriminant. All tests for validity were found to be satisfactory. Extensive data on these studies can be found in the manual.

Alpha coefficient reliabilities were computed for both forms. Both were found to be suitable. Coefficients for the Elementary Form studies were .76–.88. The Secondary Form had a median of .86 with a range of .76–.93.

### Mathematical Attitude Inventory

The *Mathematical Attitude Inventory* (MAI) (Sandman, 1979) is designed to measure the attitudes of students in grades 7 through 12 towards mathematics. The MAI consists of 48 statements about the study of mathematics. After reading each statement, the student indicates whether he or she strongly agrees, agrees, disagrees, or strongly disagrees with the statement. The items are divided into six scales measuring six constructs of mathematics attitude. Those constructs are:

1. *Perception of the mathematics teacher:* A student's view regarding the teaching characteristics of his or her mathematics teacher.
2. *Anxiety toward mathematics:* The uneasiness a student feels in situations involving mathematics.
3. *Value of mathematics in society:* A student's view regarding the usefulness of mathematical knowledge.
4. *Self-concept in mathematics:* A student's perception of his or her own competence in mathematics.
5. *Enjoyment of mathematics:* The pleasure a student derives from engaging in mathematical activities.

6. *Motivation in mathematics:* A student's desire to do work in mathematics beyond the class requirements.

Construct validity was supported by a factor analysis of the item scores from 5,034 students. The factor easily fell into the six constructs that the instrument was designed to measure. The alpha coefficients for the six scales ranged from .68 to .89.

### Inventory of Teacher Concern

The *Inventory of Teacher Concern* (Cawley & Cawley, 1981) is composed of two parts. The first part helps the teacher identify or screen children in the class who concern the teacher (either by their problem behavior or special talents). An individual inventory is used in the second phase to identify combinations of positive and negative characteristics of the targeted individuals according to 34 category descriptors. The teacher can then establish concern priorities based on the data obtained and plan his or her intervention strategies accordingly.

## SUMMARY

In this chapter characteristics of general classroom behaviors, social/emotional factors, and attitudes were described. In addition, assessment techniques such as the ecological approach, informal methods, and a sampling of the limited norm-referenced/published instruments available were discussed. Continued training and exposure of teachers to the types of methods presented here will better ensure more effective identification and subsequent programming for the learning-disabled student.

### REFERENCES

Balla, D. (1967). *Class notes.* Lawrence, KS: University of Kansas.

Blackwood, R. (1970). The operant conditioning of verbally meditated self-control in the classroom. *Journal of School Psychology, 8,* 251–258.

Bornstein, P., & Quevillon, R. (1976). The effects of a self-instructional package on overactive preschool boys. *Journal of Applied Behavior Analysis, 9,* 179–188.

Brown, L. (1983). Evaluating and managing classroom behavior. In D. Hammill and N. Bartel, *Teaching children with learning and behavior problems.* Boston: Allyn & Bacon.

Brown, L., & Hammill, D.D. (1978). *Behavior rating profile.* Austin, TX: PRO-ED.

Brown, V.L. (undated). *How to assess and teach independent study behaviors.* Austin, TX: PRO-ED.

Cawley, J.F., & Cawley, L.J. (1981). *Inventory of teacher concerns.* Glenview, IL: Scott, Foresman.

Dawson, L., McLeod, S., & Mathews, S. (1976). *Behavior checklist for middle schools.* Madison, WI: Madison Metropolitan Schools.

Estes, T.H., Estes, J.J., Richards, H.C., & Roettger, D. (1981). *Estes attitude scales.* Austin, TX: PRO-ED.

Feagans, L. (1972). Ecological theory as a model for constructing a theory of emotional disturbance. In W.C. Rhodes & M.L. Tracy (Eds.). *A study of child variance.* Ann Arbor, MI: Institute for the Study of Mental Retardation and Related Disabilities. University of Michigan.

Glynn, E., Thomas, J., & Shee, S. (1973). Behavioral self-control of on-task behavior in an elementary school classroom. *Journal of Applied Behavioral Analysis, 6,* 105–113.

Guerin, G.R., & Maier, A.S. (1983). *Informal assessment in education.* Palo Alto, CA: Mayfield.

Haladyna, T., Shaughnessy, J., & Shaughnessy, J.M. (1982). A causal analysis of attitude toward mathematics. *Journal for Research in Mathematics Education, 14*(1), 19–29.

Hall, R.V. (1974). *The measurement of behavior.* Lawrence, KS: H & H Enterprises.

Harter, S. (1979). *The perceived competence scale for children.* Denver: Department of Psychology, University of Denver.

Ingram, C.F. (1980). *Fundamentals of educational assessment.* New York:    Van Nostrand.

Kaufman, K., & O'Leary, K. (1972). Reward, cost, and self-evaluation procedures for disruptive adolescents in a psychiatric hospital school. *Journal of Applied Behavior Analysis, 5,* 293–309.

Kroth, R.L. (1975). *Communicating with parents of exceptional children.* Denver: Love.

Lankford, F.G. (1974). What can a teacher learn about a pupil's thinking through oral interviews? *Arithmetic Teacher, 21,* 26–32.

Laten, S., & Katz, G. (1975). *A theoretical model for assessment of adolescents: The ecological/behavioral approach.* Madison, WI: Specialized Educational Services.

McLoughlin, J.A., & Lewis, R.B. (1981). *Assessing special students.* Columbus, OH: Charles E. Merrill.

Michaels, L.A., & Forsyth, R.A. (1978). Measuring attitudes toward mathematics? Some questions to consider. *Arithmetic Teacher, 26,* 22–25.

Moreno, J.L. (1953). *Who shall survive? Foundations of sociometry, group psychotherapy, and sociodrama.* New York: Beacon House.

Sandman, R.S. (1979). *Mathematics attitude inventory.* Minneapolis: Minnesota Research and Evaluation Center, University of Minnesota.

Shaughnessy, J., Haladyna, T., & Shaughnessy, J.M. (1983). Relations of student, teacher, and learning environment variables to attitude toward mathematics. *School Science and Mathematics, 83,* 21–37.

Spivak, G., & Swift, M. (1973). Classroom behavior of children: A critical review of teacher-administered rating scales. *Journal of Special Education, 7,* 55–89.

Thurman, S.K. (1977). Congruence of behavioral ecologies: A model for special education programming. *Journal of Special Education, 11,* 329–334.

Walker, H.M. (1976). *Walker problem behavior identification checklist.* Los Angeles: Western Psychological Services.

Wallace, G., & Larsen, S. (1978). *Educational assessment of learning problems: Testing for teaching.* Boston: Allyn & Bacon.

Wiederholt, J.L., Hammill, D.D., & Brown, V.L. (1983). *The resource teacher: A guide to effective practices*. Boston: Allyn & Bacon.

Workman, E. (1982). *Teaching behavioral self-control to students*. Austin, TX: PRO-ED.

Wright, H.F. (1967). *Recording and analyzing child behavior with ecological data from an American town*. New York: Harper & Row.

# Appendix 9-A

# How To Assess and Teach Independent Study Behaviors

BEHAVIORAL CHECKLIST FOR DETERMINING
MATCH OF STUDENT: CLASS/SCHOOL
(Sample adapted from Dawson, McLeod, & Mathews, 1976)

PURPOSE: The purpose of this checklist is to determine the kind of match that exists— or does not exist—between the abilities and behaviors of a student and the requirements of a specific classroom, teacher, or school.

DIRECTIONS:

_____ 1. Please glance over the categories and behaviors that are suggested. Note that there is room to add behaviors you believe are more important for your specific class or program. There is also room at the end to comment further, and to summarize information. Modify the sheet before you begin to code the behaviors and the student abilities or performance.

_____ 2. In the column called "Teacher Code" use the appropriate number to indicate how important the particular behavior is to success in your class or program. You might wish to consider the behavior in terms of students who have been very successful within your class. Rate each behavior to correspond to one of these four categories:

4 = Essential to success
3 = Important for success
2 = Helpful for success
1 = Not required for success.

_____ 3. Either (a) or (b):
(a) for *all* behaviors . . .
(b) For all behaviors coded as *3* or *4* . . .
. . . rate the student under consideration. Use the following code for the column marked as "Student Code":

4 = Meets standards adequately
3 = Somewhat within class range
2 = Has done or shown, but is inconsistent
1 = Has never shown this behavior.

*Source:* Reprinted with permission from V.L. Brown. *How to assess and teach independent study behaviors.* Austin, TX: PRO-ED, unpublished manuscript, undated.

_____ 4. Subtract the code number in the "Student Code" column from the code number in the "Teacher Code" column. Write this remainder in the "Diff" (for "Difference") column.

_____ 5. If the remainder in the "Diff" column is a $+1$, $+2$, or $+3$, then put a checkmark ($\sqrt{}$) in the "$\sqrt{}$ if Sign" (Check if Significant) column.

_____ 6. Further comment may be made in the space provided, or at the end of the questionnaire/checklist.

_____ 7. If desired or needed, summarize the data appropriately; devise a program plan; verify the information given; expand the information given through personal interviews; discuss the information with the student or other relevant people; or use the data in pre-post program evaluation.

_____ 8. Suggested formats for data summaries are provided as an Appendix to the Checklist sample.

| | Teacher Code | Student Code | Diff | $\sqrt{}$ if Sign | Comment |
|---|---|---|---|---|---|
| A. Schedule Related Behaviors: | | | | | |
| 1. Attends regularly | | | | | |
| 2. Attends on time | | | | | |
| 3. Knows what to do when<br>a. late | | | | | |
| b. absent | | | | | |
| 4. _____ | | | | | |
| B. Material/Tool Related Behaviors: | | | | | |
| 1. Has working pencil/pen | | | | | |
| 2. Has notebook | | | | | |
| 3. Has book(s) | | | | | |
| 4. Has paper suitable for tasks | | | | | |
| 5. Has miscellaneous materials related to the day's tasks | | | | | |
| 6. Knows where to<br>a. find materials/tools | | | | | |
| b. put materials/tools away after use | | | | | |
| 7. Uses materials/tools with proper<br>a. care | | | | | |
| b. skill | | | | | |
| c. safety | | | | | |
| 8. _____ | | | | | |

|  | Teacher Code | Student Code | Diff | √ if Sign | Comment |
|---|---|---|---|---|---|
| C. Group Work Behaviors: |  |  |  |  |  |
| 1. Works individually/independently |  |  |  |  |  |
| 2. Works with one other person |  |  |  |  |  |
| 3. Works in groups of a. less than 5 |  |  |  |  |  |
| b. less than 10 |  |  |  |  |  |
| c. 10 or more |  |  |  |  |  |
| 4. Appropriate interactions with peers within classroom |  |  |  |  |  |
| 5. Reacts to peer provokes appropriately when they are a. physical |  |  |  |  |  |
| b. verbal |  |  |  |  |  |
| 6. Participates appropriately in group discussions |  |  |  |  |  |
| 7. Reads material in front of group |  |  |  |  |  |
| 8. Takes on share of group project |  |  |  |  |  |
| 9. _____ |  |  |  |  |  |
| D. Behaviors Related to Presence in Class: |  |  |  |  |  |
| 1. Responds to bell by being in classroom and attending to teacher/task |  |  |  |  |  |
| 2. Enters room appropriately |  |  |  |  |  |
| 3. Sits at own desk or stays at work station |  |  |  |  |  |
| 4. Raises hand or gets attention appropriately |  |  |  |  |  |
| 5. Uses free or unstructured time well |  |  |  |  |  |
| 6. Has appropriate voice level |  |  |  |  |  |
| 7. Understands classroom "rules" |  |  |  |  |  |

| | Teacher Code | Student Code | Diff | √ if Sign | Comment |
|---|---|---|---|---|---|
| 8. Conforms to most classroom rules | | | | | |
| 9. Dresses reasonably for school/ class | | | | | |
| 10. Is reasonably groomed/clean | | | | | |
| 11. Reacts appropriately to teacher directives | | | | | |
| 12. Reacts appropriately to teacher/ peer statements | | | | | |
| 13. Leaves room appropriately a. when directed | | | | | |
| b. at end of class | | | | | |
| 14. Volunteers help to others | | | | | |
| 15. _____ | | | | | |
| E. Assignment/Project Related Behaviors: | | | | | |
| 1. Knows nature of assignment/ project requirements a. content | | | | | |
| b. format | | | | | |
| 2. Clarifies/verifies assignment or project requirements a. asks appropriate questions | | | | | |
| b. writes notes about assignments | | | | | |
| 3. Understands rationale for assignment | | | | | |
| 4. Knows how to do the assignment a. content | | | | | |
| b. mechanics | | | | | |
| c. use of appropriate resources | | | | | |
| 5. Starts assignment within reasonable time limits | | | | | |
| 6. Does assignment "neatly" | | | | | |

| | Teacher Code | Student Code | Diff | √ if Sign | Comment |
|---|---|---|---|---|---|
| 7. Verifies or checks work before handing in as completed<br>a. knows how | | | | | |
| b. does | | | | | |
| 8. Works at reasonable pace | | | | | |
| 9. Accepts constructive feedback<br>a. understands | | | | | |
| b. has good attitude toward | | | | | |
| c. uses | | | | | |
| 10. Hands in completed work/project | | | | | |
| 11. Revises product/assignment if needed<br>a. knows how | | | | | |
| b. completes revision | | | | | |
| 12. Able to deal with grades received<br>a. has appropriate attitude toward | | | | | |
| b. knows procedure for changing | | | | | |
| c. uses appropriate change procedures | | | | | |
| 13. Is responsible for work missed<br>a. knows how to find out what to do | | | | | |
| b. makes up work | | | | | |
| 14. Seeks extra-credit assignments | | | | | |
| 15. _____ | | | | | |
| F. Behaviors Related to Test-Taking: | | | | | |
| 1. Studies content on a daily basis with tests in mind<br>a. knows appropriate study methods | | | | | |
| b. uses appropriate study methods | | | | | |

| | Teacher Code | Student Code | Diff | √ if Sign | Comment |
|---|---|---|---|---|---|
| 2. Shows appropriate attitude toward tests | | | | | |
| 3. Understands various test formats<br>a. multiple choice | | | | | |
| b. true/false | | | | | |
| c. short answer | | | | | |
| d. fill in blanks | | | | | |
| e. matching | | | | | |
| f. essay | | | | | |
| g. identifying parts of diagrams | | | | | |
| 4. Can study according to formats<br>a. multiple choice | | | | | |
| b. true/false | | | | | |
| c. fill in blanks | | | | | |
| d. short answer | | | | | |
| e. matching | | | | | |
| f. essay | | | | | |
| g. identifying parts of diagrams | | | | | |
| 5. Knows how to prepare for tests<br>a. with appropriate review | | | | | |
| b. with adequate physical energy | | | | | |
| c. with good planning of time use | | | | | |
| 6. Can use alternatives to written tests<br>a. knows alternatives available | | | | | |
| b. makes arrangements for alternative | | | | | |
| 7. Is responsible for missed tests<br>a. knows how to find out what to do | | | | | |
| b. makes up test | | | | | |

| | Teacher Code | Student Code | Diff | √ if Sign | Comment |
|---|---|---|---|---|---|
| 8. Able to deal with grades received | | | | | |
|   a. has appropriate attitude toward | | | | | |
|   b. knows procedure for changing | | | | | |
|   c. uses appropriate change procedures | | | | | |
| 9. Uses returned tests as feedback<br>  a. for anticipating future formats | | | | | |
|   b. for anticipating future content | | | | | |
|   c. for anticipating future study needs | | | | | |
| 10. Asks for help appropriately | | | | | |
| 11. _____ | | | | | |
| G. Behaviors Related to Obtaining Content: | | | | | |
|   1. Able to attend to class activity for appropriate length of time | | | | | |
|   2. Maintains attention toward teacher or leader-directed activity | | | | | |
|   3. Listens to lectures/discussions | | | | | |
|   4. Able to copy notes or other information<br>    a. from board | | | | | |
|     b. from overhead | | | | | |
|     c. from books | | | | | |
|     d. from misc. sources | | | | | |
|   5. Uses IMC resources appropriately<br>    a. understands range of resources | | | | | |
|     b. uses appropriate resources | | | | | |

| | Teacher Code | Student Code | Diff | √ if Sign | Comment |
|---|---|---|---|---|---|
| 6. Picks up information through<br> a. reading/studying independently | | | | | |
| b. observation of demonstrations or A-V materials | | | | | |
| c. "doing"—projects/products | | | | | |
| d. listening to teacher/leader | | | | | |
| e. discussion | | | | | |
| 7. Has experience with content area<br> a. from reading/studying | | | | | |
| b. from hands-on or first-hand experience | | | | | |
| 8. Maintains interest in class/topics | | | | | |
| 9. Persists in trying to learn skill/content | | | | | |
| 10. Tries to use or apply content outside of classroom situation | | | | | |
| 11. ————————— | | | | | |
| H. Behaviors Related to Self-Expression: | | | | | |
| 1. Has adequate writing skills<br> a. handwriting | | | | | |
| b. typing | | | | | |
| c. spelling | | | | | |
| d. grammar | | | | | |
| e. vocabulary | | | | | |
| f. uses appropriate formats | | | | | |
| g. organizes material appropriately | | | | | |
| 2. Has adequate speaking skills<br> a. grammar | | | | | |
| b. content vocabulary | | | | | |
| c. organizes material appropriately | | | | | |

| | Teacher Code | Student Code | Diff | √ if sign | Comment |
|---|---|---|---|---|---|
| 3. Has adequate performing/demonstration skills <br> a. performs relevant aspects of procedure | | | | | |
| b. uses performance as a way to show what is known | | | | | |
| 4. _____ | | | | | |
| **I. Study Related Behaviors:** | | | | | |
| 1. Knows how to use/plan time wisely <br> a. understands how to plan | | | | | |
| b. uses time management plans | | | | | |
| 2. Uses appropriate notetaking skills <br> a. knows appropriate formats | | | | | |
| b. takes notes | | | | | |
| c. reorganizes notes for various study purposes | | | | | |
| d. maintains note files | | | | | |
| 3. Keeps adequate records of study, e.g., notebook | | | | | |
| 4. Relates new to old information | | | | | |
| 5. Knows study routines, e.g., SQ3R <br> a. understands how to use | | | | | |
| b. uses consistently | | | | | |
| 6. _____ | | | | | |
| **J. Building Related Behaviors:** | | | | | |
| 1. Walks in halls | | | | | |
| 2. Appropriate noise level in halls | | | | | |
| 3. Has pass when in halls <br> a. knows how to obtain pass | | | | | |
| b. shows pass as required | | | | | |

| | Teacher Code | Student Code | Diff | √ if Sign | Comment |
|---|---|---|---|---|---|
| 4. Does not peer or shout into classrooms or offices | | | | | |
| 5. Moves from one room to another within reasonable time limits | | | | | |
| 6. Responds appropriately to adult-initiated interactions | | | | | |
| 7. Talks appropriately to building personnel | | | | | |
| 8. Stays in appropriate school areas | | | | | |
| 9. Able to sit quietly in office area | | | | | |
| 10. Interacts appropriately with peers while in non-classroom areas<br>a. verbally | | | | | |
| b. physically | | | | | |
| 11. Uses behaviors appropriate to area(s) | | | | | |
| 12. Knows how to use appropriate resource personnel in the school | | | | | |
| 13. Leaves building within reasonable time limit<br>a. when instructed | | | | | |
| b. when bell rings | | | | | |
| 14. _____ | | | | | |
| K. Behaviors Related to Participation in Extra-Curricular Activities: | | | | | |
| 1. Knows range of extra-curricular activities | | | | | |
| 2. Shows interest in some extra-curricular participation | | | | | |
| 3. Participates in extra-curricular activities | | | | | |
| 4. _____ | | | | | |

Behaviors that are not related to success in the classroom, but cause some concern on behalf of the student:

### MATCH-MISMATCH CHECKLIST: WORKSHEET FOR SUMMARY AND PLAN

| Rank | Major Mismatch Concerns | Suggested Plan for Follow-Up |
|------|-------------------------|------------------------------|
|      |                         |                              |

Use of Positive Matches

**Appendix A: Sample Formats for Data from Match-Mismatch Checklist**

Questions:
1. How does an individual student fare across teachers?
2. What is the range of differences in various classes?

Student _____

| Behaviors | Teacher # | Interpretation |
|---|---|---|
| (List behaviors or code letters/numbers for behaviors used in the check list.) (Only significant behaviors might also be listed.) | | May examine mean or modal extremes of teacher expectations; mean or modal extremes of student behaviors; or significant difference scores. |

| 1 | 2 | 3 | 4 | 5 | 6 |
|---|---|---|---|---|---|
| T/D | T/D | T/D | T/D | T/D | T/D |
| S | S | S | S | S | S |

Question:
1. What is the range of student match-mismatch in any particular classroom?

Teacher _____

| Behaviors | Student # | Interpretation |
|---|---|---|
| May list all or only significant behaviors in this column. Note Teacher Code. | | Examine range. |

| 1 | 2 | 3 | 4 | 5 | . . . |
|---|---|---|---|---|---|
| *Codes for students here* | | | | | |

Question:
1. What resources do we have to deal with significant problems of mismatch?

Behavior of Concern: _____
No more than two related behaviors (if there are any): _____

In each case, consider resources immediately available + resources available *if* X, Y, or Z were changed:

Money:

Space:

Time:

Personnel:

Materials and Supplies:

Curriculum Content:

Curriculum Methodology:

# Chapter 10

# Assessment of the Severely Impaired Mathematics Student

*Anne M. Fitzmaurice Hayes*

Billy was seven years old and in the first grade. He had spent two years in kindergarten in a school system that included the reading of the numerals 1–10 among its kindergarten objectives. After a few months in first grade, Billy's inability to meet the demands of the first grade curriculum in mathematics indicated the need for referral for assessment. As part of that assessment a mathematics consultant spent some time in the classroom observing Billy. During her lesson that day, the teacher wrote the numeral 3 on a card and asked Billy to tell what the number was. Billy looked puzzled, and finally said "em." The teacher repeated the activity for other numbers. In each case Billy's reply appeared to stem from a random selection of a letter name or a number name. Billy's written work also indicated an inability to produce a numeral to name the number of members in a set.

The mathematics consultant decided to spend some time working with Billy on a one-to-one basis. From the ensuing activities, it became apparent that in spite of his seeming inability to deal with number symbols, Billy had developed the concepts of more and less, and he could conserve number. Further, when Billy was given ten strips of paper, each of a length different from the others, and asked to line them up from tallest to shortest, he did so efficiently and unerringly.

Jill was a young girl in a self-contained, combination LD-EMR junior high school classroom. From a sense of frustration her teacher had asked for assistance in working with Jill. When the math consultant visited the classroom to observe the child, the teacher wrote a row of single-digit numerals on the chalkboard. He asked for a volunteer to point to the number 4. Jill's hand went up, and the teacher called on her. She confidently approached the board and pointed to 7. The teacher asked Jill to point to other numerals after he named them. In each case, Jill made an incorrect choice. During a conversation with the consultant later on, the teacher said that Jill seemed unable to correctly identify numerals, in spite of having received much instruction and drill and practice in that skill. Jill was able to identify letters of the alphabet, and she could read. Also, if asked orally to show four fingers, she could respond correctly.

Sal, a sophomore in college, was spending his third semester in AMB 101, the first half of a pre-calculus course designed to be taught in two semesters. Sal was quite frank about his difficulties in coping with mathematics, but the degree requirements included both semesters of the pre-calculus course, and his intended major required an additional course in calculus. More often than not, however, the symbols didn't mean anything to him, and remembering the sequence of operations necessary to solve an equation such a $4(3x+7) = \frac{1}{2}x + 9$ was sometimes impossible. Operations with signed numbers became possible for him only when a teacher showed him how to perform such operations on a calculator.

Mary was a graduate student in special education. Her difficulties with mathematics were the result of an automobile accident in which she had suffered an injury to her head. She spoke of her frustration when faced with a multiplication example such as $234 \times 63$. She said that in her head she knew how to do the example, but she could not transfer the process to symbols on paper.

Each of the individuals described above has a special problem in mathematics. In each case, with the exception of Billy's, the problem was one that had resisted many types of instructional intervention. In each case, the disability was one that seriously hindered progress in acquiring other competencies in mathematics. Yet which of the difficulties described would be considered serious impairments? At what level does one regard a difficulty in mathematics as a severe disability? What is the role of assessment in making such an evaluation? In the following pages, each of these questions will be examined in turn.

## WHAT IS A SEVERE DISABILITY IN MATHEMATICS?

The problem of functional illiteracy has received increasing attention during the past several years. Illiteracy in mathematics, a very limited ability to use the language of mathematics to deal with quantitative relationships, is a dilemma that has been the object of much less attention.

Nonetheless, mathematical illiteracy can pose insurmountable obstacles to the attainment of the skills necessary to lead a normal daily existence.

Imagine yourself in a world where printed numbers and signs of operation had no consistent meaning, carried no meaningful message. How does someone function who cannot do even the simplest calculation mentally? What is it like to be unable to compare quantities? How does one perform simple tasks when he or she has trouble dealing with such positional concepts as up/down, left/right, in front of/behind? While the presence of all these problems in one person would be unlikely, some individuals do suffer from one or more such difficulties. Such problems have come to be labeled as dyscalculia. Estimates of the number of individuals with such symptoms vary, but the phenomenon is real.

What causes such disabilities? Gerstmann (1957), Cohn (1968), and Kosc (1970) recognized some sort of neurological impairment as underlying the disorder. Kosc (1970) focused on developmental dyscalculia.

> Developmental dyscalculia is a structural disorder of mathematical abilities which has its origin in a genetic or congenital disorder of those parts of the brain that are the direct anatomico-physiological substrate of the maturation of the mathematical abilities adequate to age, without a simultaneous disorder of general mental functions. (p. 192)

Billy's case, described earlier, might well be one of developmental dyscalculia.

Dyscalculia might also be the result of some trauma incurred as a child or as an adult. Such an injury might serve to destroy or damage previous learning and prohibit further development in one area of mathematics or another. Mary's disability was the outcome of such an accident.

Poor instructional practices might also be cited as a cause of serious disability in mathematics. In this latter case impairment would be, as it were, imposed from without, rather than originating from within the individual. Sal's difficulties in mathematics may have been caused by faulty or improperly timed instruction. He may also have had a developmental deficit compounded by poor instructional practices.

Regardless of the cause, a severe learning disability in mathematics is defined here as any impairment in the capacity for learning mathematics, inconsistent with one's general level of ability and resistant to ordinary instruction, which seriously hinders one's ability to lead a normal daily existence and/or to achieve realistic career goals, that is, career goals consistent with one's general level of intellectual functioning. This definition implies that serious mathematics disability may exist alongside other problems, such as mental retardation. Jill's overall development in intellectual functioning was somewhat delayed, but her achievement level in mathematics was remarkably lower than her achievement level in other areas.

Note that the definition also implies a primary mathematics disability, to use Kosc's term (1974). Many learning-disabled children experience difficulty in learning mathematics because of the obstacles posed by problems such as dyslexia or hyperactivity. Here the impediment would seem to be less related to the content and language of mathematics itself than to the vehicles through which instruction is frequently carried out. There is no intention here to belittle such problems; the effort is only to distinguish them from a primary mathematics disability.

## THE ROLE OF ASSESSMENT

The determination of whether or not a serious learning disability in mathematics exists for a particular individual is an important matter. The earlier such knowledge can come to light, the better. One child may come to the attention of a teacher because of bizarre responses to mathematical exercises. Another child may stand out because his or her achievement in mathematics is not on a par with progress in other areas of the curriculum. Yet a third child may exhibit behavior patterns during instruction in mathematics that do not accompany other school activities. Whatever the reason, serious problems in mathematics merit closer examination, an examination that should have all the characteristics of a thorough diagnostic search.

This endeavor should consist of at least three components: a content search, an algorithm search, and a systematic arrangement of different modes of interaction to determine efficient instructional strategies for that student. In some cases, neurological and/or psychological examinations may be necessary.

### The Content Search

Bizarre behaviors in one area of mathematics may mask real achievement in other areas. In Billy's case, described earlier in this chapter, the inability to read and write numbers hid the concepts he had developed. The content search component of the diagnostic effort is designed to ferret out whatever skills and concepts a child has attained. Such a content search must have at least these qualities:

1. It should cover different areas of mathematics: arithmetic, geometry, and measurement at a bare minimum. Some children are ready for instruction in geometry before formal teaching in arithmetic. A content search may bring to light capacities and achievement in areas that may not receive emphasis in the curriculum.
2. It should allow for different forms of input and output. That is, a content search should not consist solely of paper and pencil tasks. Sal, the sophomore in college, performed much better on tests when he was allowed to dictate all his work to the instructor, who would record Sal's responses on paper.
3. A content search should consist of items sequenced in such a manner that successive items represent very small steps in concept development or skill attainment.

These three demands are easier to meet when one realizes that the range of content to be covered can be limited. That is to say, the young child suspected of having a severe disability is not likely to have achieved a wide range of skills in any of the areas mentioned. The older child who appears to have very poorly developed arithmetic skills will probably exhaust these abilities in a relatively short time. Further, if the purpose of the diagnostic effort is the initiation of appropriate instruction, the content search may focus on only those areas of content likely to receive instruction during the immediate future.

Perhaps the most difficult criterion to meet is the need to find gaps between successive items of a content search. Some sources are available for guidance. *SRA Diagnosis—An Aid to Instruction* (1975), Level A or Level B, offers both a survey test and probe tests to provide closer examination of problems evident from performance on the survey test. Although pencil-and-paper instruments, the probe tests provide good examples of how items should be sequenced for a diagnostic effort. Scope and sequence charts from mathematics programs, properly analyzed, can also provide sequencing information. Examples of different skills can be derived from the programs themselves.

Mathematics curriculum committees in many school systems have developed their own sequenced lists of objectives in different areas of mathematics. These can serve as a frame of reference for the development of a content search. If an objective criterion-referenced picture of a child's level of achievement is to be obtained, such a content search is necessary.

### The Algorithm Search

An algorithm can be defined as a computational rule or set of rules. Many children develop computational rules of their own, but they give them up when they learn the correct rules. Some children with learning disabilities in mathematics develop quite bizarre rules, and never change them. Other dyscalculic children never create any consistent patterns of behavior with respect to arithmetic calculation. A good diagnostic procedure should serve to provide a picture of what algorithms a child has developed.

Some faulty rules may be simple and understandable alterations of conventional algorithms. One youngster, for example, was observed doing a division example thus:

$$\text{Example:} \quad 3\overline{)639}$$

$$\text{Step 1:} \quad \frac{3}{3\overline{)639}}$$

$$\text{Step 2:} \quad \frac{13}{3\overline{)639}}$$

$$\text{Step 3:} \quad \frac{213}{3\overline{)639}}$$

When given the example $3\overline{)279}$, the child operated in a similar manner, writing the digit 3 in the answer first, and then the 9. With the following example, the consistency of the procedure became evident:

$$\text{Example:} \quad 5\overline{)425}$$

$$\text{Step 1:} \quad \frac{5}{5\overline{)425}}$$

$$\text{Step 2:} \quad \frac{85}{5\overline{)425}} \; 2/5$$

Such an algorithm has both advantages and disadvantages. The major disadvantage lies in the fact that, given the appropriate set of circumstances, the procedure results in a correct answer. In other words, the procedure results in random reinforcement after the learning has taken place. On the other hand, the origin of the procedure is easily grasped: in addition, subtraction, and multiplication the traditional algorithms are based on a right-to-left sequence. The child has overgeneralized this pattern. Alternate algorithms, such as repeated subtraction, can be introduced to the child.

Kosc (1974) cited the example given by Green and Buswell (1930). The example and solution were $86 - 4 = 81$. The ". . . student approached the task $86 - 4$ as follows: 'Six and four equals ten; ten and eight equal eighteen.' Then he wrote his answer backwards: 81" (p. 50).

The example provides a good argument for the need to conduct an algorithm search through the use of the interview. Only after listening to the student's explanation of his procedure could an examiner appreciate the strategy being used. Without such an interview, one might have assumed there was a simple error in subtraction facts ($6-4=1$).

The interview procedure is a simple but effective device. The Buswell-John (1925) *Diagnostic Chart for Fundamental Processes in Arithmetic* offers a protocol for such an approach. The examiner presents a number of examples in one arithmetic operation to be completed by the student. The examiner observes the student performing the task and notes in writing any observable behaviors, using a checklist for common errors and listing any behaviors not found in the checklist. Such behaviors would include counting on fingers, using tally marks, left-to-right computation, and so on. When the student has completed the exercises, the examiner asks the student to describe the procedures used for selected examples, including those with correct responses and those with incorrect responses. The student's explanations are recorded for future reference.

From such an interview the examiner can derive information providing answers to questions such as the following:

1. Does the child possess any algorithms as guides to computation?
2. Does the child use any one algorithm consistently for a given operation?
3. Is the algorithm appropriate? That is, does its use result in correct answers all the time?
4. If inappropriate, can the child's algorithm be modified to result in correct answers?

The answers to such questions can provide valuable guidance for future instruction.

**The Interaction Analysis**

The third component of a diagnostic search requires a systematic analysis of the combinations of instructor/learner interactions for an individual student for the purpose of determining which combinations are most efficient for that student. This analysis should help to provide answers to questions of efficacy and efficiency. Which combinations of input and output are best? The severely impaired mathematics learner has, in all probability, already lost time in learning mathematics. Future efforts at instruction must serve to make up for lost time, and to make the most effective use of the learner's strengths.

The Interactive Unit (IU) (Cawley, 1984) provides a model for such an analysis. The content to be imposed on the model can and should be selected by the examiner. The content should be selected so that the child can be taken through the 16 combinations of the IU at least twice. Three times would provide more reliable information and would allow patterns to begin to emerge. The first selections of content should represent material with which the student is totally familiar. For example, if the child is familiar with the names of the geometric shapes circle, triangle, and square, these three shapes might be selected as the basis of the 16 activities to match the 16 cells of the unit. A second selection of content should include material that the child would be ready to learn. If the geometric shapes described above are used, the introduction of the trapezoid shape might be a reasonable choice of unfamiliar material the child is ready to learn.

The use of material with which the child is familiar is intended to provide a picture of the combinations that cause the child difficulty even when the content does not. The use of new material should result in an indication of which modes of interaction work best for the child when he or she is attempting to extend his or her level of knowledge.

A sample set of activities for the content triangle is presented below. Note how easily the procedures can be adapted for other shapes.

Input:     Manipulate
Materials: Several thin strips of paper or popsicle sticks for examiner and
           student. Cards resembling those illustrated in Figure 10-1.

The examiner lays out representations of triangles, making them with the popsicle sticks or the thin strips of paper, while the child watches. The examiner asks the child to

1. use strips of paper or popsicle sticks to make figures like those the examiner made.
2. identify from Card A those shapes like the ones the examiner made.
3. name aloud the shapes the examiner made.
4. either write the name of the shape or select the name from the list on Card B. The examiner may also choose to ask the child to draw a picture of the shape the examiner made.

Input:     Display
Materials: Card C, several popsicle sticks  or thin strips of paper for the
           student, Card D.

**Figure 10-1** Sample Cards To Be Used during Interaction Analysis

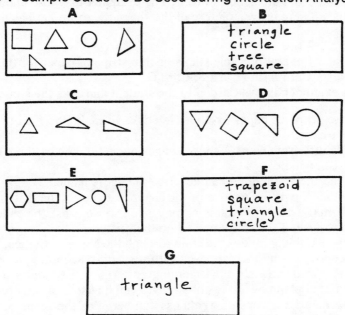

The examiner shows Card C to the student and asks the student to

1. use strips of paper or popsicle sticks to make figures like those on the card.
2. identify from Card D those shapes like the ones on the card the examiner is showing.
3. name aloud the shapes shown on the card.
4. either write the name of the shape or select the name from the list on Card B. The examiner may also choose to ask the child to draw a picture of the shape the examiner has on the card.

Input: Say
Materials: Several thin strips of paper or popsicle sticks for the student, Cards E and F.

The examiner says the word *triangle* and asks the student to

1. use strips of paper or popsicle sticks to make the figure the examiner has named.
2. select from Card E pictures of the shape the examiner named.
3. describe the shape the examiner has named orally.

4. either write the name of the shape the examiner named or select the name from the list on Card F. The examiner may also choose to ask the child to draw a picture of the shape the examiner has named.

Input:    Write
Materials: Several popsicle sticks or thin strips of paper for the student, Card A and Card F, Card G.
The examiner shows Card G to the student and asks the student to

1. use strips of paper or popsicle sticks to make the figure named on the card.
2. identify from Card A those shapes named on the card the examiner is showing.
3. read the word aloud and describe the figure named.
4. either to write the name of the shape or to select the matching name from Card F. The examiner may also choose to ask the child to draw a picture of the shape named on the card.

As the examiner guides the child through the above activities, he or she may record the child's responses with respect to accuracy, level of confidence, speed, and so on. Emerging patterns will serve as a guide to instructional planning. Areas of strength can be used for the presentation of new material. Areas of weakness can serve as the focus of remedial efforts.

The model for diagnosis described above yields little in the way of norm-referenced information. For the severely disabled student, such information is of little use. His or her standing among peers is evident. The goal of instruction for such a student is the maximization of potential, as it is for every child. However, for the severely disabled youngster, mathematics instruction must be designed even more carefully to meet the peculiar and particular needs of the particular disability present. Only in that way can the impact of the impairment on daily living and the attainment of legitimate career goals be minimized.

---

**REFERENCES**

Buswell, G.T., & John, L. (1925). *Diagnostic chart for fundamental processes in arithmetic.* Indianapolis: Bobbs-Merrill.

Cawley, J.F. (1984).

Cohn, R. (1968). Developmental dyscalculia. *Pediatric Clinics of North America, 15,* 3.

Gerstmann, J. (1957). Some notes on the Gerstmann syndrome. *Neurology, 7,* 866–869.

Kosc, L. (1970). A contribution to the nomenclature and classification of disorders in mathematical abilities. In Russian with English summary. *Studia Psychologica, 12,* 12–28.

Kosc, L. (1974). Developmental dyscalculia. *Journal of Learning Disabilities, 7,* 164–177.

# Chapter 11

# Evaluating Student Growth and the Effectiveness of the Mathematics Program

*Raymond E. Webster*

Devoting time to evaluate the impact of a program is often viewed negatively throughout the educational system. Many believe that evaluation is a waste of time because the results are of little or no practical use. Some argue that evaluation is a tactic used by administrators to make themselves look good or to secure grant monies. Still others believe that evaluation is inane because many of the products of effective teaching or a strong curriculum cannot be measured. These kinds of comments suggest apprehension and anxiety. Program evaluation is often seen as a direct assessment of one's personal competence. The intent of evaluation is seen as pointing out what is "wrong" with staff in a program.

Yet program evaluation is one of the most important components of education. It is difficult if not impossible to determine subjectively whether a certain teaching style or curriculum is effective or even useful. Maintaining objectivity is difficult as the degree of personal involvement increases.

Without good measures for student progress that clarify the relationship between student learning outcomes and teaching styles or strategies education becomes at best a haphazard trial-and-error process. Teachers receive little feedback, positive or negative, about the appropriateness of their curriculum and teaching. There is no opportunity for real professional growth because no one can say confidently what works and what fails. People can make these decisions on the basis of their feelings about an approach or a program. But feelings are subject to change daily according to the feedback emitted from the setting. Without program evaluation there is no confidence in what is happening, no way to know how to program for students who deviate even slightly from expected performance levels or where future efforts should be directed. The consequences of a lack of clear direction are immense for staff morale, professionalism, allocation of fiscal resources, and fulfilling responsibilities for students served. Further, federal statutes require that states must ensure the effectiveness of programs for handicapped children. Effectiveness is ensured by annual evaluation of both the IEP and the classroom program.

The information from a valid data-based evaluation is of great significance in addressing these areas of concern. The remainder of this chapter discusses ways to assess student progress in mathematics and evaluate it on a group level.

## ISSUES IN EVALUATION

The purpose of educational evaluation is to collect data about student academic progress and to make decisions for future programming efforts. Evaluation can occur at two levels as depicted in Table 11-1. At Level I the goal is to determine the individual characteristics affecting learning and achievement. The results from the evaluation are used to make individualized program recommendations based on these data. Level II evaluation is more global and examines the impact of a program or approach on learning and achievement for a group of students. Typically, the focus is on instruction, curriculum, or both. The data collected from Level I may be used as part of the Level II evaluation. The procedures and techniques used at one level influence the data, conclusions, and procedures at the other. Defining techniques at each level to evaluate the mathematics program requires that attention be given to the issues of (1) distinguishing between learning gains and achievement levels, (2) mathematical reasoning and problem solving, and (3) basic mathematical skills competencies.

### Learning and Achievement

Learning describes the process of gaining information. It includes the student's modality-specific learning styles, short-term memory capacity, and how information is organized during learning (using memory devices

**Table 11-1** Levels of Educational Evaluation

| Level | Evaluation Target | Purpose | Staff | Areas Assessed |
|---|---|---|---|---|
| I. | Students | Student Individualized Programming | Direct Service Staff | Academic Achievement, Behavioral Skills, Cognitive Competencies |
| II. | Classes, Programs, Projects | Project Impact | Middle-Management Staff | Teaching Styles, Curriculum Strategies, Management Tactics |

like mental imagery, mnemonics, or narrative chaining). Learning indicates the rate at which a student acquires information relative to these variables.

Achievement is the end product of learning. It is a level identified using grade equivalent scores, percentiles, developmental age, or some other standard unit of measure at which a student is functioning. It does not refer to the factors describing how the information was acquired. Achievement is a numbering system that ranks student performance relative to a normative group. It is usually reported as a grade level equivalent score when using norm-referenced tests. Actual grade level scores are based on the standards developed by the publisher of a curriculum.

Using either type of data in an evaluation provides very different kinds of information about the student or program. Learning data reveal student performance patterns in acquiring knowledge. For special education students this knowledge may be presented as annual goals and instructional objectives in the IEP. The data compiled might be the number of trials to criterion to master an objective or the total amount of time needed to learn several related objectives.

Achievement test data appear to be more objective because they quantify student performance. These data allow individual and group comparisons to be made easily using group standards. The limits of these data concern the validity of their scores. Grade level equivalents do not necessarily indicate where a student is actually functioning in a subject. This is often the case with LD students. The criteria and standards for grade levels vary among publishing companies. A 6.2 grade level on the *WRAT* does not mean the same as a 6.2 on the *KeyMATH Diagnostic Arithmetic Test*. The authors of each test define the skills associated with a 6.2 grade level differently.

The format used on achievement tests allows a student to attain an overall grade level equivalent in several different ways. The test is constructed using a spiral omnibus format. This means that each item is more difficult than the preceding one. In theory, a student will pass all items up to some point. Then the student will fail all consecutive items. The total number of items passed corresponds to a predetermined grade level equivalent. In practice this does not occur often, especially with LD students. These students often show gaps in some areas and unusual strengths in others. It is possible to get an overall grade level score by failing some items that are below that grade level and passing other items that exceed it. Table 11-2 shows three different sets of skill competencies that a student can demonstrate to attain a grade level equivalent of 3.9 on the Arithmetic subtest from the *Wide Range Achievement Test,* Level II. The *WRAT* was

**Table 11-2** Three Ways To Attain Grade Level 3.9 on the *WRAT, Level II*

| *Number of Correct Items: 14* | *Grade Level: 3.9* |
|---|---|
| *Student* | *Skills Student Could Do* |
| I. | Count from 1–15; identify three single-digit numbers; identify two two-digit numbers; mental subtraction of two single-digit numbers; mental addition of two single-digit numbers; addition of single-digit and two-digit numbers; subtraction of two-digit numbers; multiplication of three-digit number with a decimal point by single-digit number; subtraction of two three-digit numbers. |
| II. | Count from 1–15; identify three single-digit numbers; identify two two-digit numbers; mental subtraction of two single-digit numbers; mental addition of two single-digit numbers; addition of two mixed numbers; addition of four numbers ranging from two to four-digits; converting feet expressed in mixed number form to inches; multiplication of a three-digit by a two-digit number. |
| III. | Count from 1–15; identify three single-digit numbers; identify two two-digit numbers; mental subtraction of two single-digit numbers; mental addition of two single-digit numbers; converting decimals to percents; dividing a four-digit number by a single-digit number; solving an algebraic equation using addition and subtraction; subtraction of two three-digit numbers. |

selected to show this point because of its popularity as an individual achievement test with the learning disabled.

Student I shows a performance pattern consistent with the way the test was designed. As the skills tested get more difficult this student cannot solve problems beyond subtraction of two three-digit numbers. Students II and III show more erratic profiles typical of many LD students. The errors made on earlier items may have involved numeral transpositions, failure to keep numbers in the proper columns during computations, result from lack of knowledge, or be due to an inability to apply information successfully learned during class. Such patterns are not uncommon among secondary-level LD students. Only further probing by the teacher can locate the precise causes for the items failed.

All three students in this example made the same grade level equivalent on the test. Yet, each student shows significant variation in the kinds of skills mastered and possibly in their ability to use skills they have learned. In general, norm-referenced tests are insensitive to the skill-based competencies of students.

The more severely learning disabled the student the more likely that achievement test scores will not provide accurate estimates of current level of performance in mathematics. Learning data describing the number of goals and objectives mastered, rate of acquisition presented in trials-to-criterion or time needed to learn, and the teaching procedures that enhanced learning will be the most meaningful for evaluating the effectiveness of the mathematics program. With mildly learning-disabled students achievement test scores used to supplement learning data are appropriate.

## Reasoning and Verbal Problem Solving

Mathematics is an applied tool used to solve problems. These problems may have little similarity to the classroom conditions under which original learning occurred. In addition to basic mathematics computational skills students are taught logical and orderly thinking, analytic reasoning, and how to generate a variety of reasonable ways to arrive at a solution. A valid assessment of the mathematics program must examine the degree to which students acquire such reasoning skills. Some areas to examine are:

- Applying mathematics skills to real problems and situations
- Kinds of problems (vocational, financial, academic) students can solve using mathematics
- The amount of teaching time devoted to practical applications
- The success levels of students in solving various kinds of real-life problems
- Types of situations outside the classroom where students are successfully involved in using mathematics to solve problems

The data that relate to these issues may consist of a narrative description of activities and a detailed listing of how mathematics was used. More quantified data can be presented on the number of in-school or out-of-school situations students were involved in using mathematics or the level of accuracy shown by students in these activities. Supporting data on higher levels of attendance or lowered levels of disruptive behavior during a particular unit serve to further confirm the effectiveness of the program. Narrative data should not be seen as inferior to quantified data. When used together both offer very meaningful information about what is happening in the program.

**Basic Skills Competencies**

Program evaluation should examine the number of basic skills and concepts learned by students during the year. Performance in these areas can be assessed using both criterion-referenced and norm-referenced testing. Several behavioral objectives lists in mathematics are also available for use as items in a teacher-constructed criterion-referenced test (see, for example, PRIMES, 1971). Most skills and concepts needed by LD students are those taught in grades 1 to 8.

## TESTING STRATEGIES TO ASSESS STUDENT PROGRESS

Two basic test formats used to assess student performance are norm-referenced testing and criterion-referenced testing. Norm-referenced testing (NRT) compares one student's score with the scores obtained by a group of individuals of the same age referred to as the norm group. Criterion-referenced testing (CRT) compares a student's performance with some predetermined behavioral level of competency. With NRT the focus is on rating the student's test performance relative to other students. In CRT the purpose is to bring the student's performance up to desired standards. Both types measure the student's knowledge and skill in a content area. It is how this performance is interpreted where the major distinction lies.

The student's overall performance on NRT is reported as a grade level equivalent, percentile rank, and/or standard score. For CRT, performance may be reported as the total number of objectives achieved, number of behavioral competencies attained, or number of items correctly done in a teacher-developed test.

In theory, both NRT and CRT should be related to teaching objectives. In practice, typically the CRT is more directly linked to specific teaching objectives. Both formats provide useful information about student learning and achievement patterns and each type should be included in the mathematics program evaluation. The items making up the CRT can come directly from the student's IEP and teacher's lesson plans. The only modification needed is presentation of the content so that basic skills, reasoning, and problem-solving abilities are tested using several different kinds of problems to measure these behaviors.

Using NRTs to evaluate the impact of a program on students requires that the evaluator know something about the limits of these instruments. Ignoring these limitations often results in collecting data that are either meaningless, irrelevant, or contradictory to the purpose of the program evaluation. If you know what kinds of information these tests are able to provide you identify and control potential variables that could obscure the evaluation results. The major limitations concern:

1. Scoring and administration
2. Test levels
3. Interpretation of grade level equivalent scores

## Scoring and Administering Tests

The purpose of testing is to get an objective measure of a student's performance. All tests should be administered according to the instructions outlined in the test manual. All students should be tested in the same way, preferably under physical conditions that are closely similar. The effects of the surrounding environment, facial responses of the examiner, time of day for testing, and other situational variables on student performance have been well documented. Once there is variation among students in how the tests were administered there are no statistical procedures or experimental designs to overcome these problems. In short, the data become meaningless.

Test procedures should be well organized and conducted by appropriately trained professional staff. If possible, the same examiner should be used to give tests to all the students. Finally, scoring procedures must be identical for all students.

## Test Levels

Tests used to measure student progress must be selected according to the academic and intellectual characteristics of the group being tested. If student progress in an upper-level trigonometry course is to be assessed using a test dealing with basic whole number operations, one can expect that most students will get nearly all items correct. It will be impossible to measure student progress in the course because this test does not give room for growth, nor do its contents relate to trigonometry. On the other hand, using a test that is too difficult or too advanced so that only two or three students get a few items correct provides no information about student progress or level of performance. Ideally, the tests used should spread out student performance or result in most students scoring around the middle of the range of possible scores.

With CRT the issue of test level is usually not a problem, provided that teaching objectives are consistent with the student's capabilities and the methods used to measure performance behaviorally. Objectives must be task-analyzed in sufficient detail and presented in the most effective teaching sequence.

To avoid using tests that are too difficult or too easy, tests should be selected according to the known achievement levels of students. With LD students it may be necessary to examine achievement using the IEP and group and individual test data in conjunction with teacher analyses of present level of functioning. Finally, with NRT the students should be examined using tests that compare their performance with a norm group of the same age. If a child is in the sixth grade and tested with an instrument developed for fourth graders, that test should include normative tables for sixth graders so that their performance can be interpreted appropriately.

**Interpretation of Grade Level Scores**

Grade level equivalent scores from NRT are widely used to examine program impact on student progress. In the typical evaluation model students are tested in the beginning of the year and again at the end of the year. Differences between the two grade levels attained are interpreted to reflect growth or regression. The problem with using these scores is that they often are not sensitive to the kinds of gains produced by a program. A grade level of 7.0 on one test may not be equivalent to a 7.0 achieved on a second test. Moreover, a 7.0 attained on the same test by several different students does not mean the same thing for each one. This point was illustrated in Table 11-2 using the WRAT. Because of this, it is easy to misinterpret the grade level score to mean something it is not. Also, grade level scores on NRT are often calculated using statistical projections from the norm group pattern of performance. This means that a grade level of 8.0 on a test does not necessarily indicate how students at actual grade level 8.0 performed on the test. In fact, it is possible that no eighth graders ever even took the test.

NRT data form an important part of any program evaluation. The data from these tests in a pretest-posttest design can be very meaningful if used appropriately. Grade level equivalent scores should not be included as part of the program evaluation to indicate student learning in a causal way. The raw scores obtained from NRT should be converted into standard scores. The standard scores corresponding to each raw score can be easily gotten from the test manual. The mean standard scores from pretesting and posttesting may then be converted to percentile ranks. Now a comparison can be made by subtracting the mean pretest percentile or standard score from the mean posttest percentile or standard score. The difference between scores suggests the degree of academic progress attained by the group.

An example showing this process is presented in Table 11-3. Comparing only the grade level scores from September to May shows that Ben gained 2.6 grades in nine months of school. This is highly unlikely even if Ben became extremely motivated and had the benefit of an extraordinarily talented teacher. Examining the standard scores and percentiles shows that Ben did make substantial gain in mathematics. He is still below his expected level of achievement in his present class placement. But the gap between his performance and that of his peers has been closed a good deal. In fact, his performance in May is now consistent with that for students in his age group functioning slightly below average. The *WRAT* has a mean standard score of 100 and a standard deviation of 15. This means that a standard score in the range of 85 to 115 can be considered within the expected age level of performance.


## SELECTING TESTS TO MEASURE PROGRESS

With the cautions listed above in mind the next step in preparing a program evaluation is to select specific tests to use in assessing student performance. The kinds of information tests provided determine the validity and usefulness of the evaluation results. Program evaluation data should come from both CRT and NRT instruments.

There are a variety of NRT instruments available in mathematics. These tests provide an overall estimate of the student's level of achievement expressed using a grade level equivalent score. Table 11-4 lists some widely used tests.

Any of these tests are appropriate for program evaluation as long as the mean grade level scores used in group data analysis are converted into standard scores and percentile equivalents.

---

**Table 11-3** Differences in Pretest-Posttest Achievement on the *WRAT* Arithmetic Subtest

*Student: Ben Smith*

---

| | |
|---|---|
| *September, 1983* | Age: 12-9 |
| Raw Score: 14 | Standard Score: 75 |
| Grade Score: 3.9 | Percentile Rank: 5 |

---

| | |
|---|---|
| *May, 1984* | Age: 13-5 |
| Raw Score: 21 | Standard Score: 89 |
| Grade Score: 6.5 | Percentile Rank: 23 |

**Table 11-4** Some Widely Used Norm-Referenced Tests in Mathematics

| Test | Publisher/Date | Grade Levels |
|------|----------------|--------------|
| California Achievement Test | California Test Bureau, 1970 | 1–9 |
| Iowa Test of Basic Skills (Arithmetic) | Harcourt, Brace & World, 1956 | 1–12 |
| KeyMATH Diagnostic Arithmetic Test | American Guidance Service, 1971 | 1–8 |
| Metropolitan Achievement Tests | Harcourt, Brace & World, 1963 | 3–9 |
| Stanford Achievement Tests | Harcourt, Brace & World, 1964 | 1–10 |
| Stanford Diagnostic Mathematics Test | Harcourt Brace Jovanovich, 1976 | K–8 |
| SRA Series in Arithmetic | California Test Bureau, 1964 | 1–9 |
| Wide Range Achievement Tests (Arithmetic) | Guidance Associates, 1965 | K–Adult |

CRTs provide the teacher with curriculum-specific information about the skills mastered during a given time period. These skills are usually expressed in terms of instructional objectives and annual goals on the IEP or lesson plan. The teacher is free to construct a CRT oriented to what is being taught. There are several commercial CRTs available, as listed in Table 11-5. These instruments give a reference source from which teaching objectives for a particular unit can be taken. Such packages save the teacher a great deal of time and effort in developing the data-based aspects of mathematics programming. The teacher must be creative in developing items that assess verbal reasoning, problem-solving skills, and basic computations in a variety of ways.

**RECORDING STUDENT PROGRESS**

One of the more tedious aspects of compiling data on student performance is collecting and recording the information. Ease of administration, scoring, recording, and relevance to the mathematics curriculum offered should be major factors in selecting tests. The best test ever developed may not be used if the teacher must spend three hours administering it individually to 15 students twice yearly.

Using an NRT means that students must be tested twice, once at the beginning of the program and once at the end. It is worth looking for an NRT that is easy to give and readily interpretable. The test manual should include conversion tables for raw scores and their standard score and

**Table 11-5** Some Criterion-Referenced Tests in Mathematics

| Test | Publisher/Date | Other Information |
|------|----------------|-------------------|
| Buswell-John Diagnostic Arithmetic Test | Buswell & John, 1926 | No objectives; for basic whole number computations. |
| Diagnosis: An Instructional Aid: Mathematics | Science Research Associates, 1974 | 2 levels; 581 objectives in 5 areas. |
| Diagnostic Mathematics Inventory | CTB/McGraw Hill, 1976 | 7 levels; 325 objectives for grades 1–8; with teaching guides and activity books. |
| Maryland Diagnostic Arithmetic Test | Emporium, University of Maryland, 1976 | 1–8. |
| Mastery: An Evaluation Tool: Mathematics | Science Research Associates, 1976 | K–9 in 10 areas. |
| Mathematics: IOX Objectives-Based Tests | Instructional Objectives Exchange, 1976 | 2 levels, K–6 and 7–9 in 7 areas. |
| Objectives-Referenced Bank of Items and Tests: Mathematics | CTB/McGraw Hill, 1975 | K–Adult; 507 objectives in 18 areas. |
| One Step at a Time | EMC Publishers, 1977 | 1–8. |

percentile equivalents. Recording these data is a direct transfer of scores to a sheet listing student name, date of testing, and all scores for both individual subtests and the total score, if applicable. These same sheets can be used again to record data from the second testing. When dealing with naive consumers of tests student performance can be discussed using grade level scores. Standard scores and percentiles will be used in the overall program evaluation where greater precision and technical sophistication are needed.

Recording performance on CRT instruments is a little more complicated, especially at the group level. The number of skills taught may vary considerably among students. These data can be recorded using the number of objectives achieved during the year by each student and then listing them as shown in Exhibit 11-1. This chart presents an easy-to-read summary of individual student and total class progress while comparing the number of goals actually mastered with the number of goals written in the IEP. The column labeled "Goals Attained Level" indicates the actual number of goals mastered as a percentage of those developed for the

**Exhibit 11-1**  A Recording System for Instructional Objectives Achieved by Students

| Class ——— Dates of Testing ——— Teacher ——— | | | | |
| Student | Number of Objectives Mastered | Number of Goals Mastered | Number of Goals on IEP | Goals Attained Level |
| --- | --- | --- | --- | --- |
| Bill | 46 | 11 | 11 | 100% |
| Joe | 12 | 3 | 4 | 75% |
| Frances | 19 | 5 | 8 | 62% |
| Mary | 17 | 9 | 10 | 90% |
| Angela | 31 | 12 | 12 | 100% |
| Susan | 27 | 10 | 10 | 100% |
| Philip | 42 | 10 | 10 | 100% |
| John | 30 | 9 | 10 | 90% |
| Frank | 34 | 8 | 10 | 60% |
| Anne | 25 | 6 | 10 | 60% |

*Frequency Summary*

| Number of Goals Mastered | Number of Students | % of Class |
| --- | --- | --- |
| 0–1 | 0 | 0 |
| 2–4 | 1 | 10% |
| 5–8 | 3 | 30% |
| 9 or more | 6 | 60% |

student at the child study team meeting. These data complement that provided by NRT. The degree of detail in Exhibit 11-1 can be increased according to the desired degree of specificity. These data are easily communicated to colleagues, supervisors, and parents.

Testing for mastery of objectives occurs on an ongoing basis throughout the year. The actual test need be only a three-to-five-minute test to see if the student has mastered the objective according to criterion.

## EVALUATING PROGRAM IMPACT

Planning is the most important aspect of all evaluations. Decisions made during this phase affect both the quality of data collected and its relevance to the program. Three items that should be addressed during the planning phase concern factors external to the evaluation process itself. These are:

(1) Are school system personnel prepared for and receptive to involvement in an evaluation? Most evaluations generate a variety of feelings of suspicion, apprehension and anxiety for those involved. This is so even if the evaluation is limited to one class in mathematics. When the evaluation extends to more than one class because of coordinated programming such feelings can become magnified. Program evaluation is not necessarily oriented toward evaluation of an individual's performance and competence. Yet, many see evaluation as a highly personal experience that critically examines competence.

(2) What are the practical, logistical limitations affecting the evaluation either directly or indirectly? Obvious ones include district and union policies, cost and time available to conduct the evaluation, staff available to work on evaluation, student scheduling for testing, or pressures from community groups.

(3) Do you wish to compare the performance of one group with another used as the control or are you interested in the progress of only one group of students? From a research perspective the use of a control group is highly desirable for determining the impact of a program. In practice, this is difficult to implement because of ethical reasons with respect to the student selection process and problems in matching groups on pretest measures. In systems using a variety of delivery options to offer mathematics to LD students it may be possible to make such between-group comparisons. The major disadvantage is that students will not be matched on pretesting and then randomly assigned to one of several delivery system options.

The replies to these questions determine the kind of evaluation model used. The more precision desired in the evaluation, the more sophisticated the procedures necessary to examine program impact. When evaluating the impact of instructional or curricular strategies one is concerned with the relationship between these activities and actual student learning outcomes. Experimental rigor is something that should be sought. It is important to select a model that is appropriate to the purposes for the evaluation and that as much scientific rigor as possible be maintained.

**Norm-Referenced Model**

The norm-referenced model is appropriate when no control group is available to compare the effects of the program. In this model one compares the actual performance of students during a given time period with the expected level of performance of students in a norm group. Students must be tested twice yearly using NRT. The rate of growth as shown by these tests is compared with the expected rate of growth based on the standard deviation for the test used. All raw scores are converted to standard scores. A difference of one-third of the standard deviation or greater is commonly accepted as indicating significant educational improvement. Exhibit 11-2 illustrates this procedure, presenting the pretest and post-test data for 22 LD students participating in a mathematics class co-taught by a mathematics and special education teacher. The students were tested twice using the *WRAT* arithmetic subtest. These data are depicted in the top half of Exhibit 11-2. The mean scores computed for each test date reflect growth adjusted for age increases. These data show that students in this class improved from the third to twelfth percentile ranks in mathematics performance on this subtest.

"Projected Performance of Students" indicates the expected levels of growth using the normative data in the test manual. It is assumed that the growth rate of students would be the same had they not been given the special mathematics program. This is reflected in the same standard score and percentile ranks in the two testings. Even though the grade level equivalents show growth of 0.4 grades, this growth is not substantial given the increased age for the group. This growth would be expected and is not the result of the impact of the mathematics instruction.

The final step is to compare the actual growth rate of the students in the program with these expected growth rates. The difference between the standard scores in the post-testing is 11. The standard deviation for the *WRAT* standard scores is 15. One-third of this is 5. The difference between the expected and actual standard scores in the posttesting greatly exceeds this number, thus providing support for the observation that the co-teach-

**Exhibit 11-2** Evaluation of Student Growth in Mathematics Using a Norm-Referenced Model

| Actual Performance of Students | | |
|---|---|---|
| | September | May |
| Number of Students Tested | 22 | 22 |
| Mean Age at Testing | 11–2 | 11–11 |
| *WRAT* Arithmetic Subtest | | |
| Mean grade level score | 2.20 | 4.10 |
| Mean raw score | 10.50 | 14.50 |
| Mean standard score | 71 | 82 |
| Mean percentile | 3%ile | 12%ile |

| Projected Performance of Students (If not given special mathematics program) | | |
|---|---|---|
| | September | May |
| Mean grade level score | 2.20 | 2.60 |
| Mean raw score | 10.50 | 11.50 |
| Mean standard score | 71 | 71 |
| Mean percentile | 3%ile | 3%ile |

ing of mathematics by a mathematics and special education teaching team produced greater educational progress than the traditional approach.

This model is probably the easiest and most direct to use for assessing program impact. The data provided relate only to the overall level of achievement of students. If the NRT used is not sensitive to the variety of academic areas where growth may have occurred, large amounts of information are lost. This model also does not evaluate the impact of specific processes used during the innovative program. Feedback is given only once—at the conclusion of the post-testing. The model is highly cost-effective, requires minimal time to compile and analyze data, and is well suited for programs that are directly linked to the NRT instruments used to assess student progress.

### Single-Group Pretest-Posttest Model

The single-group pretest-posttest model is used when no control group is available and more detailed information about program impact is desired than that given by the norm-referenced model. This model expands the previous model by using NRT, CRT, and instructional objectives to assess effectiveness. Achievement gains with NRT are determined using the procedures described in the first model.

CRT instruments are administered twice to each student. The first occurs prior to the unit in which the material is to be taught. The student's performance, as indicated by total number of items correct, serves as the baseline or pretest data. After the unit has been completed, the test is administered again. This score is the post-test data. The group mean scores for each testing are computed. The greater the difference between the two the larger the academic gain in terms of the skills tested.

Test results can also be displayed using a frequency distribution chart in which the numbers of students attaining 50, 60, 70, 80 percent and so on of the items correct are compared. This chart offers added clarification of the growth made by students. It can be as simple as the one shown in Exhibit 11-3.

These data show that almost none of the students in this group could correctly divide using mixed numbers with any consistency prior to the unit. Two months later almost all students had mastered this skill at the 80 percent level or higher. Clearly, the teaching unit on division using mixed numbers was very successful with this group.

The third source of data using this model is the number of instructional objectives and annual goals on the IEP mastered. These data reflect con-

---

**Exhibit 11-3** Frequency Distribution Chart, CRT Scores

TEST: Division Using Mixed Numbers
NUMBER OF TEST ITEMS: 40

| Percent Correct | January (pretest) | March (posttest) |
|:---:|:---:|:---:|
| 0–25% | 17* | 0 |
| 26–49% | 11 | 0 |
| 50–59% | 11 | 0 |
| 60–69% | 1 | 0 |
| 70–79% | 0 | 1 |
| 80–89% | 0 | 5 |
| 90–99% | 0 | 19 |
| 100% | 0 | 5 |

*Numbers of students in the category

tent that anchors the mathematics program during the year. As such, they indicate the degree to which the program is achieving its purpose of educating LD students. Once again, frequency charts seem to be the most useful and direct way to display the data. Data can be shown as the numbers of students attaining various proportions of the total objectives and goals listed in the IEP. The chart would be similar to that presented to show CRT results except that only two columns are needed. The first would be for the percent of goals or objectives attained and the second for the numbers of students at each level.

These kinds of information on student educational progress are more detailed than that using only norm-referenced testing. The thrust of the evaluation is on both grade level achievement scores and actual teaching for specific skills. This model requires greater amounts of data to be collected and analyzed.

Either of these models is appropriate for use by a teacher or supervisor to examine the impact of a class grouping or teaching innovation on student educational progress. Although more detailed and time consuming, the single-group pretest-posttest model provides a great deal of information about the program. This information is more meaningful than that from the norm-referenced model because it is directly related to both how teaching is proceeding and its results. In general, neither model is especially difficult to implement, nor will excessive or even great amounts of time be devoted to data collection, analysis, and interpretation. The criterion in deciding which one to use is how much information one wants about the program being evaluated.

## Matched-Groups Posttest Model

One final model is presented. This model differs from the preceding two in several ways. The greatest difference is that two groups of students matched along a number of characteristics are involved. This model allows one to compare the effects of a program innovation with those of the typical program. The model will probably be of interest to administrators who are responsible for doing overall program evaluations and who have some influence over the placement of students into specific types of programs.

The matched-groups posttest model involves randomly placing students by pairs into either the innovative program or the typical (control) program. Students are pretested in mathematics and paired according to those with about equal mathematics skills. The specific tests used to pair students can be NRT or CRT. Whichever is used it is important that some criterion be selected to pair students in a consistent and objective way. Once the two groups are selected, students in each can be given the remaining set of NRTs and/or CRTs prior to beginning the actual treatment phase, which is participation in the innovative mathematics program for one group and involvement in the typical program for the control group.

At the conclusion of the treatment phase students in both groups are tested again using those instruments from the pretesting. NRT scores are converted into standard scores. The mean and standard deviation for each group are calculated for both the pretest and posttest measures. The resulting posttest scores of each group are statistically analyzed using a t-test for matched groups. The computational formula for this procedure can be found in any introductory test. Using a one-tailed probability it can be determined whether there are statistically significant differences between the two groups on the posttest measures. If significant differences are found, the greater progress of the treatment group can be attributed to the program's impact. In addition, the treatment group's scores from the pretesting can also be statistically analyzed using this procedure to see if significant changes did occur.

This model is quite suitable because of its sound experimental and statistical bases. The major limitation of the model is that it requires that students be matched on the skill in question and then randomly assigned to one group or the other. In practice, there may be ethical and professional considerations that mitigate against this kind of selection process.

## SUMMARY

Evaluation is an important part of any educational program. It allows staff to assess the effectiveness of current programs to determine if new program alternatives are needed. It provides concrete information about how well present teaching methods and curricula are meeting student needs. There are a variety of obvious and hidden aspects involved in all program evaluations. The readiness of the system as a total organization and the preconceptions held by individuals within the system need to be examined before one even considers doing an evaluation. Once organizational willingness and individual receptivity are determined, one must look at the goals of the evaluation and select ways of representing, collecting, compiling, and analyzing data to best achieve these goals.

This chapter reviewed the types of data collection options available and offered recommendations about which options may be more appropriate for students with varying degrees of learning disability. Three models that analyze these data in substantially different ways were presented. Program evaluation should be viewed as an objective process and product that allows educators to become more effective in their job roles by instilling confidence in practices that work and identifying transient approaches that appear effective but lack impact on student educational growth and progress.

---

**REFERENCE**

Primes: Mathematics content authority list: K-6. (1971). Harrisburg, PA: Pennsylvania Department of Education.

# Index